ORWELL AND THE POLITICS OF DESPAIR

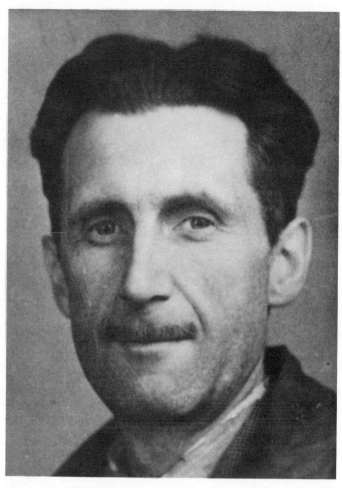

George Orwell, 29th December 1943. This picture appeared on Orwell's National Union of Journalists card. (Reproduced by courtesy of the Orwell Archive, the Library, University College London).

ORWELL
AND THE
POLITICS OF DESPAIR

A critical study of the writings of George Orwell

ALOK RAI

*Reader in English at the University
of Allahabad, and Senior Fellow at the
Nehru Memorial Museum and Library, New Delhi*

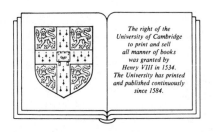

The right of the
University of Cambridge
to print and sell
all manner of books
was granted by
Henry VIII in 1534.
The University has printed
and published continuously
since 1584.

CAMBRIDGE UNIVERSITY PRESS
Cambridge
New York   New Rochelle   Melbourne   Sydney

Published by the Press Syndicate of the University of Cambridge
The Pitt Building, Trumpington Street, Cambridge CB2 1RP
32 East 57th Street, New York, NY 10022, USA
10 Stamford Road, Oakleigh, Melbourne 3166, Australia

First published 1988

Printed in Great Britain at the University Press, Cambridge

British Library cataloguing in publication data
Rai, Alok
Orwell and the politics of despair: a
critical study of the writings of George Orwell
I. Fiction in English. Orwell, George,
1903–1950. Critical studies
I. Title
823'.912

Library of Congress cataloguing in publication data
Alok Rai.
Orwell and the politics of despair.
Bibliography.
Includes index.
I. Orwell, George, 1903–1950 – Political and social
views. 2. Political fiction, English – History and
criticism. 3. Despair in literature. I. Title.
PR6029. R8Z575 1988 828'.91209 88–2847

ISBN 0 521 34519 7

to my parents

CONTENTS

PREFACE AND ACKNOWLEDGMENTS

On 25 March 1945, Eileen Blair wrote to a Mrs Cocking of the BBC, expressing her inability to sign any contracts on her absent husband's behalf. Orwell was at that time, she informed Mrs Cocking, in Europe, reporting the *après-guerre* for David Astor's *Observer*. But he was, Eileen volunteered, 'due home in the latter half of next month and he is a curiously reliable man'. Four days later she died during an unconscionably postponed operation for a suspected malignancy – and her 'curiously reliable' husband, bereaved, hurried back to England sooner than he had planned. This odd, sad episode – with its intimate, irreducible paradox – suggests some of the difficulty that attends all attempts at getting the measure of this famously 'reliable' writer.

This book started life as a doctoral dissertation, but much effort has been expended in the intervening years towards overcoming the handicap of its origins. This was done not merely for the selfish reason that in these degenerate anti-intellectual times, alas, people do not fall over each other to read doctoral dissertations: I felt that the argument that I had tried to make, the issues I had sought to address, were too important to remain immured within the dread dialects of academia. Thus, my book takes the form of a literary–critical account of George Orwell's work and its relationship to his life. But implicit in that account – and not only implicit – is a wider argument, not just about Orwell but about Orwell's world, and ours, and about the ways in which it is possible to understand one and the other, or one *through* the other.

It would be disingenuous of me to pretend that my pressing of a particular reading of Orwell is politically neutral: I am aware, not least due to his own critical example, that particular ways of reading

Orwell are tied to particular ways of 'reading' the world. Orwell is, as I see it, an important guarantor, as he was one of the makers, of what I think of as the Cold War consensus – that powerful and flexible explanatory system in which we are, still, effectively imprisoned. As such, any radical reinterpretation of Orwell is bound to have implications well beyond the domain of literature and literary criticism, disturb whole ranges of corollary equations, rake anxieties, stir antagonisms.

In the course of this study I have, of course, drawn upon all the published writings of George Orwell. In addition, I have drawn upon the unpublished materials in the Orwell Archive at University College London; and also upon its invaluable holdings of Orwell's uncollected writings, and of secondary materials *on* Orwell. Apart from these sources, I have also consulted the newly discovered Orwell papers in the Written Archives of the BBC – whence comes the Eileen Blair letter quoted above – as well as the papers in the Berg Collection in the New York Public Library. I have also tried to make my coverage of the secondary material as complete as possible: including, and even a little beyond, the Great Fuss of 1984. No one who writes on Orwell can afford to ignore the mould of his fame, to disregard altogether the politics of his reputation. From what I know of their writings, I know that there will be many Orwell scholars – and readers of Orwell – who will find much of what I have to say sympathetic; others, no doubt, will find themselves in passionate, angry disagreement. That is one of the occupational hazards of writing on this 'curiously reliable man'. However, whereas I have indicated specific attributions in the appropriate places, I have, in the main, tried to avoid a running engagement with Orwell critics.

The burden of gratitude which it is my pleasure to acknowledge here must seem disproportionate to its modest vehicle. A large number of persons and institutions have helped, in different ways and at different times, in making this book better than it might otherwise have been, and I am pleased to be able to acknowledge their help publicly, formally, finally.

My greatest debt is to Dan Jacobson of University College London: such virtues as my book might possess are due in considerable measure to the sustained, affectionate and deeply gratifying attention which he has lavished upon the book and its author. The number of people who have discussed Orwell's work with me, have read and commented on the numerous drafts that sections of this book have gone through and/or have made bibliographical and critical material available to me is too great for anything more than a simple alphabetical listing to be possible here. I am pleased to acknowledge the assistance of: Rukun Advani, David Astor, Jasodhara Bagchi and her colleagues at Jadavpur, Anil Bhatti, Tom Chalmers, Basudev Chatterji, Bernard Crick, Terry Eagleton, Claire L'Enfant, David Farrer, Brian Finney, T. R. Fyvel, Richard Hoggart, Sudipta Kaviraj, Ravinder Kumar, Arvind Mehrotra, Robert Meister, Martin Moir, Paul Potts, Harriet Raghunathan, Mahadev Saha, Peter Sedgwick, John Sutherland and Ian Willison. Ruchira Chatterji, Geetam Tiwari and Tasneem Usmani helped out with materials in the final stages of revision.

Anyone who works seriously on Orwell must incur an unredeemable debt of gratitude to Janet Percival and her colleagues at the Orwell Archive in University College London: I am proud to be in their debt. Special thanks are also due to Jacqueline Kavanagh and her colleagues at the Written Archive Centre of the BBC. And to all the people who made it a pleasure to work at the British Library; the Senate House Library; the India Office Library; the New York Public Library; the Nehru Memorial Library. I have also received crucial assistance from the American Center Library in New Delhi and the American Studies Research Center in Hyderabad: many thanks. I am also pleased to acknowledge the assistance, at different times, of the Commonwealth Scholarships Commission; the Cassel Trust; the Inlaks Foundation; the University Grants Commission. The Indian Council of Social Science Research generously awarded me a Fellowship so that I could shed teaching responsibilities and work on the final manuscript; and the University of Allahabad allowed me to do so.

The author and publishers are grateful to the late Sonia Brownell Orwell and to Secker and Warburg Limited for use of certain quotations.

Finally, I would like to thank my wife, Rajul. She has been steadfastly supportive throughout the time that Orwell has been an odd, demanding third in our *ménage*. But it must be our daughters, Tia and Tanvi, who have, really, made the writing of this book possible – if only through forbearing to exercise, over extended periods, their considerable capacity to make it impossible!

1

INTRODUCTION: THE ORWELL PROBLEM

Orwell's image of Dickens is well known:

the face of a man of about forty . . . He is laughing, with a touch of anger in his laughter, but no triumph, no malignity. It is the face of a man who is always fighting against something, but who fights in the open and is not frightened, the face of a man who is *generously angry* – in other words, of a nineteenth-century liberal, a free intelligence.

(1, 460)

The resemblance between this figure and Orwell himself has not been missed.[1] Orwell's image of Dickens *is* near enough to the truth about himself to be seductive – but it is also, I hope to show, ultimately misleading. He is, precisely, distinctively, a *twentieth-century* liberal: in his own words, 'someone who is a Socialist by allegiance and a Liberal by temperament'.[2] Orwell is a liberal who endorses and owes allegiance to the socialist critique of liberalism and capitalism; and his career is, in its particular form, a working through of that contradiction. Consider, for example, the terms in which Orwell praises Thomas Mann. Mann, he writes, is not 'the kind of liberal who sees no further than political "freedom" and is quite content to leave the world in its capitalist shape. He sees clearly the need for Socialism.'[3] Orwell's ideological allegiance to socialism is, we know, significantly qualified. He points with insight and persistence at a crucial and terrifying area of darkness at the heart of socialist, and particularly Marxist–Leninist, theory and practice. However, Orwell does something else as well: he wrestles with the crisis at the heart of twentieth-century liberalism itself.[4] Orwell's work engages with – 'enacts' – the crisis which is both indicated and generated by the widening gap between the ideology of liberalism and the reality produced by its institutions: put simply, the hiatus between the free market and the receding possibilities of human freedom and fulfilment that were its supposed justification.[5]

There is another respect in which Orwell is, allowing for differences of scale, similar to his own Dickens: he, too, is 'one of those writers who are well worth stealing' (1, 413). All manner of people have raided his work for all kinds of meanings – meanings religious, reactionary, radical. Orwell is, transparently, many things to many men. He is appropriated with equal facility by the New Left, which is drawn to his prickly, stubborn radicalism; and by the ideologues of the Institute of Directors, who see the dread shadow of 'totalitarianism' in the merest gestures of social regulation. To one interpreter, Orwell is 'a genuinely socialist thinker and critic, a lonely figure moving tentatively' towards the 'absent centre' of British socialism.[6] To another, Orwell is a propagandist in the cause of 'free trade, free enterprise and free markets'.[7] One critic's Orwell, 'frustrating . . . reader expectations' in his early novels, sounds like a proto-post-modernist; another's is a sort of ecology-buff, as good as 'Green'; yet another's is a neo-conservative, as good as Jeanne Kirkpatrick.[8]

But if Orwell bears a certain resemblance to his Dickens, he is also, in his inescapable but also strangely elusive presence, a little like Big Brother. The famous lined, life-scarred visage, 'full of power and mysterious calm', the all-knowing 'hypnotic eyes . . . that follow you about when you move', alert to the least shadow of deviousness, relentless and unforgiving in the pursuit of disingenuousness – this, too, is a precisely composed image. If Orwell-as-Dickens describes one aspect of, one response to his work, Orwell-as-Big Brother is not less relevant in that it helps to crystallise the manner in which Orwell, despite the meagreness of his purely *literary* achievement, dominates a certain range of the modern consciousness.

There is an apparent amorphousness in Orwell's writing. The corpus is a paradoxical collocation of heterogeneous elements from which, with a little judicious editing, particular, selective interpre-tations might be coaxed. On the other hand, a mere listing of the diversity, a descriptive taxonomy of its particularities, a catalogue of its contradictions, is also not adequate to our experience of reading Orwell.[9] A conceptually linear approach such as this is, I suggest, unsuited to the task of understanding the obsessive, repetitive, *locked* quality of Orwell's writing. There is indeed a great deal of paradox and contradiction in Orwell that resists being reduced and fused into one whole; but there is also the sense of a deep coherence, an intuitive recognition of an underlying unity. This unity, this sense of a 'master form' is, necessarily, missed by a casually or conscientiously dia-chronic, more or less picaresque account of Orwell's career.

To take one not quite random example: Bernard Crick is emphatic that *Nineteen Eighty-Four* neither was, nor was intended as, a 'last testament': 'it was simply the last major book he wrote before he happened to die'.[10] This may well be true, but those others who see *Nineteen Eighty-Four* as a sort of 'last testament' are not altogether wrong.[11] Orwell might well have written other books if he had lived – his long-projected family saga, perhaps. But the critical intuition that *Nineteen Eighty-Four* represents 'the end of a movement',[12] the fulfilment of some kind of logical–ideological development, this too cannot be denied. In this intuition lie the seeds of a recognition of that pattern of necessity – the 'master form' – that underlies the diversity and the apparent contradiction. It is here, I suggest, that we will need to look for an explanation of Orwell's formidable cultural presence.

Orwell's preferred figure for a writer's career was that of a parabola. 'Any writer who is not utterly lifeless', he wrote, 'moves upon a kind of a parabola, and the downward curve is implied in the upward one' (I, 457). The parabola is, as it happens, a tightly controlled curve in which, as Orwell wrote,' the end is present in the beginning'. (The commonest example of a parabola is, ironically, the path described by an inert projectile!) A critically adequate account of Orwell would, in my opinion, be one which would not only be faithful to the apparent heterogeneity, but would also incorporate the sense, which the parabolic metaphor implies, of a controlled, internally logical development – further, a development which constitutes a unity but which is also complex enough, like the parabola, to allow for an apparently radical change of direction.

Much of the critical writing on Orwell testifies, in one way and another, that it is difficult to focus critically on the writings themselves, difficult to constitute Orwell as an object of critical enquiry. As one critic has remarked: 'it is curious that a writer whose prose style is consistently praised as a model of clarity, appropriate to the honesty and commonsense it is assumed to express, should be so elusive'.[13] Part of the difficulty, at any rate, derives from the very clarity of the prose: it is a typically Orwellian paradox that the prose which aspires to the ideal clarity of a windowpane reveals nothing so much as it does Orwell himself. As critics we do not look through the window upon the larger world, but rather *into* it, and discover the writer at work on his most durable creation, 'Orwell'. That is, of course, if we are careful to exercise a degree of critical intelligence, to defend oneself against ingratiating candour with scepticism.[14] Otherwise, quite unconsciously, the apparent transparency of the prose, its 'obviousness', gets translated or naturalised into invisibility. And then, quite simply, there is the 'honest' Orwell:

Orwell was fair, honest, unassuming and reliable in everything he wrote.[15]

It is this Orwell who may be said to tell us 'the truth'.

Orwell's writing does not really lend itself to traditional literary analysis – he appears to foil by his disarmingly available presence the elaborate tools that literary criticism habitually deploys:

His novels were direct and fairly simple narratives in an old tradition. Their meanings are mainly on the surface. Orwell posed no riddles, elaborated no myths, and manipulated no symbols . . . There is not much to do with Orwell's novels except read them.[16]

His meanings are, one feels, not recondite, waiting to be discovered by the analysis of deep structures, of clusters of images and the mysterious intercourse of symbols. Orwell's meanings appear, and this must be rated an achievement of prose style and perhaps even of moral daring, emblazoned on the polished surfaces of his work. But the traditional tools of literary criticism were not, I believe, designed to deal with the obvious. This is not to suggest that literary–critical methods of textural and structural analysis are of no value in studying Orwell, but simply that the manner of their use has to be adjusted to the particular, peculiar nature of the materials.

In a sense, of course, a critical perspective has to be struggled for in the case of all literature. But Orwell presents some rather special problems. In the case of literature that might plausibly be assumed to inhabit an 'aesthetic' domain into which one is lured, one can also, by the same token, find a location outside that domain. But contemporary political literature appears to be coextensive with a historical world, and reaches out to the reader/critic importunately or imperiously with suggestions as to how that historical world and consequently itself – the literature – ought to be read.[17] Again, with many authors, though not always justifiably, it is possible, and this is the strategy of much traditional literary criticism, to isolate the author from the historical and social continuum of which he is a part. Indeed, the possibility of this kind of significant isolation is the philosophical ground on which the initial attempt to write on an 'author' rests.[18] However, such a conventional act of isolation is particularly unsuited to Orwell. His work itself demands that we reach out, as *it* does, beyond the confines of personality and even of literature, into history and politics, into the Spanish Civil War and the Cold War; demands that we should both find and lose ourselves in necessary alleys and by-ways, and streets that lead suddenly to arguments of often insidious intent. These detours from the straight and narrow path of *literary* criticism, these lapses from the vows of 'textuality', are, I suggest, ineluctable. They might even, unless we exercise due caution, prove seductive. Much of the bulk of Orwell criticism bears involuntary testimony to the processes whereby the unwary eye glances off the polished, transparent prose and, before too long, one is deep in the soothing noise of contemporary civilisation, the clash of clichés and stereotypes, the vehement and familiar clamour of complementary prejudices.

The critical strategy, as I see it, is to insist on maintaining the critical distance which the urgent contemporaneity, the flaunted topicality, of the work seems determined to obliterate. However, such an insistence on the autonomous and factitious nature of literature – particularly literature of the kind that is my theme – would appear to merit the criticism that, I believe rightly, attaches to the critics who, inveigled by the autotelic and self-referential aspect of art, surrender all notion of its social presence.[19] An over-emphasis on the factitious-ness and the 'made-up' nature of art, while intended to offset the naive literalism of less sophisticated critics, can, in practice, be so overdone as to suppress the notion of truth and historical reference altogether. There might, so to speak, be no way back from the Palace of Art, even if it is renamed the People's Palace. I would, therefore, like to distinguish my own recourse to the notion of factitiousness in dealing with Orwell, my insistence that despite the foregrounded historical markers, there is in the work a mediating, shaping, consciousness at work. My 'autonomism' is tactical, a heuristic strategy, an attempt to create a critical space within which one might regard the literary work itself without being swamped instantly by the crowding urgencies of our history.[20] Such a critical space is essential if we desire to see the work at all, because it is only too easy to see through the work, the famously transparent prose, and engage directly, as it were, with the urgencies of which it is a product.

It would require little effort, for instance, to start out discussing Orwell and slip almost instantly, imperceptibly, into discussing post-war European politics. Orwell criticism is rife with examples. Lionel Trilling's 'George Orwell and the politics of truth' (1952) is a highly regarded piece of critical writing. And, be it said, the account that

Trilling gives of what happened to Orwell in Catalonia is accurate enough, if a little simplified. But the real default is that he is unable to focus his critical lens on the book at all. Orwell's text has become simply transparent, a neutral filter, a mere window on a tragic corner of contemporary history. And all Trilling can do is to assert, repeatedly, in what sounds like a state of admiring stupefaction, how true it all is: 'He told the truth . . . He was interested only in telling the truth . . . And what matters most of all is our sense of the man who tells the truth.'[21] But the *politics* of 'truth' escapes his attention altogether. Such criticism aspires, adapting Pater, to the condition of paraphrase: to saying what, it must be assumed, the 'truthful' work has said already. This kind of criticism, to put it bluntly, *finds out nothing* about Orwell's writings, although it is very free with opinions about international history, political theory and, above all, the strange, sodden career of the Russian Revolution. Irving Howe, in 'The idea of the political novel', offers involuntary testimony to the difficulty of focussing on the literary dimension of contempory political literature:

The chapters on Stendhal and Dostoyevsky contain a far heavier stress on the literary side of things than do the chapters on Koestler and Orwell . . . In a book like *Nineteen Eighty-Four* politics has achieved almost total dominion, while such works as *The Possessed* and *The Charterhouse of Parma* cannot be understood without using traditional literary categories.[22]

The obvious implication is that *Nineteen Eighty-Four can* be understood directly, without the mediation of literary categories, because, it is implied, it wears its meaning on its surface. Much of the vast bulk of Orwell criticism is in fact a victim of this difficulty of focussing on the literary and so factitious nature of the work – and such criticism is, I suggest, condemned to justifying its initial assumption of critical superfluity.

It is not only the deceptive transparency of Orwell's writings, or their imbrication with a known and passionately perceived historical world, that lies at the root of the critical problem. It is also the fact that Orwell's writing, since it is essentially in the form of a para-biography of the evolving mythical persona, 'Orwell',[23] necessarily incorporates suggestions and injunctions on how the writings ought to be read. It is useful to recall, at this point, the two ghosts who, the American critic Sheldon Sacks reports, obstructed his work *Fiction and the Shapes of Belief*: the first obstructed him by saying that a writer had *no* beliefs, only aesthetic ends; but the other obstructed him just as much by insisting that a writer's beliefs were what the writer said they were.[24] The first, 'aesthetic' ghost is easily disposed of in the case of Orwell. One might, with a certain heroic irrelevance, attempt to write on, say, Orwell's water imagery – drawing upon, perhaps, the ruined pool in *Coming Up for Air*, 'The moon under water', and the fragment of coral embedded in 'rainwatery' glass in *Nineteen Eighty-Four*, to say nothing of the stubborn aspidistra that Comstock neglects to water; but the absurdity of this 'aesthetic' enterprise will be pointed up by the evidently polemical nature, the urgent 'invitation' of the works themselves. Sacks's second ghost, however, is less breezily vanquished. After all, what use are we to make of the evidence which the writer offers about himself, the author's self-interpretations, the conceptions which he himself offers for understanding him?

The problem arises in an acute form, for instance, when one tries to locate Orwell in the context of the 1930s. On the one hand, Orwell is a part of the movement of consciousness that is associated with the literary radicals of the 1930s. On the other hand, Orwell has himself, particularly in 'Inside the whale', created a powerful and persuasive framework of misunderstanding.[25] It is a particularly delicate matter deciding how to deal with Orwell's dismissive account of the thirties. It would of course be naive to treat Orwell's account as the plain, historical truth. But it is also insufficient merely to demonstrate that Orwell's retrospective account of his literary contemporaries is biassed and inaccurate. Beyond the local truths (and the local falsities) of his assertions, there is the fact of Orwell's offering a particular *interpretation* of a cultural–historical conjuncture which, in my view, helped to make him the writer he became. This interpretation, which thus inevitably implies self-interpretation, must itself be read critically, seen to be part of the 'problem' even though it appears in the guise of an explanation. When, for example, Orwell writes in 1946: 'Every line of serious work that I have written since 1936 has been written, directly or indirectly, *against* totalitarianism and *for* democratic Socialism' (I, 5), he is clearly 'inviting' us to read him in a particular way. But, I believe, serious criticism must decline the invitation; it must preserve its distance and independence, its right to scrutinise critically the invitation itself. What does Orwell mean when he makes a statement such as the one quoted above? Is it true? Is it adequate to explain the range and change, from *The Road to Wigan Pier* to *Homage to Catalonia*, from *Homage to Catalonia* to *Coming Up for Air*, from *Coming Up for Air* to *Inside the Whale*, and *Inside the Whale* through *The Lion and the Unicorn* to *Animal Farm*? Of course, the commitment to 'democratic Socialism', *and* his view of that commitment in 1946, must be given due recognition in any explanation, but we must be wary of trusting an author too far simply because we like what he says.

Orwell raises in a peculiar form that which is known as 'the problem of belief' in literary criticism. The traditional solution to this problem is to think in terms of a 'suspension of disbelief', a mode of hypothetical assent which allows the object under analysis to do its work.[26] This has, moreover, an obvious relevance to Orwell's work when one considers the angry and insensitive reviews of *Animal Farm* and *Nineteen Eighty-Four* by early reviewers with communist sympathies.[27] However, when dealing with political, polemical literature in which, by definition, the 'belief' is not incidental, the circumambient element in which the work crystallises, but substantive rather, itself the 'work', it would seem that a mere suspension of disbelief would be an inadequate critical strategy. As John Wain has argued persuasively, Orwell's work is *essentially* polemical,[28] and criticism must find a way of engaging with, while not being swamped by, that polemical quality. Irving Howe's warning is apt:

For both the writer and the reader, the political novel provides a particularly severe test: politics rakes our passions as nothing else, and whatever we may consent to overlook in reading a novel, we react with almost demonic rapidity to a detested political opinion.[29]

The problem is, of course, not confined merely to 'detested' opinions, but also to ones that are held deeply. The mere suspension of disbelief, whether conscious or unconscious, would allow the work, the polemic, an easy and uncritical passage. I suggest, therefore, that in addition to a suspension of disbelief, a *suspension of belief* too is essential.

The alternative to this suspension of belief is, I suggest, hagiography, admiring *ad hominem* panegyric where one, legitimately, expects to find criticism. Such 'criticism' moves disconcertingly from the excellence of Orwell the man to the excellences of his writing, and back again, in an ascending spiral at the end of which we are confronted with St George, the 'wintry conscience of his generation',[30] 'the sea-green incorruptible of the Left, a knight of commonsense illumining a dark dishonest decade'.[31] On such hagiographic criticism, it is difficult to disagree with the cool sobriety of I. R. Willison:

such a mode of description is too transcendental and inflexible to account for the outstanding characteristic of Orwell's work when viewed as a whole, its prodigal and apparently conscienceless heterogeneity.[32]

The problem, as I understand it, reduces itself ultimately to the question of Orwell's 'plausibility': the process which underlies the critical recognition of 'honesty' and 'truth'. Considered at an abstract level, the experience of plausibility appears to be constituted by a three-term relationship between a *recipient*, a *reality*, and an *account* of that reality which mediates it to the recipient. However, it is of the very nature of plausibility that one of the terms, the mediating account or, variably, the mediating *persona*, should tend to become transparent and thus disappear. This suggests the possibility of an investigation into correspondent realities and recipient subjectivities, but the immediate critical task, the *problem*, in fact, is to focus on the mediating account itself, the vanishing middle term: to assimilate critically the paradox of the fictional character – 'Orwell' – who tells the 'truth'. The pre-condition for being able to do this is, in a sense, to refuse the experience of plausibility, and fix one's attention on the authorial consciousness which mediates realities with such disarming transparency. The alternative is, as I have said, celebratory paraphrase. With work that is as subtly ingratiating as Orwell's, criticism must become an act of violence, delicate or brutal as the need arises, but determined anyway to seize that which the work itself is reluctant to yield, instead of politely or gratefully accepting what the work is profferring anyway, and so declining into superfluity, mumbling about 'truth'.

I would suggest, further, that one is able to do this to the extent that one can displace, destabilise, or, more modishly, 'defamiliarise' and 'deconstruct' the basis on which the polemic is itself constructed. Because, to be lured into controversy with the work which one is trying to criticise – lured, that is, into arguing with Orwell – is, once again, to obliterate the necessary critical distance. Clearly, anyone who wishes to write on Orwell must be willing to be both 'aesthetic' and 'political'. I find, however, that in trying to cope critically with the urgent invitation of Orwell's writing – an invitation to assent or controversy – I have sought to preserve my critical distance by, to put it schematically, responding 'aesthetically' where the work itself invites a 'political' response, and 'politically' when the work is itself 'aesthetic'. If we can master the plausibility in this way, instead of ourselves being disarmed by it, we might be able to think about it to some critical advantage, whether in respect of Orwell or in respect of those who read Orwell and the world in particular, innocent, ways. Because I believe that this plausibility, although it presents itself initially as a critical problem, or trap, does, after all, indicate something of importance about Orwell's *œuvre*. It reinforces the sense which reading Orwell engenders, that underlying the diversity, the heterogeneity and the paradox, there is a kind of unity. Implicit in the experience of plausibility is the intuitive sense of a sympathetic whole, greater than the sum of its variable and sometimes indifferent parts.

Implicit, and so presumably accessible through it. Robert Martin Adams, writing about 'authenticity' in a sense close to my own 'plausibility', throws out an intriguing suggestion:

One needn't be a hard-boiled sceptic to sense that authenticity is a state of mind in the hearer, quite as much as a condition of what's being said. It is a *provisional complicity*, a moment or more of assent; and assent, it goes without saying, is generally given on the basis of evidence much more complex than the verbal strategy of the propounder.[33]

The American theorist Hayden White, comparing historical and fictional modes of narration, points out that the difference between the two is not reducible to one of *correspondence* as against *coherence:*

Every history must need standards of coherence no less than those of correspondence if it is to pass as a plausible account of 'the way things really were'.[34]

In the case of Orwell's fictional narratives, we may note *en passant*, it is the truth of their 'correspondence' with a troubled and ambiguous history that has been much emphasised. I propose, eventually, to examine the truth of their 'coherence': a cultural phenomenon that must encompass the master narrative, 'Orwell', itself.[35]

Any person who tries to write on Orwell must, sooner or later, come up against a sense that, in addition to being a writer, Orwell is also a figure of social myth. In the words of one commentator: 'If Orwell had not existed, it might have been necessary to invent him. But, of course, that is exactly what did happen.'[36] It has been argued that myths, which might be 'historically true, legendary, or invented', serve to 'maintain and preserve a culture against disruption and destruction'.[37] Myth is, in this sense, a shared semantic system, a framework of explanation, wherein one orders the anarchy of circumstance, penetrates and humanises the indifferent self-absorption of the physical world: the real purpose of myths is not pleasure, but rather the alleviation of perplexities. In the words of Sir Maurice Bowra, myths 'help to break down the barriers between men and the intractable mass of phenomena which surround them'.[38]

It follows therefore that the power of myth will be directly proportional to its ability to provide satisfactory (or plausible) explanations over a *range* of social experience: proportional, that is, to its flexibility and adaptability. Frank Kermode has argued that the fictions that we live by must be complex enough to speak to our condition, intricate and ironic so as to seek out the hidden loci of our distress: 'without paradox and contradiction our parables will be too simple for a complex poverty, too consolatory to console'.[39] Myths, of course, are the fictions that whole cultures live by. In a powerful speculation on the nature of what he calls the 'mass cultural text', Fredric Jameson has argued:

if the ideological function of mass culture is understood as a process whereby otherwise dangerous and protopolitical impulses are 'managed' and defused, rechannelled and offered spurious objects, then some preliminary step must also be theorised in which these same impulses . . . are initially awakened within the very text that seeks to still them . . . [It] must necessarily involve a complex strategy of rhetorical persuasion in which substantial incentives are offered for ideological adherence.[40]

Durable social myth cannot afford to be innocent. Its power depends upon the risks it takes, the subversive emotions that it domesticates, the unassimilable polarities that it reconciles.

Myth is a cultural construct: it is also a part of that essential skeleton which enables a culture to hang together *as* a culture. Myth may seek to establish its credibility through an appeal to history – and may, therefore, be criticised on that count. But, it has been observed, 'historical myth . . . resists rational criticism because it is emotionally satisfactory'.[41] One may note in this context, for instance, the extraordinary resilience of the myth of the (always/already?) lost 'organic community' in the face of specific historical disproof. The relevant dimension in which myths need to be understood (and criticised) is in terms of their *functions*, in terms of the experiences and perceptions which they process and articulate in particular ways and to particular ends. They must be understood, that is, not only in terms of the specific dispositions *within* the structures of coherence but also in terms of what lies outside, and under, and beyond these necessary structures. The myth of 'Dunkirk' in wartime Britain – whether true or false – served the needs of trans-class mobilisation in a bitterly politicised, hierarchically divided society; the myth of the socialist utopia legitimises – or *seeks* to legitimise – a destiny of queuing for bread and potatoes. It may also inspire the *peon* to take up arms against a Somoza or a Duvalier. A critical understanding of social myth, therefore, must encompass not only what the myth permits or enables, but also what it inhibits or suppresses.

Reviewing a film called *Western Union* – a 'western' and *not* a premonition of NATO – in 1941, Orwell wrote of the 'psychological need in a world which grows constantly more dangerous but also more regimented', of the myth of 'the lonely traveller on his horse, with no protection save his revolver and his skill in using it'.[42] Is it possible that Orwell is himself, in his mythical dimension, that 'lonely traveller', a tweed-jacketed Lone Ranger for politically conscious adults? Or does the myth of Orwell work, appear truthful and plausible, by speaking both to that sense of extremity which the experience of our time evokes and – in the finished shape of his career, his 'parabola' – to that feeling of impotence which is produced by the oppressive realities of our world? Can the myth of Orwell, properly analysed, be made to yield knowledge about the cultural totality of which it is an integral part? We may recall here the words of Arthur Koestler in 1943:

Myths grow like crystals . . . as soon as a suitable core is found, they group themselves around it and the crystal is formed . . . The question, of course, is who makes a suitable core. Obviously, it must have some affinity with that vague, diffuse sentiment, that craving for the right type of hero to turn into a myth; obviously he must express something which is the unconscious content of that craving.[43]

To return to the perception from which we started: it may well be the case that there is an incommensurability between Orwell's purely literary achievement and his undeniable cultural importance. But, instead of being embarrassed by this disproportion, we might recognise in it an opportunity for a more wide-ranging, a more penetrating investigation into the modes, the processes whereby a social and cultural order expresses and learns to recognise itself.[44] Raymond Williams has directed attention towards the

deep structures of consciousness and pressure that were producing the shifts during the thirties and forties which in Orwell's case resulted not in an isolated major individual, but in what was to be a widely imitated style.[45]

He has enlarged the scope of necessary enquiry to encompass 'not Orwell writing, but what wrote Orwell'.[46] Because, of course, finally it is 'Orwell' that is the text, and Orwell is only *one* of its authors.

2

TOTALITARIANISM, ETC.

the false secondary power, by which
In weakness, we create distinctions, then
Deem that our puny boundaries are things
Which we perceive, and not which we have made.
(Wordsworth, *Prelude* (1805–6), book ii, 221–4)

There is a crucial matter of *terminological* clarification – and not, I insist, political theory or revisionist historiography – which must be attended to *before* one can go on to develop an adequate critical account of Orwell. We must first deal with what one exasperated commentator described as 'that blessed word "totalitarian".'[1] Surprisingly, considering the dust of contention that hangs about it, there is a quite precise sense to the word 'totalitarianism'. It was the name of the philosophy of the unitary state, developed by Mussolini's Hegelian philosopher, Giovanni Gentile, tireless in pursuit of the self-realising Idea. Gentile ended up in the Fascist Social Republic set up by the Germans in Salo after Mussolini's fall, and was made president of the Accademia d'Italia (in which post he served until he was killed by Communist partisans on 15 April 1944). In addition to identifying Gentile's constitutional philosophy, the word 'totalitarian' also had a precise formal sense deriving from that conception: it was used to designate a party which did not attempt to ratify its mandate by participating in elections. The earliest use of this sense of the word, recorded by the *OED*, appears a little ironic in retrospect:

1928. *Contemp. Rev.* Apr. 453 Fascism renounces its function as a totalitarian regime and enters the electoral field on equal footing with its adversaries.

Gentile's term was subsequently appropriated by people on the political Left. It was employed to criticise the bureaucratisation of the

Russian Revolution and its related suppression of dissent by pointing out the resemblance to that to which it claimed to be an alternative – the *Fascist* transcendence of the problems of capitalism. Karl-Dietrich Bracher mentions 1928 as the original date for this development.[2] This polemically directed embarrassing similarity between Fascism and Communism gradually merged into identity in the theory of totalitarianism. Fascism and Communism became but two instances of an underlying malignity, immanent and transcendent, anti-democratic Evil Itself. One of the earliest books in which the transformation might be observed is Franz Borkenau's *The Totalitarian Enemy* (1940). The precise moment of this transformation, the original thunderclap, so to speak, wherein and wherefrom the fully fledged monster of totalitarianism was born, is explicitly identified by Borkenau to be the signing of the Nazi–Soviet Non-Aggression Treaty in August 1939 – the primal scene of this political conception.[3] Later historians have pointed out the complicated and comprehensively dishonourable history surrounding that episode, but in the imaginations of Borkenau and others, Fascism and Communism became permanently bonded in the theory of totalitarianism, and their correspondent realities merged into the composite horror of 'totalitarianism'. (Orwell came to know Borkenau around this time, and wrote a favourable review of Borkenau's book: see 11:8). The monster of 'totalitarianism' was, so the theory went, implacably opposed to what, by miraculous retrospective conflation and absolution, had become, simply, 'the democracies'. One might have expected that the epic (and tragic) proportions of the Second World War, which was, mainly, a war between the entities which colluded so cosily in the theory of totalitarianism, would destroy the theory also. However, as Dr Frankenstein discovered, and the post-war development of the theory revealed, monsters too, once begotten, have a life of their own.

In the aftermath of the Second World War, the theory of totalitarianism, which had primarily been a weapon of the libertarian Left, was appropriated, with suitable modifications, by the resurgent Right – in America, as the ideological cornerstone of the Pax Americana, the American Century – and, more generally, by the restorative forces of the old order throughout Europe.[4] Fear of the monster of 'totalitarianism' and the promise of protection therefrom provided the requisite ideological cover, the fig-leaf necessary for the 'democratic' affirmation of developed capitalist societies, condemned by the logic of factors too immense to be squeezed into parentheses to intervening internationally on the side of privilege and traditional injustice. This fear provided (and provides) the rationale for the kind of 'open door' policy which developed capitalist economies need in relation to their miserable 'Third World' adjuncts. It is an invaluable and perhaps irreplaceable weapon in what Conor Cruise O'Brien once called 'the real cold war',[5] between the 'developed' and 'under-developed' parts of the capitalist world, between 'North' and 'South'.

There is, additionally, a national dimension to the appropriation of the theory of totalitarianism by the Right. Nationally, the fear of 'totalitarianism' – not the monster but the malignant regulatory spirit that animates it – is used to contain an activist State which, paradoxically, developed capitalism itself needs. The stridently in-culcated fear of 'totalitarianism' functions, in this respect, like a blind man's leash on his guide dog.[6]

These are, admittedly, controversial matters, although, ironically, a great public silence surrounds them. Still, this much at least is unarguable: that the theory of totalitarianism, which simply asserted that Fascism and Communism were but two manifestations of a single, evil idea,[7] was used as an ideological weapon in the Cold War between the West and the rest.[8] Bracher refers somewhat coyly to 'the occasional misuse of the term in the service of Cold War and other propaganda'.[9] However, a later scholar, who is not committed to the theory in the way that Bracher clearly is, says unambiguously that the theory *became* 'a powerful weapon in the Cold War'.[10]

Then, as historical events unfolded, as the 'East' mysteriously thawed, then froze, and the 'democracies' could no longer suppress the awareness of their undemocratic affiliations, the theory of totalitarianism – in which 'totalitarianism' monotonously confronts 'democracy' – began to look rather frayed. Then again, growing historical research into the regimes which were supposed to embody the malign spirit of 'totalitarianism' showed that the identity (or significant similarity) on which the theory rested was factually insecure and critically unspecific.[11] Lastly, because of its incorpor-ation into the ideological apparatus of states, the term began to show the usual signs of distortion and fatigue, and thus became un-serviceable for serious use. One commentator has described its function in modern political discourse as being similar to that of Luther's 'reason': 'a conceptual harlot of uncertain parentage, belonging to no one but at the service of all'.[12] Another has observed the vagueness of its definitions, ranging 'from the policy of economic planning and Popper's social engineering to Buchheim's colourful but ridiculous malapropism "the creeping rape of man"'.[13] he also cites a Sovieto-logist who, 'in his despair at the methodological sloppiness and dishonesty of many of the protagonists of the theory has remarked that "totalitarianism" is little more than "a 'boo' label on a 'boo' system of government"'.[14] With a certain fitness, albeit adding to the prevalent confusion, Herbert Marcuse and others chose to apply the term 'totalitarianism' to describe advanced capitalist – 'democratic' – societies themselves.[15] The entire development is summed up thus by John Mander:

Totalitarianism was a valuable concept in the Forties because it described certain apparently quite new phenomena. But the new concept rapidly became a slogan, not least thanks to Orwell's *Nineteen Eighty-Four*. And, as a political slogan in the Cold War, it ceased to be a working concept and became a substitute for thought.[16]

By now, one may safely conclude, the theory of totalitarianism has fallen into disuse among serious historians and social scientists. Maurice Cranston dropped *totalitarianism* from his *Glossary of Political Terms* (1966)[17] and the historian D. C. Watt, writing the entry on *totalitarianism* in the *Fontana Dictionary of Modern Thought*, used a confident past tense:

A theoretical view of Nazism, Fascism and Soviet Communism which sees them as examples of a political system dominated by a single party and an ideology . . . This view was much current in the 1930s–1950s period.[18]

A contributor asks the question 'Is totalitarianism a meaningful concept?' in *A Dictionary of the Social Sciences* (1964) and answers his question in an unambiguous negative.[19] The entry on *totalitarianism* in *The International Encyclopaedia of the Social Sciences* (1968) notes that the first *Encyclopaedia of the Social Sciences* (1930–5) had contained no such entry. It then describes the confusion and political mendacity surrounding the concept, and expresses the hope that the next encyclopaedia, like the first, will not list *totalitarianism*. Finally, the historian Walter Laqueur, in *The Fate of the Revolution* (1967), notes the passing away of the theory:

Some of the theories of the fifties have already been almost forgotten, for instance the concept of unchanging totalitarianism which arose under the impact of the late Stalin period. Events have since disproved it.[20]

This obituary is, however, a trifle premature. For the strange fact of the matter is that, although the concept is demonstrably defective and unproductive of knowledge, it continues to be used. Factual disproof may be inconvenient, but it is hardly decisive, because the real strength and durability of such ideological conceptions derives from their ability to provide psychologically satisfactory explanations. I am not, here, referring to conscious mendacity and hypocrisy – the hollow rhetoric of the 'Evil Empire'.[21] The concept continues to be used, in all innocence, by people to whom the idea of 'totalitarianism' is an essential part of their explanatory equipment. To take one random example: an eminent English professor was recently taken to task by a correspondent:

It seems that Professor Frank Kermode's political touch is far from certain. He dredges up an old piece of Cold War theory by stating that there was little difference between the totalitarianisms of Stalin and of Hitler . . . Fascism is a possibility of advanced capitalism and Stalinism a possibility of socialism. We can only began to guard against them both by being very clear in our definitions as to what they are.[22]

I would suggest, then, that the theory of totalitarianism is not only a weapon of mystification in the ideological cold war, it is all too often the form in which people 'mystify' themselves, since a false explanation is still preferable to none at all. The theory of totalitarianism lives, even after its clinical death, because it fulfils a certain need – perhaps even sets of needs. Thus, the word is used by dissident East European writers to describe their experience of 'actually existent socialism': even though their heroic persistence in the face of official discouragements is itself disproof of the gloomy theory. For Western liberals, I hope to show, totalitarianism occupies the space vacated by the liberal doctrine of human becoming under the impact of the realities of 'actually existent capitalism': it provides the negative utopia that substitutes for the eroded humanist aspiration of classical liberalism. For East Europeans, no doubt, it performs different functions: it is, variably, an ideological password, a cleansing expletive, an emotive metaphor for their uniquely tragic post-war destiny. Edward Said argued in *Orientalism* (1978) that while the theory of 'Orientalism' is not deeply illuminating about its ostensible subject, 'the Orient', it does in fact tell us much about the people who propounded, developed and held to the theory. Similarly with totalitarianism, its supersession as a tool of historical explanation merely makes it available as a key to the thinking of those who believed it to be such a tool, those who found 'true' the 'explanation' it provided.

One can, of course, only use it in this way if one chooses to do so. One might still go on pretending that the theory is in good health and, with William Steinhoff, say, 'take the view' that 'Orwell's development as a writer coincided with his growing knowledge and hatred of totalitarianism.'[23] What Steinhoff is doing here is hardly unique; indeed, I believe it is the besetting sin of much Orwell criticism: he is simply *assuming* that which needs to be *explained*. Because he obliterates or is unaware of the distance (or distinction) between the theory and historical actuality, Steinhoff is unable to see that the grip of a theory, the apparently irresistible and progressively stronger appeal for Orwell of a particular way of 'reading' the world around him, is not an explanation, it is the 'problem' that critical explanation must seek to address. Steinhoff's error is the one that is indicated in the Wordsworth epigraph at the head of this chapter: he has mistaken a theory for a thing, a material fact. This lapse, it will be seen, merely recreates the persistent difficulty with writing on Orwell: the fact of his plausibility, the disarming process whereby he tends to disappear as an object of critical attention and reappears instead as a wonderfully honest and therefore transparent and invisible 'reporter', a mere window upon a sordid world.

To summarise, then, I shall use the term *totalitarianism* and its derivatives in the following way.

(a) Totalitarianism (without inverted commas) refers to the theory of totalitarianism in its post-war incarnation. Fascism and Communism are, as explained above, manifestations of a single Evil, mysteriously erupting, or, in Hannah Arendt's influential formulation, a 'subterranean stream', breaking out.[24] (The earlier senses are either subsumed in this one or, as in the case of Gentile's theoretical contributions, have become irrelevant.) One of the long-term effects of this theoretical 'eruption' has been to blur and perhaps bury under its ash the subversive significance of what the capitalist crisis of the 1930s had revealed.

(b) 'Totalitarianism' (with inverted commas) refers to that which is the notional object of the theory of totalitarianism, the monster State, with its awesome apparatus, ruthlessly making itself and the world, according to Arendt, 'consistent'. It might be urged by apologists of the theory that there are distinct and remarkable (and not infrequently remarked) similarities between 'totalitarianism' and certain historical societies – Hitler's Germany and Stalin's Russia, for example. However, I shall use the alternative available descriptions of these societies since, if I wish to gain a critical perspective on totalitarianism, I must take my descriptive categories from outside the domain of the theory itself. In addition to designating the State which is the object of the theory, 'totalitarianism' is also used to denote the supposed dynamic principle of this State. I cannot on my account, it will be evident, take issue with anything that the theorists of totalitarianism aver about the nature of 'totalitarianism' since the latter is, crucially, *their* creature, to be moulded howsoever they will – in other words, I have no desire to *correct* the theory. Where I baulk is when the theorists start taking short cuts to historical reality, and the conceptual monster, 'totalitarianism', suddenly solidifies, 'reifies', into an allegedly material thing. Consider, for instance, this statement from Arendt's book, *The Origins of Totalitarianism* (1951), itself an important source book on the intellectual origins of the theory of totalitarianism:

The aggressiveness of totalitarianism springs not from lust for power, and if it feverishly seeks to expand, it does so neither for expansion's sake nor for profit, but only for ideological reasons: to make the world consistent.[25]

Such a statement is, within its conceptual limitation, unobjectionable. However, as an explanation of, say, Soviet actions in Eastern Europe during the period 1945–50, or of the German quest for *Lebensraum* at the expense of weaker nations, it is, at best, useless.

(c) Those who subscribe to the theory of totalitarianism are called, somewhat perversely, 'anti-totalitarian'. However, I felt that the confusion would be deeper if these adherents, like Borkenau and Koestler, were called, simply, totalitarians – which, on my terms, they are. This category, 'anti-totalitarian', in fact covers a large range, from the libertarian Left to the far Right. My own concern, particularly apropos Orwell, is with the Left adherents of the theory.

3

INVENTING A FORM

It is relatively easy to construct a smooth, harmonious account of Orwell's development as a writer. Characteristically, it is Orwell himself who provides the means by which this may be done. In 1946, from the achieved perspective of a (then) moderately successful career, Orwell wrote:

From a very early age, perhaps the age of five or six, I knew that when I grew up I should be a writer. Between the ages of seventeen and twenty-four I tried to abandon this idea, but I did so with the consciousness that I was outraging my true nature and that sooner or later I should have to settle down and write books.

(1, 1)

The way he tells it in 'Why I write' is that Orwell, returning from Burma when he was twenty-four, settled down to 'write books' and become the writer he became. Looked at from the perspective of 1946, and perhaps more particularly when looked at through the author's eyes, the development appears 'natural', mere manifestation of an existential and artistic destiny. We recognise Orwell's authentic voice in statements such as this:

My starting point is always a feeling of partisanship, a sense of injustice. When I sit down to write a book, I do not say to myself, 'I am going to produce a work of art.' I write it because there is some lie that I want to expose, some fact to which I want to draw attention, and my initial concern is to get a hearing.

(1, 6)

On the other hand we recall Orwell's letter to Brenda Salkeld, apropos *Keep the Aspidistra Flying*: 'I want this one to be a work of art' (1, 148). However, my contention is that the appearance of naturalness, the retrospective inevitability of the career suppresses, albeit with the author's connivance, the wide range of choices and emphases, the inner and finally creative contradictions which his notion of a 'writer' contained within itself, and so elides out of the story the *drama* of the making of George Orwell which is crucial to an understanding of this familiar, elusive 'writer'.

Orwell's influential repudiation of the literary radicalism of the 1930s in 'Inside the whale' makes it only too easy to see his development in an a-historical, decontextualised manner. As John Wain has argued, Orwell's later pronouncements on the phenomenon of 1930s literary radicalism tend to obscure the degree of his own complicity in it.[1] However, in order to comprehend the distinctive, paradoxical, embattled quality of Orwell's achievement, it is essential to situate Orwell in the cultural–literary context in which he was formed – and which he, too, helped to form. We have to recontextualise Orwell, despite the fact that even prior to those repudiations, Orwell was, always, an awkward and ill-fitting part of the necessary context in which he needs to be understood.

The single most decisive event which might be said to have produced 'the catastrophic impasse of the 'thirties'[2] happened, of course, in 1929, before the decade itself got under way. But in England, at any rate, it was not the Wall Street Crash which brought home the sense of crisis; it was rather the 'National' Coalition Government of 1931 which was cobbled together in an attempt to find a way out of the conditions that followed in the wake of the Great Crash. Persons as different as Harold Macmillan and John Strachey have testified that in 1931 they began to feel that they, and their country, had reached the end of a road. Macmillan, who was a Conservative back-bench MP at the time, wrote:

Up to 1931 there was no reason to suppose that [changes] would not, or could not follow the same evolutionary pattern which had resulted from the increased creation and distribution of wealth throughout the 19th century . . . Now, after 1931, many of us felt that the disease was more deep-rooted. It had become evident that the structure of capitalist society in its old form had broken down, not only in Britain but all over Europe and even in the United States. The whole system had to be reassessed. Perhaps it could not survive at all: it certainly could not survive without radical change . . . Something like a revolutionary situation had developed, not only at home but overseas.[3]

John Strachey has described the process of awakening to a sense of crisis:

The collapse of the second British Labour Government in the year 1931 was for me the decisive event. It was necessary for me to see with my own eyes and at close range the mingled impotence and treachery of social democracy in action.[4]

The means whereby the general socio-economic crisis worked itself into the aesthetic consciousness must have been complex and manifold. However, there was one fairly obvious level at which the larger crisis obtruded itself – by affecting the middle-class intellectuals who were the bearers of that aesthetic consciousness. Thus, Orwell offered a succinct explanation of the phenomenon: 'Middle-class unemployment' (1, 514). About six years prior to Orwell, Edgell Rickword wrote:

What had actually happened was that the licensed amenities mentioned [The pursuit of pleasure, the enjoyment of wit, the exercise of a sceptical intelligence, all the licensed relaxations of a prosperous economic dictatorship . . .] were no longer available even to the small number of the middle-class who had before been allowed access to them. Pleasure, and even wit, had by means of the film and heavily-capitalised publishing, irretrievably become *commodities*, and even the pose of 'cultural values', which had persisted through Matthew Arnold's lifetime, was no longer seriously kept up . . . In material ways, the economic crisis has very definitely worsened the conditions for the intellectual worker. There are fewer periodicals in which he can place articles, and the tendency to concentrate all a firm's selling power on a few best-sellers makes it almost impossible for him to get more than a pittance from book sales.[5]

Michael Roberts expressed the same moment of consciousness – the shoe beginning to pinch the middle-class wearer – somewhat more dramatically (but less analytically) in the 'Preface' to *New Country* (1933):

It is too late for a letter to *The Times*, Carlton House Terrace must go to the highest bidder, and the National Trust can never buy the whole of England. What is the use of isolated protests? You can't control exploitation for private profit in this piecemeal fashion, even though you bother only about the amenities of a cultured leisured class. It is time that those who would conserve something which is still valuable in England began to see that only a revolution can save their standards. It's past the stage of sentimental pity for the poor, we're all in the same boat.[6]

Noreen Branson and Margot Heinemann have summarised the process thus:

The years after 1931 undermined what remained of the long-standing sense of stability in British middle-class and intellectual life. The once-ordered society turned out to be disordered, immoral and dangerous. It was this, rather than any upsurge of romanticism, that led to the radicalisation of many intellectuals, and a crisis of outlook reflected in every aspect of art and culture.[7]

Orwell is among the writers who have expressed, and embodied, most clearly this sense of an aesthetic crisis:

The writers who have come up since 1930 have been living in a world in which not only one's life but one's whole scheme of values is constantly menaced. In such circumstances detachment is not possible. You cannot take a purely aesthetic interest in a disease you are dying from . . . Literature had to become political, because anything else would have entailed mental dishonesty.

(II, 126)

One cannot be too careful in speaking about 'a sense of crisis' in literary contexts. In one way and another, the expression seems relevant to a consideration of most literature – and modern literature in particular certainly appears to be propelled by an obscure dynamic of crises. The 1930s radicals, in a moment of perceived crisis, tried to reach beyond the metaphysical anguish of T. S. Eliot; but Eliot and Pound, loosening with urban ironies the suffocating embrace of Georgian pastoralism, were themselves self-consciously located at a point of perceived crisis in civilisation. Similarly, no doubt, the 'Apocalyptic' poets of the 1940s and the Angry Young Men of the 1950s saw themselves as writing out of critical historical moments. (Thus, one of the essays in the Angry Young Volume, *Declarations* (1956), was entitled, predictably, 'A sense of crisis'.)

However, despite this degree of general applicability which renders the expression somewhat blunt and unserviceable, it is still possible to say that the Great Crash of 1929 and the ensuing Depression brought home a sense of crisis to large numbers of people and gave to that amorphous 'sense' a hard, material content – expressed and confirmed it in highly visible images of social dysfunctioning. The sense of crisis which runs like an ironical leitmotif through the literature of our time suddenly acquired an irrefutable political dimension, an ineluctable physical presence. One no longer had to be sensitive to notice that something was very wrong – one had to be blind not to. Although it crystallised with relative suddenness, it is possible to detect adumbrations of this crisis in certain advanced quarters some years before 1929.

Writing in *The Calendar of Modern Letters* in July 1925, Edwin Muir explained the significance of James Joyce's *Ulysses* thus:

in the history of literature . . . the principle of selection sometimes becomes a conventional, an arbitrary one . . . therefore it is at rare times necessary for the artist to put himself in a position where a fundamental act of selection becomes compulsory, and where he feels that every decision, whether to include or reject, is significant not only on traditional grounds but is made by his own unconditional volition and as if for the first time. *Ulysses* not only raises the problem of selection again, in part it answers it by bringing into literature things banished from it . . .[8]

Edgell Rickword, in an important essay, 'The returning hero', sounds a similar note of aesthetic restlessness:

The literature of disillusionment is reaching the last stage; it is becoming popular with the reading public. Mr Strachey and Mr Huxley have Ruskin and Carlyle. No doubt, too, all young men of poetic ambition have their version of *The Waste Land* in their wash-stand drawer . . . Though we are not likely to cut any new ideals for a good many years, being hardly convalescent from the wholesale extractions of the last century, we cannot imagine the poets remaining content to cultivate the drugget-fields of genteel discontent. A Hero would seem to be due, an exhaustively-disillusioned Hero (we could not put up with another new creed) . . . who has yet so much vitality that his thoughts seize all sorts of analogies between unrelated objects . . . *The form of him is naturally still in question*, but we can be pretty sure that he will not be a Watts horseman in shining armour. Possibly he will be preceded (I should say that he is being preceded) by some tumbling, flour-faced harbingers to the progress . . . just as the death-facing wire walker in the circus is led into the ring by clowns who mime his tragedy.[9]

At the time this was written, it is interesting to note, Orwell was still in Burma. It is nevertheless possible to say that he was eventually to become, in some respects, the 'exhaustively-disillusioned Hero', a 'death-facing wire walker' who fashioned a vocation out of seeing through 'creeds' – 'smelly little orthodoxies', he called them. However, we should not forget, also, that for Orwell, returning in 1927 with a somewhat romantic conception of 'Art', his attempt to become a writer, in and of the thirties – to find his form – was bound to involve a struggle, not least with himself.

By 1930 social issues had become substantially more pressing and undeniable than they had appeared to the writers in *The Calendar of*

Modern Letters. In 1930 Herbert Read, reviewing Siegfried Sassoon's *Memoirs of an Infantry Officer*, rebuked Sassoon in unusual and significant terms: 'the aim is nothing but literary . . .'[10] In his 'Preface' to *New Country* (1933) Michael Roberts was even more explicit in his rejection of the 'literary':

Perhaps . . . 'literary' writing is tolerable in a time of stable tradition, but it is not tolerable at present. The writers in this book are trying to make something, to say something as clearly as may be, to express an attitude which this preface can only adumbrate. They are no more concerned with making 'literature' than Plato was, or Villon, or Wilfred Owen: 'The poetry is in the pity.'[11]

In October 1930 the *New Adelphi* was reincarnated as the *Adelphi* with the addition of Richard Rees to the editorial board. The first number of the new magazine, in which Orwell published a significant proportion of his early writing, carried, possibly under the influence of J. Middleton Murry, a pompous but significant statement of policy:

The first principle we desire to see governing the contents of this magazine is the apparently very simple one summed up in the phrase 'a sense of reality' . . . It is because so much of the literature of our day wears the mask of cynical indifference, superficial wit, or otiose amiability that we desire to react against the current tendency by seeking a sense of values commensurate with the glory of life and the majesty of death.[12]

Cambridge Left, a short-lived periodical of the early 1930s, carried this simple, typical epigraph on its cover:

> Now future's traps
> Challenge inertia;
> Choose buttercups
> Or hunger-marcher[13]

However, in the same issue of *Adelphi* in which Herbert Read rebuked Sassoon for being merely 'literary', Orwell chided Priestley in a markedly different accent:

a novelist is not required to have good intentions but to convey beauty . . . the indefinable, unmistakable thing we call beauty.

(1, 25, 26)

Orwell's earliest book reviews, wherein, so to say, his literary *principles* are revealed in contrast to his *practice*, are in fact surprisingly 'aesthetic' and Pateresque. Thus, Lewis Mumford is criticised for over-explaining Melville:

It was much better to have discoursed simply on the form, which is the stuff of poetry, and left the 'meaning' alone.

(I, 20)

Orwell goes on to describe Melville:

More important than this strength, he had – what is implied in real strength – passionate sensitiveness; to him seas were deeper and skies vaster than to other men, and similarly beauty was more actual and pain and humiliation more agonising . . . a man who felt more vividly than common men, just as a kestrel sees more vividly than a mole.

(I, 20–1)

The mature Orwell displayed a fine contempt for the literary Paris of the 1920s, in which so many Americans got 'lost':

when dollars were plentiful and the exchange-value of the franc was low, Paris was invaded by such a swarm of artists, writers, students, dilettanti, sightseers, debauchees and plain idlers as the world has probably never seen. In some quarters of the town the so-called artists must actually have outnumbered the working population.

(I, 493)

However, we should not allow this retrospective contempt to blur the fact that in 1928, somewhat belatedly but also at the beginning of his own literary apprenticeship, Orwell made essentially the same pilgrimage – he went to Paris to become a 'writer'. Ruth Pitter, who was closely involved with Orwell's early attempts to establish himself as a writer, remembers the change in him on his return from Paris. He appeared markedly more confident, and looked formidable in a broad-brimmed hat that he had picked up on the Left Bank,[14] reminiscent (curiously enough) of Joyce's Stephen Dedalus (who made a similar pilgrimage, then later mocked himself: 'My Latin Quarter hat, God, we simply must dress the character'[15]). It is true that although Orwell went to Paris for vaguely 'aesthetic' reasons, he mingled with and wrote about not the expatriate writers and artists but rather the disreputable citizens of 'rue du Coq d'Or'. Still, a letter which Orwell wrote from his sickbed in 1948 to Celia Kirwan gives one an idea of how much the Paris of the 1920s, tidily dismissed in *Inside the Whale*, had really meant to him:

It's lucky for you you're too young to have seen it in the twenties, it always seemed a bit ghost-like after that, even before the war. I don't know when I'll see France again.

(IV, 402)

It is strange to think of Orwell, who is in many respects the perfect symbol of the gritty, socially committed 1930s, as having started his apprenticeship in the Paris of the 1920s, about which Cyril Connolly wrote with his customary exuberance:

What we mean by the Twenties is a climate of dandyism and artistic creation which came to a head in 1922, year of *The Waste Land*, *Ulysses*, Valéry's *Charmes*, Rilke's *Elegies*, *Jacob's Room* and the *Forsyte Saga*. Proust was at his zenith, Bloomsbury buzzed, Huxley and the Sitwells scintillated; Lawrence was still respectable. Hardy, Conrad and Moore were still alive. France was cheap to live in, demobilised fugitives from prohibition or the family business reinforced Montparnasse. The Diaghilev ballet flourished. Paris went expatriate.[16]

The detail which brings out sharply the oddity of Orwell having even a part of his roots in 'expatriate' Paris is, in fact, the year which Connolly selects as being especially significant – 1922. Because it was in 1922 that Orwell went out to colonial Burma to become a policeman.

It is a delicate methodological problem how much stress one should lay on missed experiences, on absences. I would like to suggest nonetheless that not only did the fact that Orwell spent the years 1922–7 as a policeman in Burma endow him with a rich store of experience which, I hope to show later, immigrated into hidden and surprising corners of his personality, his implicit absence at a critical time from the Europe of his adult activity also contributed to that attitude of 'estrangement' which is so identifiably a part of Orwell's creative matrix.[17] Orwell's Burma years, perhaps, contributed negatively as well as positively to his air of being slightly anachronistic, a sort of Rip Van Winkle who had been not quite asleep, but awake in another country. It is, I believe, this experience of displacement which enables Orwell, who was after all a participant in the history he was describing, himself affected by the fashions and changes of perspective which affected those he was writing about, to adopt in 'Inside the whale' a cool, mediatory tone, valedictory, above the fray, distanced alike from the 'tragic sense of life' of the 1920s and the 'social purpose' of his contemporaries.

The English originals of Orwell's early Paris articles are, apparently, lost – and one has to make do with retranslations from the French. These retranslations certainly lack the precise flavour of the originals, but at any rate they allow one to see what the apprentice writer was up to. The first of these articles was on censorship in England, and was published on 6 October 1928 in a paper called *Monde*, which was edited by the Communist Henri Barbusse. Later, Orwell wrote a three-part article for *Le Progrès Civique* – this was entitled 'The great misery of the English worker' and consisted, somewhat ironically, of sections on the unemployed, the tramps and the beggars of London. These early articles indicate clearly that interest in hitherto-neglected areas of reality, the lives of the forgotten and the disinherited, which is associated with the literary radicals of the 1930s. In the terms of the *Cambridge Left* epigraph quoted earlier, Orwell was evidently one of those who, albeit with some ambivalence, 'chose' the 'hunger-marcher'. Indeed Orwell is of the thirties not merely in his choice of subjects but also, precisely, in his aesthetic anxieties and un-certainties, his experimental forays on the borders of literature and politics. Thus, the necessary counterpoint to the assertiveness of the epigraph is the following statement from the *same* issue of *Cambridge Left*:

Those who are left in their politics have to face certain problems as writers of prose or verse, but to formulate them successfully would be to have solved them. So it is most profitable to try and solve them by trial and error.[18]

Most literary rebellions march, somewhat confusingly, under the banner of 'reality' – against what is only apparently real, or is conventionally accepted as real, in favour of some reality which is, strangely, perceived to be 'more' real. There is, of course, no obvious sense in which a Wordsworthian countryman is more 'real' than one of Pope's perfumed ladies, or an unemployed miner's home more 'real' than the room which Prufrock is hesitant but ultimately not unwilling to enter, where the women talk of Michelangelo. To some extent, no doubt, these claims and counterclaims are explicable on the grounds of fashion, the jostling and elbowing of competing artists for a place in the sun. However, in their more serious forms, the moments of aesthetic crisis are merely aspects of a profounder crisis, and the apparent 'problematisation' of the 'real' is merely an incidental effect of a realignment of forces within the social body – 'reality' – itself.[19]

This radical challenge is felt, in the first instance, in the area of literary conventions. These conventions are, at one level, conventions of form, of what are, most generally, the appropriate shapes and strategies of literature. However, these conventions are also, in-evitably, conventions of content as well – bearing not only upon the appropriate shapes but also, through them, on preferred areas of experience. This might appear abstract, but a little consideration reveals that formal innovations are invariably accompanied by new content and might, indeed, be themselves necessitated by the pressure of a new content straining for recognition. The challenge of the literary radicals of the 1930s, therefore, was along the axes of both form and content. Bourgeois literature was attacked as meretricious and artificial. Isherwood's Philip Linsley (apparently a somewhat exaggerated portrait of Stephen Spender) 'temporarily abandoned Mayfair' to concentrate on the 'realler' reality to be found in North Kensington:

How he gloated over it! By the time he had finished with the district, there wasn't a window left unbroken; every pair of lace curtains was faded, every aspidistra was dusty, every venetian blind was falling to pieces.[20]

Orwell sneered at the literature of the 'well-fed':[21]

Some people, it is felt, justify their existence simply by possessing complicated emotions. They toil not, neither do they spin but their reasons for marrying and divorcing one another are more subtle than those of bricklayers.[22]

And complained further that:

people able to write books simply cannot get into contact with real life . . . [they] can't make contact with the manual workers, even if [they] want to.[23]

'History', Edward Upward wrote, using the word in a sense very close to 'reality':

was once in the castle on the cliff, in the sooty churches, in your mind; but it is abandoning them, leaving them only the failing energy of desperation, going to live elsewhere. It is already living elsewhere. It is living in the oppression and hustle of your work, in the sordid isolation of your lodgings.[24]

Such a fundamental challenge cannot be confined merely to literary modes – it is directed also against the life which finds its appropriate form within them, against what are perceived to be the bland surfaces of bourgeois life, hypocritically concealing 'reality', themselves mysteriously 'unreal'. A challenge as potentially radical as this involved, for Orwell as for his contemporaries, a struggle at the roots of the mind – because what they sought to combat was not, in its most significant aspect, externally imposed but, rather, internalised, imprinted and ingrained in the gestalt of the mind. Cecil Day Lewis wrote of a sense of inhibition and difficulty at the beginning of his career:

These nineteen-twentyish germs must be expelled from my system. Who are they to tell me that I must not preach? But it's difficult.[25]

There is indeed a further sense in which the sanctions *are* external – they work through the pressures which the middle-class audience – the only available audience – exerts even on a writer who seeks to locate himself outside its ambit.[26] As Orwell said in a broadcast discussion on the subject of proletarian literature:

So long as the bourgeoisie are the dominant class, literature must be bourgeois.

(II:14)

Such an assertion should not, however, lead us to obscure the subversive intention of Orwell's own literary endeavours, but merely alert us to the inherent difficulty of the project. Thus, consider this minor exhibit: Orwell is describing his fellow-sleepers in a kip in the Southwark Bridge Road. One of them was, Orwell tells us, a pale and consumptive youth, 'evidently a labourer, who was devoted to poetry. He repeated:

> A voice so thrilling ne'er was 'eard
> In Ipril from the cuckoo bird
> Briking the silence of the seas
> Beyond the furthest 'ebrides

with genuine feeling. The others did not laugh at him much' (1, 54). To whom, one asks, is the last sentence addressed – *ideally*, for 'Hop-picking' is only a diary fragment? I suggest that Orwell is sharing a joke with the derided 'well-fed' who *would* laugh at Wordsworth in a working-class accent, and would no doubt have found Keats's Cockney hilarious. In an unpublished letter to Dennis Collings, written on 27 August 1931 from a lodging house, Orwell again mentions the Wordsworth-reciting labourer and writes: 'I should love to hear him recite "O holy hope and high humility".'[27] One should not be too harsh on this, but one can hardly help noticing that the precise effect is achieved by keeping a foot in both worlds, not merely the obvious one in the sub-world of the derelicts, but a less obvious one in the world of middle-class literati.

This schizoid affiliation – to literati and to tramps, or, *mutatis mutandis*, to received aesthetic notions *and* to his recalcitrant experience of his time – holds the key to the sense of formal difficulty in Orwell's early writings. The formal incongruity, the critical and perhaps unavoidable ambivalence, is perhaps best illustrated, here, by looking at the 'deformation' of his early novels by the ingrained pressures of traditional literary modes.

It seems likely that Orwell, fresh from the experiences which had compelled him to abandon a safe career in the colonial police, *intended*, in *Burmese Days* (1934), to write a novel which could be a vehicle for his critique of imperialism. Years later, in 1942, Orwell wrote that *Burmese Days* contained 'the whole history' of his anti-imperialism (II, 228). Some six years before this, in *The Road to Wigan Pier*, Orwell expressed the opinion that his novel was really about Burmese landscapes (*The Road to Wigan Pier*, 110) but this seems to me merely a perverse misrepresentation of his novel and his intentions.

The action of *Burmese Days*, summarised briefly, is as follows: the protagonist, Flory, is a discontented timber agent who is both lonely and violently resentful of his fellow-colonials and of the colonial reality in which his life is cast. He has a Burmese mistress, Ma Hla May, whom he is getting tired of, and a Tamil friend, Dr Veraswamy. Dr Veraswamy is obsequious and verbose, but Flory's friendship with him is upsetting the wily Burmese magistrate U Po Kyin, who realises that in order to rise in the local hierarchy, he must get ahead of Dr Veraswamy, and in order to do that he must first destroy his white patron, Flory. Flory, meanwhile, falls in love with the husband-hunting Elizabeth Lackersteen who, after a brief idyllic phase, discovers that Flory has a mistress, and breaks off relations with him. There is a curious episode at the Club house, where the colonials are gathered, anxiously arguing about how to circumvent an official directive which requires them to admit a token 'native', Dr Veraswamy, as Club member. The Club house is attacked by a 'native' mob and Flory, who has failed earlier to make a stand on behalf of Dr Veraswamy, rises manfully to the stereotyped occasion. Flory tries, again, to regain the affections of Elizabeth, but she spurns him. Then, in a powerful final scene, when the colonials are gathered in the church for the police chief's funeral. Flory's mistress, also spurned, breaks into the church and humiliates herself – and so Flory – before the assembled multitude. Flory blows his brains out, Dr Veraswamy is disgraced, and U Po Kyin is made the token member.

In obvious ways, Orwell's novel is located deliberately athwart the conventions of colonial fiction. A protagonist such as Flory, weak and dissolute, can only be a calculated departure from the traditional heroes of colonial fiction, who are 'all sunburn and stern renunciation'.[28] Then again, by showing the whites of the colonial station off-duty, so to speak, Orwell punctures with deadly effect the mystique of the pioneers of civilisation, the myth of 'the white man's burden' and of 'the Frontier' beyond which lurk the forces of native barbarism. Mrs Lackersteen is a furiously parodic reincarnation of a traditional stereotype. The necessary counterpoint to the Strong White Man in colonial fiction had been his equally staunch mate – not rough and unmaternal, but transformed by the spirit of sacrifice into something far above mere human weakness. In Ollivant's *Old For-ever* (1923), for example, Marion Oliver loses her only son because she is away in the wilds helping her husband to cope with the oddly murderous business of 'civilisation'. When she learns of her son's death, she brushes away an unseen tear and shrugs her shoulders in stoical resignation to higher duty. Mrs Lackersteen, too, accompanies her husband into the malarial jungle, but only in order to prevent him from drinking and fornicating. Orwell's protagonist is indecisive and maundering, his fellow-colonial are drunks and lechers, the narrative is interlarded with anti-imperialist diatribes in which the persona of the fictional Flory is barely maintained – but even so, a close examination suggests that the sheer stress of writing a 'novel' exerts a powerful drag towards traditional resolutions.

Although the overtly stated sympathies are clearly anti-imperialist, the actual references to Burmese nationalism, which constitutes the political background, are consistently contemptuous and belittling, and the 'natives' are caricatures drawn from the traditional mode of colonial fiction. The newspaper in which Mr McGregor is vilified is the *Burmese Patriot*, and when Orwell describes the imprisonment of its editor, the division of sympathy, or more precisely, the balance of antipathy, is evident in the juxtaposition of these sentences:

His arrest had provoked a small riot in Rangoon, which was suppressed by the police with the death of only two rioters. In prison the editor went on hunger strike, but broke down after six hours.

(*Burmese Days*, 111)

Orwell's ambivalence is mirrored in the ambivalence of his relationship to his protagonist, Flory. At one level, clearly, Orwell approves of the sensitive and thoughtful qualities with which he has endowed Flory, and which differentiate him from the 'dull louts' who congregate at the Club. The authorial concurrence is clear in the accents of Flory's speculations on imperialism:

What was at the centre of all his thoughts now, and what poisoned everything, was the ever bitterer hatred of the atmosphere of imperialism in which he lived. For as his brain developed – you cannot stop your brain developing, and it is one of the tragedies of the half-educated that they develop late, when they are already committed to some wrong way of life – he had grasped the truth about the English and their Empire.

(*Burmese Days*, 68)

It is interesting to observe, however, how the vehemence of this outburst is contained. After railing against his narrow-minded, boring, bigoted compatriots and *their* 'Bonzo'-based culture, Flory rounds it off with a surprising *mea culpa*: 'God have mercy on us, for all of us are part of it' (*Burmese Days*, 33). By switching abruptly from 'them' to 'ours' and 'us', Flory's anger is defused, quenched in a vague, passive complicity. Unquenched, it would have forced the author up against the inertial strength of the traditional shapes of colonial fiction – forced him either to endorse his protagonist's perceptions and constitute the novel's action on the basis of that endorsement, or else to abandon him. Consider, for example, the 'formal' function of Flory's birthmark. At one level, it is the formal analogue of his difference from the others. At another, it is symbolic also of his abnormality, and serves to discredit the sentiments voiced through him. Each time Flory acts or, more accurately, thinks of acting on his principles, he becomes aware of his birthmark, and his voice goes 'flat and guilty' (*Burmese Days*, 63; 235). The symbolic significance of his birthmark becomes clearer through his death:

With death, the birthmark had faded immediately, so that it was no more than a faint grey stain.

(*Burmese Days*, 282)

Symbol of that which was alive in him, the birthmark is barely visible after he is dead, merged as it were with the common body. It is thus implied – by Flory (*Burmese Days*, 72–3) and by his author – that 'his criticism is a function of his isolation, his desperate need to be understood, which is in turn a function of his bachelorhood, and that of his disfigurement'.[29] This is remarkably similar, as a formal device, to the red hair (symbolic of Irishness) or Jewishness (dark hair, big nose, etc.) which was used, in traditional colonial writing, to discredit anti-colonial sentiments. For instance, the anti-colonial Donald McGregor in Gordon Casserly's *The Elephant God* (1920) is, we are told in a significant aside, only a 'Hebrew Highlander', a false Scotsman.[30]

A crucial part of the action of *Burmese Days* is predicated upon the friendship between Flory and Dr Veraswamy. This is clearly anti-conventional – but, by the same token, Orwell's failure to make a man of the good doctor, to suggest a basis on which such a subversive relationship of equality could rest, is also significant. Although the fact of the relationship subverts the tradition, Dr Veraswamy keeps slipping helplessly into the stereotype of the 'comic native', with his convoluted English and his ingratiating mannerisms – a stereotype which derives precisely from the tradition that the author is seeking to subvert. This is why when, towards the end of the novel, Dr Veraswamy rushes to minister to his friend, and finds him dead, we find his natural grief unexpected, abrupt and embarrassing (*Burmese Days*, 282). Interestingly enough, when Dr Veraswamy speaks on this occasion, it is not with the conventional accents, the stressed sibilants and the serpentine syntax of the 'comic native':

I will tell Mr McGregor that it happened accidentally while he was cleaning his revolver . . . Your master was my friend. It shall not be written on his tombstone that he committed suicide.

(*Burmese Days*, 282)

(On earlier occasions – pages 43 and 256 – 'was' had been 'wass'.) Even the simple dignity of his last words strikes us as uncharacteristic because Orwell has not prepared us for a real human being.

In his essay on Charles Dickens, Orwell suggested an interesting test of a writer's attitudes:

One thing that often gives a clue to a novelist's real feelings on the class question is the attitude he takes up when class collides with sex. This is a thing too painful to be lied about, and consequently it is one of the points at which the 'I'm not a snob' pose tends to break down. One sees that at its most obvious where a class-distinction is also a colour-distinction.

(I, 437)

Trans-racial heterosexual liaisons were notoriously difficult territory for colonial writers. In the early part of the nineteenth century when, as it happens, Englishwomen were scarcer in the East and British dominion was surer, there was no stigma attached to these liaisons.[31] Even earlier, trans-racial liaisons were actually encouraged and the Court of Directors of the East India Company even provided a subsidy for the purpose.[32] But from about mid-century, such unions began to be looked upon with disfavour. As a consequence, the native mistresses of fictional colonials began dying off in large numbers. (The

Suez Canal, opened in 1869, has a lot to answer for!) In *Fitch and His Fortunes* (1898) by G. Dick, the 'fair Indian' Savitra Bai commits suicide. In *Self and the Other* (1901) by 'Victoria Crosse', Narayanah Chandmad, the 'heaven-sent guest' of Francis Heath, is removed in time by the plague. In *The Jewel of Malta* (1927) by Donald Sinderby, Kamayala enters a convent and thus 'saves' Sir John Bennville. In *The Scorpion's Nest* (1929) by Joan Angus and Hope Fielding, Anarculli, who is determined to marry John Ferguson, is killed in a fight. In Kipling's 'Without benefit of clergy', the child of the union of Holden and Ameera dies first, and further miscegenation is prevented by the invention of a cholera epidemic which kills Ameera. Maud Diver in *Far To Seek* (1921) does 'allow' a successful marriage between Lilamani Singh and Sir Nevil Sinclair, but only on certain conditions – the former converts to Christianity, and the couple live in England to avoid further contamination.[33] In an article entitled 'The Indian mutiny in fiction', published in *Blackwood's Edinburgh Magazine* in February 1897, we can observe the conventions of handling trans-racial liaisons in colonial fiction in an interesting state of flux. Commenting on Colonel Meadows Taylor's novel *Seeta* (1872), in which Cyril Brandon marries Seeta, who has fought alongside her husband against the mutineers, the reviewer complains:

the reader is beginning to anticipate Seeta's conversion to Christianity, and a long happy life for her with Brandon, when she is mortally wounded while giving the alarm during a sudden attack. This sudden and violent ending to Brandon's difficulties strikes us as akin to the action of the player who upsets the chessboard because he can see no way of winning.

Eventually, Brandon marries a nice English girl.

Some related inhibition seems to be at work in Orwell's realisation of Ma Hla May. Almost till the last scene, she is little more than a convenience which Flory has employed but has now outgrown. At the very end, however, Ma Hla May, harrying Flory, hurt and unforgiving in the twilight, explodes into humanity. In the last scene, stripping herself before the shocked mourners, forcing them (and us) to look at her, she acquires – through the author – a sluttish dignity for which we have not been prepared – again, by the author. Orwell would, at the level of 'plot', have us believe that she is merely a puppet subserving U Po Kyin's machinations. However, and this is in some paradoxical sense almost despite the author, there is more 'anti-imperialism' in the way in which the exploitative personal relationship, itself symbolic of the larger colonial one, erupts into Flory's dream of domesticity, than there is in all of Flory's authorially underwritten and self-doubting diatribes. Still, there *is* one sense in which, despite everything, the colonial tradition regarding trans-racial liaisons is significantly modified by Orwell: in *Burmese Days* it is not the woman but the man who dies!

It is, finally, with some sense of shock that we realise how heavily the 'mob scene' of Orwell's anti-colonial novel draws upon the traditional mainstream of colonial writing. It is true that Orwell does not lose all sense of proportion and transform the hitherto mocked characters into heroes and heroines. But, that notwithstanding, the dominant tone of the writing is far from mock-heroic, and Flory's act of single-handed courage against insuperable – but 'native' – odds draws unashamedly on the tradition that grew out of (and perhaps into) legends like those of Clive at Arcot and Gordon at Khartoum. Not only is this sudden heroic dimension psychologically incredible in the maundering Flory, there are other details as well which suggest that there might be some traditional interference at work in the anti-colonial inspiration. Thus, from the beginning, Ellis is presented as the very type of the bigoted racist – a fact that is the cause of some fine comedy in the scene between him and the young Verrall. Ellis thinks Verrall, a relative stranger, should not have kicked the butler: 'You're not even a member of this club. It's our job to kick the servants, not yours.' The insolent Verrall offers to kick him as well (*Burmese Days*, 208). But in the mob scene, not only is it Ellis whom Flory volunteers to defend, but Ellis is accorded a dignity which strikes one as gratuitous: thus, while the 'native' clerk 'scooted' indoors when the stones began to fly, Ellis merely 'disdained to run' (*Burmese Days*, 243). Aung has suggested[34] that for this scene Orwell was probably drawing upon an incident in which he had himself been involved. The young police officer had been taunted by some schoolboys and he had resorted to violence against them. Aung has written that he was himself one of those schoolboys. If Aung is right then Orwell's personal complicity in the memory might have been transformed into sympathy for Ellis in the fictional scene which drew upon that memory.

There is a telling little incident in the aftermath of the riot which encapsulates, as it were, the limits of at least Flory's rebellion. After the mob disperses, Flory discovers that Dr Veraswamy has been beaten up in attempting to pacify the rioters. As he holds out his damaged knuckles for Flory to see, U Po Kyin enters, in 'studious neglige', angling to get a share of whatever credit might be going. Flory tries, not very effectively, to speak on behalf of the doctor. By this time, however, they have arrived at the Club gate, and this, one must remember, is the *only* time in the novel that the three principal characters are shown together:

At the Club gate all three men halted. It was now extraordinarily dark . . . Low overhead, just visible, black clouds were streaming eastwards, like a pack of hounds . . . All three men turned and hurried for shelter, the Orientals to their houses, Flory to the Club. It had begun raining.

(*Burmese Days*, 255)

They divide, finally, along racial lines, and Flory, deserting his friend, finds sanctuary in the bosom of that community which he professes, with conviction, to despise. It seems clear to me that Flory's suicide – his 'voluntary' abdication from the scene – allows Orwell an easier, cleaner conclusion to his 'anti-imperialist' novel than would otherwise have been possible. If Flory had not died, the novelist would have been compelled to alter the fictional–colonial reality to accommodate him.

It is perhaps not necessary to look at *A Clergyman's Daughter* and *Keep the Aspidistra Flying* in similar detail in order to illustrate the formal difficulty and incongruity, the process of 'deformation', in Orwell's early novels which I am trying to establish. We might recall, in this context, a remark which Orwell made in a letter to Julian Symons, written while he was revising *Nineteen Eighty-Four*:

I am not a real novelist anyway . . . One difficulty I have never solved is that one has masses of experience which one passionately wants to write about . . . and no way of using them up except by disguising them as a novel.

(IV, 422)

The word 'disguising' suggests the difficulty that I am indicating – that is, the novel as conceived by Orwell in traditional terms is not the natural form that his experience takes.

The urgency of the reality of pain and suffering outside a narrowly circumscribed range, ignored alike by bourgeois art as by the bland banalities of bourgeois social intercourse, the felt pressure of life unlived and only partly lived, which drove Orwell, and others, beyond the confines of what was traditionally available as literary material, and also beyond conventional ways of thinking about the social crisis in which their lives were cast, might be seen at work even in a potboiler like *A Clergyman's Daughter*. It is the sense of life unlived which causes Dorothy's breakdown. *A Clergyman's Daughter* starts off conventionally enough, with a heroine in a country rectory. But the novel's energy derives from her discontent with that life. Therefore she is rather crudely 'translated' to the areas which Orwell 'passionately wants to write about', displaced from the country rectory in Suffolk to her experiences on the road. A new and undomesticated content has broken up the inadequate former, formal, home. The 'disguise' is thin, but not non-existent, and the very necessity of 'disguise' generates pressures which force Dorothy back to the life from which she had fled with Orwell's connivance. The patched-up, 'novelistic' resolution, the awkward affirmation at the end of *A Clergyman's Daughter* – 'doing what is customary, useful and acceptable' (*A Clergyman's Daughter*, 319) – is essential to the novel as it stands. The interesting but open question is whether the affirmation causes the novel to end as it does or whether the reluctance to break the traditional formal moulds in turn generates the affirmation as its necessary justification.

The protagonist of *Keep the Aspidistra Flying*, again, elects to break from conventional middle-class life – a safe career in advertising, raising a family – in quest of states of meaning which are perceived to be unavailable within it. The action and substance of the novel is provided by Comstock's rebellion against the 'money-code'. His criticism of contemporary society is represented with considerable rhetorical energy and conspicuous authorial sympathy. However, there is a crucial ambivalence in the inspiration, and the 'conventional', feeding off that ambivalence, affects both the form and substance of the novel. Thus, while one part of Orwell is in sympathy with Comstock's petulant and romantic rejection of his society, another part also judges the rejection as callow and self-indulgent, perhaps even wrong. Come novel-end, Comstock must be brought back to the once-rejected world of petty-bourgeois gentility. It is this conflict which provides the novel's energy but which also, ultimately, tears the novel apart in the manner described by Dorothy Van Ghent:

the satirical energy which Orwell expends on Gordon Comstock's world is too insistent and furious to be taken as the emotion informing a comedy of manners; Gordon's peace with the aspidistra makes his revolt merely a touchingly awkward pose of youth; and the problem of maintaining moral identity in the lower-middle-class is broken in two like a surrealist cadaver.[35]

It cannot, again, be determined whether an attitudinal conservatism determines Comstock's eventual surrender to the world of
aspidistras and advertising, or whether, on the other hand, there is at
work a kind of formal conservatism – a notion, say, of 'well-rounded
action' – which resolves the conflict at the heart of the novel in a
particular way.[36] What can be said, however, is that the formal
constraints which shape the novel are at odds with the radical
energies implicit in the novel's action.

If, for instance, we compare the 'anti-imperialism' of *Burmese Days*
– consisting in the main of Flory's hysterical, self-doubting rantings –
with that of 'Shooting an elephant' (1936), we notice a surprising
maturity.

Orwell was gently mocking John Lehmann when he wondered, in a
letter written in response to Lehmann's invitation to write for *New
Writing* (1:79), if there was much 'anti-Fascism' in an account of a
colonial police officer's shooting of an elephant, but the essay is justly
famous as being a deeply felt condemnation of the imperialist
relationship. The essay is too well known to require more than the
briefest summary. An elephant has managed to unchain itself during
its periodic bout of 'madness' and is rampaging through the town. The
white police officer is, naturally, summoned to take the necessary
action – a summons which he, equally naturally, answers. Yet it is,
paradoxically, while he is playing the part of the Brave White Sahib
that the protagonist realises the futility and corruption of imperialist
domination:

it was at this moment, as I stood there with the rifle in my hands, that I first
grasped the hollowness, the futility of the white man's dominion in the East.
Here was I, the white man with his gun, standing in front of the unarmed
native crowd – seemingly the leading actor of the piece; but in reality I was
only an absurd puppet pushed to and fro by the will of those yellow faces
behind. I perceived in this moment that when the white man turns tyrant it is
his own freedom that he destroys.

(I, 239)

He is trapped in an unacceptable relationship – and the entrapment,
as well as the complex untenability of the dehumanising relationship,
is dramatised vividly in Orwell's description of the action which is the
ostensible subject of the essay. The elephant, now peaceful, beating a
'bunch of grass against his knees . . . with that preoccupied grand-
motherly air that elephants have' (I, 240), has to be shot anyway,
because that is what is expected of the Brave White Sahib in the play

which he invented but in which he is now, equally certainly, trapped. The elephant's dying, however, is not immediate – it is harrowing and prolonged, and this is registered by Orwell in precise, passionate prose:

> In that instant, in too short a time, one would have thought, even for a bullet to get there, a mysterious, terrible change had come over the elephant. He neither stirred, nor fell, but every line of his body had altered. He looked suddenly stricken, shrunken, immensely old . . . His mouth slobbered. An enormous senility seemed to have settled upon him. One could have imagined him thousands of years old. I fired again.
>
> (I, 241)

Yet it is only the third shot which brings the elephant down, trumpeting 'for the first and only time'. But even then he does not die, but merely:

> gasps, his great mound of a side painfully rising and falling. His mouth was wide open – I could see far down into caverns of pale pink throat. I waited a long time for him to die.
>
> (I, 241)

The death agony of the wounded elephant is a kind of extended reproach, a sudden and unexpected image of that colonial damage which can neither be undone nor decently, quickly, buried. 'He was dying', Orwell notes, 'very slowly and in great agony.' The sympathetic suffering of the colonial officer is intensified by the fact that, unable as he is to undo the terrible violence which he has inflicted, he is unable also, with that violence which is his sole allotted part, to reach into 'some world remote from me' where the elephant is slowly, accusingly, dying but 'where not even a bullet could damage him further . . . In the end I could not stand it any longer and went away.'

The explanation for this sudden maturity is to be found, as we shall see, in Orwell's discovery, in and through the process of writing *The Road to Wigan Pier*, of a form adequate to the knotty complexity of his response to his time: a form that did not enjoin the reductive, deformative, disjunctive violence which we have seen in the early novels. From this perspective, the formal disorder in Orwell's early writings appears as something positive, the index of a new content straining to find its appropriate form. The clumsy and awkward shifts, the creaking contrivances, the restlessness and unease, become clues to Orwell's characteristic strength and originality, and point the way to that formal breakthrough which enabled Orwell to become Orwell.[37]

We have observed at least two strategies whereby the 'problematis-ation' of the 'real' – the perception of the arbitrariness involved in conferring artistic 'reality' on selected aspects of our common, commonsensical world – might be evaded. The first is the apparently 'progressive' one whereby 'reality' is relocated among the lives of the forgotten and the disinherited, the poor, the neglected and the exploited. Orwell himself is, as we have seen, prone to this sentimental though well-intentioned strategy. The surfaces of bourgeois life are first distinguished from the reality which the protagonists seek in alternative locations, then, mysteriously – strategy two – again sanctified within the work itself with 'reality'. In this way, the reasserted dominion of the empirical, the 'given', actual, ordinary world displaces the uncertainties of philosophical scepticism as well as the radical challenge implicit in the initial secession of the protagon-ists. However, it surely must be the case that 'reality', once lost, may not simply be 'found' anywhere again, no more down a coal mine than among spiky, polished aspidistras. What is valuable in the process must be the problematisation itself, the 'defamiliarisation' of a given, everyday reality – *and* the recovery, therefore and therefrom, of the creativity as well as the responsibility of the *act* of observation itself, through a kind of willed innocence, a paradoxically canny naiveté.

Orwell is able to achieve this innocence by refusing to accept any of the convenient or available formulations – whether of the Left or Right – by forcing himself to work through a persona through whom the drama of the act of observation might be recreated. This persona is, I believe, valuable not so much for the individual findings, which are often commonplace, but rather because the persona is, in itself, a living record, like a worked-over manuscript, of the process of finding out, of the difficulties of knowledge and commitment. Orwell de-scribed one of his earliest 'literary' exploits as consisting of 'the making up of a continuous "story" about myself . . . soon my "story" ceased to be narcissistic in a crude way and became more and more a mere description of what I was doing and the things I saw' (1:1). This is, we notice, a striking anticipation of his mature literary practice as a clear-eyed observer, but one must attend also to the obvious implication that the 'mere description', even at its most apparently neutral, needs to be understood, despite the 'transparent' prose, in terms of 'a continuous "story" about myself'. However, in creating his literary persona, the man who existed at the crossroads of history, who had seen all and suffered all, who was endowed with a relentless openness to experience and an innocence of artifice, Orwell developed, in time, the perfect myth, 'Orwell': a myth which could, finally, carry the range of his disparate concerns, his passionate but uncoordinated loyalties, without formal stress. The fact that the 'transformation' of Blair into Orwell – the subsuming of Blair in Orwell, the usurpation of Blair by Orwell – was an event or process of some significance has been widely recognised by Orwell critics.[38]

Considering how crucial this aesthetic strategy – the adoption of a pseudonym – is to his overall achievement, it is chastening to discover that Orwell more or less blundered into it:

I think if it is all the same to everybody I would prefer the book to be published pseudonymously.

(I, 85)

However, 'Orwell' is obviously more than a mere pseudonym – it is also Orwell's aesthetic opportunity, a formal device, a strategy. It enables Orwell to dramatise the act of observation by embodying it in a creation which partakes of both the authority of fact and the licence of fiction, and at one remove, in the creations of that creation. Did Orwell really witness a hanging, or shoot an elephant? 'Orwell' certainly did. Orwell's work raises delicate questions of factuality because of the manner of assent it appears to demand, but it can also evade those questions with an equally delicate dexterity by invoking its aesthetic defence. The events in *Down and Out in Paris and London* have been 'rearranged', the incidents recounted in *The Road to Wigan Pier* have been sharpened,[39] but their factuality is thereby, curiously, refined rather than impaired. Did Orwell really have an unhappy childhood, although his sister suggests that he didn't?[40] Was St Cyprian's really as awful as Orwell makes it out to be in 'Such, such were the joys'? Clearly, for 'Orwell' it must have been, needs to have been.

It is in *The Road to Wigan Pier* that the pseudonym, so casually adopted for *Down and Out in Paris and London*, finally becomes an enabling persona, and it is a relief to turn from the knotted, clotted rhetoric of *Keep the Aspidistra Flying*, choking on self-hatred, to the essential fluency of *The Road to Wigan Pier*. In many obvious ways, *The Road to Wigan Pier* makes a break from Orwell's previous writings. The physical journey to the Depression-hit North of England, the structured exploration in contrast to the apparently random 'low-life' excursions of the past, where he had slipped into 'disguise' at his various 'drops', is only the most visible aspect of this. In a deeper sense, too, it was in and through *The Road to Wigan Pier* that Orwell finally discovered his precise commitment to the historical experience of his time or, what is the same thing, discovered an enabling form to experience fully and express that commitment. In *The Road to Wigan Pier*, finally, he shed 'disguises' and travelled as himself, Orwell.

There is, however, a paradox here which needs to be thought about: why does Orwell's creative imagination appear more thwarted in a fictional mode, in which he can exercise a relatively more untrammelled freedom, rather than in a quasi-realistic mode, such as *The Road to Wigan Pier* represents, in which the exercise is necessarily constrained by the resistance of the actual? One possible explanation is that the relative 'impersonality' of the novel form allows Orwell too readily to express his 'masochism' – the strenuous self-division that manifests itself in his curiously adversarial relationship to his fictional protagonists – without, as it were, having to take responsibility for it. In the novels he can torment his autobiographical protagonists, his creations, and simultaneously, so to speak, pretend to be Joyce's God, uninvolved, paring his fingernails. The resultant impression is that of a sensibility wastefully but also innocently at war with itself. In the quasi-realistic autobiographical form, on the other hand, there is an element of inhibition – in other words, Orwell can only allow his self-undermining 'masochism' free rein under cover ('disguise') of fiction. The inhibition therefore, paradoxically, frees him for utterance. However, another explanation is also possible and, to me at any rate, more persuasive. The apparent 'masochism', I suggest, is itself only an effect, a symptom. Thus, I suggest, the conservative element in Orwell's make-up which 'contains' the rebellion or breakout, be it Flory's or Dorothy's or Comstock's, the affiliation which manifests itself as a 'masochistic' deflation by the author himself of the authorially underwritten recalcitrance – this can find *independent* expression in a less organic, more open-ended, discursive form. When the antagonistic elements of the authorial personality are not forced into relation with each other, the 'masochism' disappears. (It re-appears, and to deadly aesthetic effect, in *Nineteen Eighty-Four* – see below, chapter 6: 'The roads to Airstrip One'.) The constitutive open-endedness of 'Orwell', the creature of paradox and contradiction, frees Orwell from the necessity, manifested as 'masochism', of integrating his conflicting attitudes and loyalties within a conventional aesthetic unity.

If one asks, for example, in what respect, 'Orwell' is different from, say, Comstock in *Keep the Aspidistra Flying*, the boldness of the strategy becomes readily apparent. Comstock, too, is a quasi-autobiographical character, living in society and reflecting upon it, but his dividedness, his strenuous anguish, is ultimately merely an aberration, an inconvenience which, though it is the source of such vivacity as the novel has, must also be domesticated, tamed within an alien formal intention. Comstock's hesitations, his existential uncertainties, must be subverted, shown up to be merely a form of childish self-indulgence – otherwise they would have to be shown to lead beyond both the romantic garret and the 'real' aspidistra. 'Orwell', on the other hand, is a formal principle in itself. I have said above that in 'Orwell' Orwell had found a myth which could carry the range of his concerns without stress. However, it would be nearer the truth to say that in 'Orwell' the stress is internalised, appropriated as itself the major subject, so that it ceases to be merely disruptive and reappears as the constitutive principle instead. The internal oppositions – Orwell's susceptibility to and sympathy with tradition in its many forms, *and* with the radical challenges thereto – are disabling in the fiction, functioning as a kind of insubordinate and random negative capability. However, these same oppositions could be turned to advantage within the quasi-autobiographical, quasi-historical myth which we know as 'Orwell'. The ambivalence and self-division, far from disabling Orwell as 'Orwell', become creative, and provide the existential guarantee of the latter's continuing dialectical life.

Self-division and ambivalence, though it is often disguised as dogmatism, is, I suggest, Orwell's key theme, and by working through, and simultaneously towards a mythical persona which is constituted precisely through the stress between contending elements, between contradictory yearnings and divided loyalties, Orwell is playing to his characteristic strength instead of aspiring vainly towards a wholeness – aesthetic, spiritual, ideological – which is simply not his.[41] There are several important corollaries which derive from this aesthetic of acknowledged self-division. There is, most obviously, the directness of address, of tone and language, the feeling of release which comes from having escaped the need for, to use Orwell's word, aesthetic 'disguises'. Flowing from this directness, there is also a sense of loose-limbed, wide-ranging flexibility; paradoxically enough, for someone who is escaping from the compulsion of finding unified aesthetic disguises, a kind of have-masks-will-travel quality. Indeed, most of what is most characteristic of Orwell has either its source or at least its sanction in this aesthetic of division. However, what is perhaps most remarkable is the light which this aesthetic sheds on Orwell's remarkable and much-remarked honesty. I believe that this acknowledged and confessed and avowed and proclaimed self-division underlies the *rhetoric* of Orwell's honesty – that is, in its formal aspect. The self-division itself provides a kind of all-purpose verification principle in as much as it renders Orwell, in every position, that most dependable of witnesses, an 'unwilling' one,[42] testifying against the grain of something which he has himself written elsewhere. The 'reluctance' does not of course impair the fluency, but it provides that fluency with something like moral ballast. It is amusing, nonetheless, to discover that when, towards the end of volume III of his unpublished 'Domestic diaries' (7 May 1946 to 5 January 1947), Orwell drew up a list of 'propaganda tricks', the sixth of these is the 'unwilling witness'![43]

The formal peculiarity of *The Road to Wigan Pier* hardly needs to be stressed. The first part is a fairly straightforward account of conditions in the areas described, competent but not exceptional. The second part boldly shifts focus from the scenes observed to the observer himself, his development, his thoughts on related subjects. There must undoubtedly be a certain irreducible element of personality in all reportage, be it by Cobbett or Defoe, but the candid and overt presentation of the self in *The Road to Wigan Pier* is clearly something different. I think it should be admitted outright that *The Road to Wigan Pier* is *not* very satisfactory considered simply as reportage. If one is simply interested in conditions in the North of England during the mid-1930s, then the digression, almost as long as the report itself, into personal history is bound to seem irrelevant. Still, whatever the value of *The Road to Wigan Pier* as a piece of social history, both by virtue of what it describes and by virtue of what it is, that value is for my purposes secondary to the fact that in it Orwell achieves the formal breakthrough which enables him to harness the conflicting loyalties, the self-divisions, which had merely hampered him so far. Because Orwell is able, or rather, enables himself, to forego the quest for consistency and unity within the self, his writing acquires the aura of an unselfish fidelity to the ambivalence of reality itself. This is, I would suggest, a deceptive transparency, because what appears like 'selfless' transparency is really a dissolution into many selves, and a consequent multiplication of perspectives. However, it is sufficient here to note that, as a consequence of what I consider a formal breakthrough, Orwell is able to *utilise* his self-division by reflecting it on to or aligning it with the contradictory persuasions of a complex reality.

It might be instructive, at this point, to recall John Bayley's perceptive observation about Kipling:

In such a compartmented mind, of a kind familiar to us from daily human contact but not often met with in great writers ... we experience contradictions and prejudices which do not meet and examine one another except through our presence ... the compartments act like a modern equivalent of what Keats called 'negative capability'.[44]

This has, particularly in the light of the discussion above, an obvious application to Orwell who, by inventing and working through the persona of 'Orwell', enables himself to abandon the need for consistency within the self. Thus 'enabled', Orwell can represent in a raw, 'honest' form 'contradictions and prejudices', the stuff of the complex and unsystematic response of ordinary people in ordinary situations. It is in this way, by adopting the protective colouring of the ordinary, that Orwell is able to attain the 'invisibility' and plausibility which we have remarked earlier. By freeing himself from the demands of internal coherence, Orwell achieves a sort of *external* coherence, a kind of plausibility 'familiar to us from daily human contact'.[45]

In a valuable essay on the writers of the 1930s, Arnold Rattenbury distinguished between 'writers driven by the logic of their engagement as writers to intellectual positions which in the end involve them in political action, and writers whose politics had no such profound connection to those springs of being out of which they write'.[46] Orwell, quite clearly, belongs in the former category. He is not merely seeking blue-book data in Wigan, he is also, in a curious sort of way, making himself, taking one more step along 'the road from Mandalay' (*The Road to Wigan Pier*, 123). The divisions within Orwell – between artist and rapporteur, between socialist and nostalgic sentimentalist – are no doubt *inherited* from Blair, but as 'Orwell' in *The Road to Wigan Pier*, he faces up to, and publicly acknowledges, these divisions, and derives a creative dynamic from the tension between them.

What preserves the products of this 'dynamic' from degenerating

into mere introspective mumbling, what facilitates Orwell's movement from the personal to the historical, is of course not entirely
fortuitous. The formal strategy – ultimately resting on the assumption
that an individual's experience has a general significance and is of
general interest – works because the scope and depth of Orwell's
commitment was wider than that of most people, more subtle than
the politicians', more serious than the artists'. Stephen Spender was
rebuked by a contemporary for persistently confusing his personal
struggle with the class struggle,[47] but this was not a charge that many
people would have applied lightly to Orwell. Due to a combination of
factors, some relating to the accidental circumstances of his life,
others to consciously sought experience, Orwell's voice acquired a
natural authority. It is difficult to disentangle design from accident in
this development – if only because the truly happy design is that
which transfigures the accidental retrospectively into a larger pattern
of necessity. Born in India when the slow decline of Empire had
already set in, he was, by what appears like assisted or inspired
coincidence, present in all the right places – a colonial policemen, a
tramp in the Depression, in 1930s Wigan, in revolutionary Barcelona.
'It was'. Raymond Williams writes, 'sureness of instinct, not chance,
that took him to all the critical places and experiences of his epoch.'[48]

A critic has observed of Conrad that 'with little sense of strain, he
moved from self to society; it was one of his eccentricities to myth-
ologise an historical self, to place his own life at the heart of
historical conflicts'.[49] Something similar might be said of Orwell also,
but the reason why this 'eccentricity' acquires in Conrad as well as in
Orwell the dimensions of power rather than mere whimsicality is, as
we have noted, because the selves in question actually have – by
accident, by design – been present at the turning points, the
significant historical conflicts. To put the matter simply, this aesthetic
conceit of 'eccentricity' is not similarly available to a suburban
householder. It needs the alchemy of a Wells to transform and elevate
the life of Mr Polly into something like an historical dimension. The
life of an Orwell, on the other hand, in Burma, in Barcelona, can
easily assume historical significance. Perhaps too easily.

It is ironical to reflect that someone whose most durable achievement is a unique synthesis of the 'literary' and the 'political' – at its
best, indeed, is a compelling refutation of the dichotomy itself – should
have retained, at the level of explicit theory at any rate, not only in the
early reviews but even when his own work was fully and gloriously

soiled with the dirt of history, a curiously 'pure' notion of art. Orwell's inability to free himself from an aesthetic theory which negates his whole practice as a writer is present in the numerous remarks about the 'invasion of literature by politics' (IV, 408), and in his remarks about the books he would have written if he had been born in a less clamorous time. He complains about being forced by the age into becoming 'a sort of pamphleteer' (I, 4) even though he is also of the opinion that 'the pamphlet ought to be the literary form of an age like our own' (II, 285). In an essay like 'The frontiers of art and propaganda' (II:20) one can sense the pull of aestheticist notions – 'Literature has been swamped by propaganda' (II, 123) – and also their felt untenability. Thus, in the same essay, the literary radicalism of the 1930s is commended for having 'destroyed the illusion of pure aestheticism. It reminded us that propaganda in some form or other lurks in every book' (II, 126). The somewhat defensive attitude about his own characteristic activity as a writer is present, perhaps most significantly, in his statement that he tried 'to make political writing into an art' (II, 6). At one level, clearly, this refers to the avoidance of semi-conscious assembly-line propaganda; but it is haunted also by the notion of 'art' as something superior, inhabiting a sphere above human strife; '"good art"', he wrote as late as 1940, 'is a more or less mysterious gift from heaven' (II, 6).

Orwell's achievement is made, on Orwell's testimony, against his grain. However, there is never any sense, in the words themselves, of being driven against the grain. Indeed, the opposite is more nearly the case: it is when Orwell tries to be 'artistic' that he seems lumpy and awkward, as in the famous 'Nighttown' chapter of a *A Clergyman's Daughter*. It is telling that the ludicrous comparison between this and the 'Circe' episode in *Ulysses* was, apparently, first suggested by Orwell himself.[50]

Orwell appears to have recognised this towards the end of his career:

looking back through my work, I see that it is invariably where I lacked a *political* purpose that I wrote lifeless books and was betrayed into purple passages, sentences without meaning, decorative adjectives, and humbug generally.

(I, 7)

It would be fair to say that there is an essential fluency about Orwell's mature literary practice which belies the token deference that Orwell pays to his own somewhat romantic aesthetic ideas.

In his speech to the First Conference of Soviet Writers in 1934, Karl Radek had said:

We must turn the artist away from his 'inside', turn his eyes to these great facts of reality which threaten to crash down upon our heads.[51]

This was a very important conference and the conclusions it endorsed were to be widely, if sometimes regrettably, influential over the ensuing decade. However, Radek's formulation, somewhat oddly, *assumes* the rightness of the originally romantic distinction between the 'inside' and the 'outside', although the respective values of the two entities are inverted. Orwell, in the main, rejects this polarity itself in his actual writing, although in his reflections on literature he sometimes reverts to it. But the best of Orwell's work is predicated on the assumption that the distinction is a false one; that, in fact, literature is about praxis, about happenings along that shifting and shadowy frontier where the 'inside' acts and is acted upon by the 'outside'. Even more importantly, and this enables Orwell to escape the self-contempt which seems to cripple so many of the literary radicals, for him literature itself *is* praxis, is an activity valuable in itself, and not merely as a means to the desired end of revolution. One may, however, recognise a justly Orwellian paradox in that Orwell produces his most significant artistic effects when, cleaving to the complex and knotty texture of his response to his time, he gives up the attempt to produce 'art'.

4

A KIND OF SOCIALISM

Wyndham Lewis wrote of George Orwell:

His left-wingery was probably a species of sport, as obviously as his plunge into the underworld of tramps was the act of a sportsman.[1]

A later critic demonstrated, to his evident satisfaction, that 'Orwell was never really a socialist at any time in his life.'[2] A third saw him as being initially afflicted with a 'vulgar democratic unreflectiveness' which he later overcame, thus enabling himself to 'direct his creative energies to the more vital level of insight which begins with a total revolt against all abstractions with which society traps, labels and affixes status to the individual, and whose object is the self, here and now and unique and doomed in the end to absurdity in a strange cosmos'[3] – which sounds impressive enough, but hardly like Orwell. Another critic, Norman Podhoretz, has claimed Orwell for the neo-conservatives, and averred that 'if Orwell were alive today, he would be taking his stand . . . against the Left'.[4] Yet another anti-socialist appropriator of Orwell sees his 'intellectual history' as one of 'gradual emancipation from the fog of "progressive" attitudes and stereotypes' even though, he ends regretfully, 'he died before he had quite shed them all'.[5]

There is another, relatively subtler, way of making Orwell's social-ism ('awkward' in more ways than one) disappear: by collapsing it into a general, and generally dismissive, history of 1930s literary radicalism drawing, crucially, upon Orwell's own influential repudiation of that radicalism in 'Inside the whale'. Orwell evidently resists reduction to the dimensions of the caricature literary 'helot' of the 'low, dishonest decade'.[6] But it would also, as we have seen in the context of his literary beginnings, be misleading, despite 'Inside the whale', to detach him entirely from his historical context. That said, however, it is still worth remarking that the process of becoming a socialist is, for Orwell, in a time when large numbers of people like him might be supposed to be negotiating *similar* shifts of consciousness, curiously embattled and strenuous. He is, undoubtedly, a part of what Philip Toynbee, alluding specifically to David Archer's bookshop in Parton Street, called 'the whole marvellous atmosphere of conspiracy and purpose'.[7] However, he is just as certainly a curious, angular, ill-fitting part; a participant in the history of 1930s literary radicalism, but also something of an anomaly within it.

But, for all that, Orwell's stubborn commitment to socialism cannot be wished away that easily. Any serious account of Orwell must give full weight to the fact that, through all his contradictions and confusions, through all the changes of his short but highly charged career, Orwell believed himself to be, and was, albeit with reservations, believed by others to be, a kind of socialist. His socialist commitment is undoubtedly problematic and 'awkward',[8] but it is neither dissolved or cancelled by its constitutive ambivalence, nor even superseded or transcended by his later and overwhelming anxiety about 'totalitarianism'. It is, admittedly, futile to try and arrest the restlessness of Orwell's socialism in order to shackle it with a label. But that tense restlessness is itself, I hope to show, the dynamic principle of his socialism, and of the career that embodies that tortuous commitment.

Indeed, faced with the apparent amorphousness of Orwell's 'socialism', its freedom from orthodoxy, one is tempted to ask, does it have a fundamental nature at all, or only a history? Is it anything more than a series of responses to changing historical situations?[9] Clearly, Orwell's changing political attitudes correspond to historical developments, from the experience of the Depression through revolutionary Barcelona and war-wracked Europe down to the locked and hostile post-war world – and it is part of my intention to offer an account of this trajectory. However, in addition to this, sympathetic exposure to Orwell's writings suggests that his socialism has a nature as well: a synchronic formal element that persists through the diachronic development and is, indeed, expressed and so known through the specific course of that development. Through all the evident changes there is, I suggest, the sense of 'a form moving through time'.[10]

Orwell's career is a bewildering spectacle of continuities and discontinuities. At a superficial level, there is a continuity of attitudes between the uncomplicated socialist of the early Paris articles and the mature author who unambiguously declined an invitation to address the League of European Freedom in November 1945 because the League 'claims to defend democracy but has nothing to say about British Imperialism . . . I belong to the Left and must work inside it' (IV, 30). There is, more specifically, the continuity which the author's self-interpretation foregrounds in 'Why I write' and elsewhere – the commitment to 'democratic Socialism' (I, 5). But there are also yawning discontinuities between, for instance, the infectious euphoria of *The Lion and the Unicorn* and the comprehensive antitotalitarian gloom of the last writings.

Orwell's Paris articles, to which we have had occasion to refer already, are characterised by a kind of brash and uncomplicated socialism which is not normally associated with Orwell. Thus, we are informed that 'Unemployment is a sub-product of capitalism' and that the worker must continue to 'suffer until there is a radical change in the actual economic situation'. Orwell informs his readers that 'a revolution is not far distant', but, he writes, 'in the meantime', the only 'real hope' of the aforementioned worker is that 'there will be elected a Government strong enough and wise enough to bring about this change'.[11] I am not certain, however, that anything more can be inferred from these articles than that Orwell was moving around in left-wing circles in Paris, and that he is trying out a somewhat unfamiliar rhetoric, awaiting the revolution and the next election with equal innocence.

It is, however, with a slight sense of shock that one realises how *little* there is of politics in Orwell's writings of the years 1930–5. These years were, of course, a time of deep and widespread discontent, a period during which large numbers of people, including middle-class intellectuals, found themselves driven by the logic of their experience into radicalisms of various hues. This is the time during which *New Signatures* (1932) and *New Country* (1933) were published, the British section of the Writers' International was formed, *Left Review* started publication – a time of unemployment and industrial decay and hunger marchers, in a word, the Auden landscape. Of this urgent world, there are surprisingly few and indirect hints in Orwell's writings (and letters) of this period. Even when he addresses potentially political matters directly, there is a curious and innocent timelessness about those attempts. Consider, for example, *Down and Out in Paris and London*.

In *Down and Out in Paris and London* Orwell is essaying exactly the kind of material which might have tempted into tirades a young socialist with half-baked ideas about capitalism. Instead, Orwell produced a book which might almost be a model of 'objective' observation.[12] (There is, of course, no reason to let the gratitude we reasonably feel overcome the sense of surprise which we should also feel when we see *Down and Out in Paris and London* in the context of the Paris articles I have referred to above.) In chapter 22 of *Down and Out in Paris and London* Orwell does raise, in a general way, the question of the social arrangements which require a significant proportion of the population to be confined to soulless drudgery. However, he deprives his speculations of their general applicability by withdrawing, in the last paragraph of the chapter, to the formal limitations of the fictional situation:

These are only my ideas about the basic facts of a plongeur's life, made without reference to immediate economic questions, and no doubt largely platitudes. I present them as a sample of the thoughts that are put into one's head by working in an hotel.

(*Down and Out in Paris and London*, 121)

Once, in chapter 36, Orwell suggests that tramps might be employed to grow their own food, but for the most part, he appears to take the tramps (and indeed, the whole sub-world) for granted and gives little hint of any proto-socialist desire to reorder society in such a way that there are no more tramps and derelicts wandering about ceaselessly in quest for food. Reviewing Mark Benney's *The Big Wheel* for *Tribune* on 23 August 1940, Orwell remarked on Benney's similar tendency to assume that the sub-world he described was as immutable and 'eternal as the pyramids'.[13] It is almost as if Orwell's political attitudes to his ambient society are held in deliberate abeyance, and are only rarely allowed expression such as in the clear-eyed bitterness of this observation:

Money has become the grand test of virtue. By this test beggars fail, and for this they are despised. If one could earn ten pounds a week at begging, it would become a respectable profession immediately. A beggar, looked at realistically, is simply a businessman, getting his living, like other business-men, in the way that comes to hand. He has not, more than most people, sold his honour; he has merely made the mistake of choosing a trade at which it is impossible to grow rich.

(*Down and Out in Paris and London*, 174)

Be that as it may, the coolness of the political tone is remarkable when we consider that it is the work of a man who, he wrote to a friend, would feel 'choked' if he were to live in middle-class Bayswater (I, 137).[14]

Orwell remarks, in *A Clergyman's Daughter*, that Dorothy's father, the Rector of St Athelstan's, 'lost in his golden Oxford days' (p. 36), bestows but scant cognisance on 'the age of Lenin and the *Daily Mail*' (p. 22). However, we can hardly help noticing that Orwell's Knype Hill itself exists in a time-warp, a sort of supra- or infra-historical parenthesis, a Shangri-la from which Dorothy must escape into life, by way of mental breakdown and amnesia. Despite the hop-picking and tramping and school-teaching episodes, 'the age of Lenin and the *Daily Mail*' is largely an unseen and unrealised presence in Orwell's novel. At one level, clearly, Orwell is aware that the 'time-warped' quality of Knype Hill is insane, but at another level, he is himself seduced by its air of carrying on the traditional, conventional life, sheltered by historical accident and authorial connivance from the importunate 1930s.

Keep the Aspidistra Flying (1936) is, compared to *A Clergyman's Daughter*, more historically *situated*. There is the enveloping, oppressive presence of poverty, there are the repeated visions of the unemployed, the superfluous and the 'redundant', 'the living dead':

They were just by-products. The throw-outs of the money-god. All over London, by tens of thousands, draggled old beasts of that description; creeping like unclean beetles to the grave.

(*Keep the Aspidistra Flying*, 23)

In a sense, of course, driven and stupefied multitudes have been a feature of urban experience at least since Engels observed the English working class in 1844. Thus, they are present, suitably phantom-like, in Eliot's Waste Land:

> A crowd flowed over London Bridge, so many,
> I had not thought death had undone so many.[15]

And Lawrence Ferlinghetti, adrift in modern America, wanders 'lonely as a crowd'.[16] Despite these continuities, however, the unemployed multitudes of *Keep the Aspidistra Flying* are as characteristic of the 1930s as the dole queues, the hunger-marchers and the Jarrow Crusade. Perhaps the subtlest historical marker of all, and one that enables us to observe something which is characteristic of

Orwell's political thinking, is the surprisingly important part that advertising plays in the novel. Though it is widely known that the 1930s were a time of economic decline, it is perhaps less well known that the 1930s also saw a deeply ironical boom in advertising: the system whose crisis drove millions to destitution sought to save itself by exhorting those ruined millions to *buy* with a desperate vehemence.[17] Thus, the New Albion advertising company, which Comstock spends most of the novel evading, is described as 'one of those publicity firms which have sprung up everywhere since the War – the fungi, as you might say, that sprout from decaying capitalism' (p. 65).

However, although advertising during a depression might offer an illustration of the inherent contradictoriness of capitalism as an economic system, it is also, clearly, a second-order manifestation, a symptom merely, of underlying processes of production and distribution. And to make advertising the major target of one's political critique is, quite simply, to miss the point – something like putting out a fire by blowing at the smoke. Thus, although the disgust which corrodes Comstock is undeniably strong, it is also relentlessly superficial. As a consequence, Comstock's would-be political critique of his society ends up being, at its best, aesthetic – as if the solution to the problems of modern capitalist civilisation lay in better copywriters. It would be unfair to Orwell (and perhaps also to Comstock) to suggest that his political understanding is confined entirely to an aesthetic level, but aesthetic disgust is certainly one of the sources from which he derives his political impulse. And the ugliness of the world of *Nineteen Eighty-Four*, like that of the world of *Keep the Aspidistra Flying*, is neither incidental nor coincidental.

Keep the Aspidistra Flying is instinct with that comprehensive disgust with the bourgeois world which is, so to speak, the substance out of which Orwell's mature political attitudes are formed but – and this is relevant in the present context – there is little socialism in it. There is much rhetoric about decadent capitalism and about what Carlyle had castigated as the cash-nexus of capitalist society, but the disgust which underlies the rhetoric stubbornly resists being moulded into 'socialism'. Thus, Comstock describes socialism as:

some kind of Aldous Huxley Brave New World; only not so amusing. Four hours a day in the model factory, tightening up bolt number 6003. Rations served out in greaseproof paper at the communal kitchen. Community hikes from Marx Hostel to Lenin Hostel.

(*Keep the Aspidistra Flying*, 110)

Ravelston's socialism, Orwell lets us know, is distinct from this mechanistic fantasy, but neither Comstock nor, apparently, his author, can give much credence to the alternative versions. Thus, Orwell, writing in his authorial voice, about a paper 'called the *Bolshevik*, duplicated with a jellygraph', which Comstock and his friends had published in those halcyon days *after* the First World War, says:

It advocated Socialism, free love, dismemberment of the British Empire, the abolition of the Army and Navy, and so on and so forth. It was great fun. Every intelligent boy of sixteen is a Socialist. At that age one does not see the hook sticking out of the rather stodgy bait.

(*Keep the Aspidistra Flying*, 55)

This is clearly very sour, for not only is socialism mere 'bait', but it is also 'stodgy', which indicates bad fishermen, or very perceptive fish. Orwell's next move, however, was entirely characteristic, and probably tells us something essential, in the context, about the dynamics of his temperament. Because, directly after finishing *Keep the Aspidistra Flying*, Orwell went to the depressed North to research *The Road to Wigan Pier*, attended *two* socialist summer schools[18] and, having finished the manuscript of *The Road to Wigan Pier* by the end of 1936, went to Spain to write and eventually to fight for, precisely, socialism.

However, before we turn to *The Road to Wigan Pier* and later works, I suggest that our attempt to understand the nature and dynamics of Orwell's paradoxical and tense and even ambivalent commitment to socialism will be facilitated if we pause to consider a formative but oddly neglected phase of Orwell's life – his five years as a colonial policeman in Burma from 1922 to 1927.

Although Orwell grew up in Henley and Southwold, a remark which George Bowling makes in *Coming Up for Air* about his wife's Anglo-Indian background suggests that Orwell might well have had some acquaintance with the sham world of the colonials even before he went out to Burma to become a policeman:

Do you know these Anglo-Indian families? It's almost impossible, when you get inside these people's houses, to remember that out in the street it's England and the twentieth century. As soon as you set foot inside the front door you're in India in the eighties . . . It's a sort of little world of their own that they've created, like a kind of cyst.

(*Coming Up for Air*, 136)

Eventually, of course, Orwell was to locate himself emphatically in England and the twentieth century – at the heart of their essential historical experience – but it is, once again, characteristic that he should have enabled himself to do so indirectly, by returning first to the disintegrating Indian Empire.

Why, indeed, did Orwell opt for a career in the Imperial Police? There is a passage in *The Road to Wigan Pier* in which Orwell, with characteristic honesty, hints that his motive might, in fact, have been to reinforce his insecure social position as a member of the 'landless gentry':

> The people who went there as soldiers and officials did not go there to make money . . . they went there because in India, with cheap houses, free shooting and hordes of black servants, it was so easy to play at being a gentleman.
>
> (*The Road to Wigan Pier*, 125)

There appears, indeed, to have been a marked increase in the outflow of ambitious young men to the East in the years immediately following the end of the First World War. Such, at any rate, was the view put forward in the house-history of one of the major trading companies in colonial Burma:

> Released from the burden of arms and the tensions of war, a multitude of young men rejecting a tame prospect of civilian life at home flocked to the East, some to follow a family tradition, some for adventure, some mainly intent on gaining for themselves a portion of its fabled riches.[19]

It is chastening to think that Orwell was part of this 'multitude', though it may help to explain the vehemence of his eventual rejection of a world in which 'men play at being gentlemen'.

Remembering his time as a policeman in Burma twenty years after he returned to England, in 1947, Orwell wrote that:

> at that time nationalist feelings in Burma were not very marked, and relations between the English and the Burmese were not particularly bad.
>
> (III, 403)

This is a curious remark. In 1919, as a result of the Montagu–Chelmsford Reforms, an exiguous degree of indigenisation was introduced in the colonial administration of India but, for some not quite explicable reason, the then-province of Burma was not brought within the purview of the Reforms. The Burmese, for their part, felt that they had been excluded because they had not clamoured for reforms. In the event, 1919 marks the *beginning* of serious nationalist agitation in Burma. In response to the public outcry, the British tried to make amends by empowering Governor Craddock to devise special reforms for Burma. But by the time these were introduced in 1922, it was evident that not only had too little been done too late, it had not been done very well either. As a consequence, the years after 1922 – the year Orwell, then Blair, arrived in Burma – were *particularly* tense and troubled politically. Thus, Orwell's sudden amnesia, in 1947, about anti-colonial turbulence during his time in Burma is indicative rather of the manner in which the alternative (but also, as I hope to show, strangely competitive and even antagonistic) concerns of the post-war period tended to diminish the significance of the anti-colonial element in Orwell's political make-up. In a somewhat similar fashion, in the essay in which Orwell, so to speak, 'came out' with his patriotism – 'My country right or left' – the Burmese experience, the crucial importance of which I hope to demonstrate shortly, had dwindled to merely 'five boring years within the sound of bugles' (1, 540).

By the time Orwell arrived in Burma traditional Burmese society had been crumbling under economic pressure for some time. The commercial cultivation of rice had increased several-fold since the opening of the Suez Canal in 1869, and this, coupled with the exploitation of Burmese oil and mineral resources, released forces which ensured that Burmese society was dangerously in flux. Moreover, apart from the influence of strictly economic processes, the British had antagonised the Buddhist clergy by setting up secular schools, thus depriving the monks of the basis of their traditional secular authority. The monks were, as a consequence, driven increasingly into oppositional, 'nationalist' roles – a fact which might, perhaps, account for Orwell's desire, acknowledged in 'Shooting an elephant', to disembowel a Buddhist monk (1, 236).

Sedition had become a sufficiently serious problem for the Burma Police Enquiry Committee of 1924 to recommend centralisation of the work of suppressing it.[20] Again, and significantly, the Governor set up a 'Standing Committee for the Imperial Idea' with effect from 1 July 1917. This Committee, whose brief was 'to ascertain and advise how the Imperial Idea may be inculcated and fostered in Schools and Colleges in Burma' declared in its *Report*:

It is not necessary or possible to define the Imperial Idea precisely. But the war has shown what the Empire stands for. It stands for freedom, justice and right and it rests on the organised forces of every section of it.[21]

However, the fact that the Committee, in the given context, recommended the encouragement of *boxing* as being 'likely to do the Anglo-Indian and the Burman very considerable moral good', indicates perhaps not only the paucity of its political imagination but also the measure of its desperation. This Committee also instituted (and later subsidised the publication of) a series of lectures on 'Imperialism in modern history' by Professor D. G. E. Hall of the newly established University of Rangoon. Professor Hall came to the predictable conclusion that the *British* Empire, unlike other Empires, was, in general, a good thing, since the British were merely 'trustees of civilisation'.[22] In retrospect, it sounds a little like whistling in the dark. It is perhaps worth noting here that the aforementioned Standing Committee in its *Report* singled out the folk-drama, *pwe*, as an especially malign influence and recommended that 'this is an evil which should be eradicated'.[23] This casts a new light on Flory's somewhat oblique act of rebellion in taking Elizabeth Lackersteen to one of the performances of this folk-drama (*Burmese Days*, 101–7).

The fact of widespread social and political disturbance is registered, duly, in the dramatically rising crime figures which are reported in the Police Reports of successive years. It is arguable, of course, that Police Reports give one a somewhat distorted picture of the life of a time in that they are concerned, necessarily, with breakdowns of normalcy. However, Orwell *was* a policeman – in his own words, 'part of the actual machinery of despotism' (*The Road to Wigan Pier*, 147) – and the world of the Police Reports, distorted (and distorting) as it well may have been, was Orwell's Burma. This was the world of beleaguered 'civilisers', shot through with hypocrisy and hollow rhetoric, full of contempt for their subjects and pompous self-regard, which Orwell chose to enter – and then rejected.

The biographical detail available on Orwell in Burma is, unfortunately, slight. He was only a junior police officer in obscure places, and no details about his service (apart from the barest outlines) are available in the records of the India Office in London. But the little detail that is available elsewhere suggests a fairly unremarkable tenure, at least superficially. His colleague, Roger Beadon, saw no signs of the future radical in him, and the Head of the Police Training School in Mandalay was sufficiently surprised by *Burmese Days* to threaten to horsewhip Blair if he should ever see him again.[24] Years later Orwell was remembered in Moulmein merely as someone who rode a peculiar motorcycle and who had been a skilful centre-forward in the Police football team. A schoolmistress remembered a young police officer shooting an elephant in Moulmein in 1927, and a District Collector remembered having received a brace of game birds from his subordinate, Blair, in Katha.[25] It is a futile task trying to identify the original incident which, it is presumed, Orwell describes in 'A hanging' – far too many people were hanged during Orwell's time in Burma: 59 in 1923, 71 in 1924, 84 in 1925, 136 in 1926, 144 in 1927.[26] One thing is known, however – as an ASP (Assistant Superintendent of Police) Orwell was not required to be present at any hanging and so, in what we will come to recognise as a pattern, it must have been an experience to which he chose to expose himself.[27]

There are, however, faint hints of trouble, or misgivings on the part of the authorities about Orwell, and these too should be a part of the record along with the football and the fact that Orwell was awarded a Certificate of Honour on 3 July 1926. (This, it should be emphasised, was not a rare distinction.) Roger Beadon remembers that the young police officer used to frequent 'native' churches – could it have been for the religion? Another curiosity is Orwell's statement, in a letter to Jack Common written in 1938, that as a policeman in Burma, he 'used to read anti-imperialist stuff' (1, 357). The subtlest indication of trouble is to be found in Orwell's service record. Beadon suggested that Orwell resigned from the Indian Police because he had been badly treated by a superior officer.[28] However, Aung has argued against this by pointing out that Blair's 'superior' in his last posting – Katha, which became Kyauktada in Burmese Days – was a 'promoted' Burmese official who is likely to have been too grateful for his preferment to be troublesome. But it is perhaps not insignificant that out of the tiny number of five 'native' officials who had been promoted into the higher ranks in deference to nationalist demands, no less than three should have had Blair as a subordinate.[29] Within the sophisticated code of the colonial bureaucracy, it would appear that Orwell was being singled out – for disfavour. When the MV Shropshire sailed for England from Rangoon on 14 July 1927 it carried E. A. Blair, bound for Marseilles.[30] We next see Orwell on the steps of one of the British banks in Marseilles, 'a few days before Sacco and Vanzetti were executed'[31] on 23 August 1927, watching a workers' demonstration in support of Sacco and Vanzetti. There is one further detail of some possible significance – on his way down from Katha Orwell stopped for ten days in Rangoon, and took care to have this period classified in such a way that it did not cut into his leave on average pay.[32] Such a fine sense of bureaucratic nicety does not betoken a mind at the end of its tether. However, when he resigned from the Imperial Police on 1 January 1928, he had over two months of that leave on average pay still left to run,[33] so the choice of the date appears to have been something of a symbolic act.

That his Burmese experience was of some significance was recognised by Orwell when he had occasion to reflect on the course of his development – as for instance in *The Road to Wigan Pier*. In trying to estimate what this significance might be, the temptation, following Orwell's own lead, is to blur the particularity of the story in favour of the general pattern – the innocent's exposure to the iniquities of colonial reality, the return full of anger and insight. This is how Karl Marx described the process:

> The profound hypocrisy and inherent barbarism of bourgeois civilisation lies unveiled before our eyes, turning from its home, where it assumes respectable forms, to the colonies, where it goes naked.[34]

Thus, Orwell wrote on joining the Independent Labour Party:

> For perhaps ten years past I have had some grasp of the real nature of capitalist society. I have seen British imperialism at work in Burma.
>
> (1, 337)

However, the specific individual histories within this general pattern were quite dissimilar. Leonard Woolf went to Ceylon as an innocent, and despite some ambivalence with regard to the pleasures of imperialism,[35] returned prematurely to devote a hardworking lifetime to the gradualism of the Fabian Left. For Conrad, too, Africa was a formative experience,[36] but in his case the experience of the horrific iniquities of King Leopold's vigorous efforts to 'civilise' central Africa interacted with the complicated psychology of someone who belonged to the aristocracy of a subject nation, to produce an amalgam which was very different from the moderate reformism of Leonard Woolf.

The years in Burma provided Orwell with a core of precious first-hand experience which he was able to deploy against the other leftists with their 'utter ignorance of the way things happen' (1, 357). Perhaps the most famous instance of this kind of snubbing is the rebuke which Orwell delivered to Auden for his line: 'The conscious acceptance of guilt in the necessary murder.' 'Personally', Orwell wrote:

I would not speak so lightly of murder. It so happens that I have seen the bodies of numbers of murdered men – I don't mean killed in battle, I mean murdered. Therefore, I have some conception of what murder means – the terror, the hatred, the howling relatives, the post-mortems, the blood, the smells.

(1, 516)

The detail of the 'post-mortems', of course, clearly reveals the colonial source of his knowledge. The history of Orwell's relations with that highly differentiated entity, 'the Left', is determined, and bedevilled, by a variety of factors; but it is clear at any rate that his colonial experience gives Orwell an air of superiority which he is often not greatly at pains to conceal. Because Orwell's political attitudes crystallised around a core of first-hand experience, they acquired a kind of durability which stands out in comparison with the 1930s radicals whose opinions were more lightly acquired. However, despite the stridency of the early Paris articles, it would be fair to say that the Burmese experience only gradually worked its complex way into the development of Orwell's political attitudes.

The most obvious product of Orwell's Burmese days was, of course, his anti-imperialism. The mainstream Left in Britain, perhaps unsurprisingly, was not greatly concerned about imperialism. Labour's Colonial Secretary, J. H. Thomas, writing in *The Times* on Empire Day, 24 May 1934, was not untypical:

Nothing can be more mistaken than the idea, prevalent in some circles, that Labour is hostile to the Empire and to the Imperial idea . . . Labour realises that it has good reasons to be proud of the British Empire. It knows the part that working-men have played in the building of the Imperial edifice.[37]

What is true for Labour is of course not necessarily true for the smaller parties of the Left, but even there the pull of imperialist arrogance was not unknown. Thus, when H. M. Hyndman of the Social Democratic Federation 'translated' Marx for the consumption of English audiences, he produced 'a curious amalgam of socialism and the white man's burden'.[38] In the words of a sympathetic historian, E. P. Thompson:

It is certainly true that imperialism penetrated deeply into the labour movement and even into the socialist groups; this is the tragedy of European socialism in this century.[39]

Orwell is characteristically explicit about the parochialism of the indigenous Left: 'In a prosperous country, above all in an imperialist country, left-wing politics are always partly humbug' (I, 394). He chided the Left for deliberately forgetting that:

the overwhelming bulk of the British proletariat does not live in Britain, but in Asia and Africa . . . It is not in Hitler's power, for instance, to make a penny an hour a normal industrial wage; it is perfectly normal in India, and we are at great pains to keep it so.

(I, 397)

Orwell, in stark contrast to the vast majority of the 1930s literary radicals, consistently hammered the theme that:

the European people, and especially the British, have long owed their high standard of life to direct or indirect exploitation of coloured peoples. This relationship has never been made clear by official Socialist propaganda.

(IV, 373)

The fact that the truth about the imperialist relationship was ignored provoked Orwell's ire, but it was hardly surprising in a time when the more usual complaint on the Left was that there was too much unemployment and the standard of living was not high enough. 'The attitude of the so-called left-wing in England and France over this imperialism business', Orwell complained – and the complaint has remained relevant to the post-war social democracies which ritually invoke his name – 'simply sickens me' (I, 369).

Orwell's anti-imperialism is not confined to an abstract understanding of the international mechanisms of exploitation. Watching a man on his way to the gallows sidestep a puddle, Orwell had what was, in a Joycean sense, an epiphanic vision of our common humanity. Finding himself at the repressive end of the colonial machine, Orwell broke through to the splendid democratic affirmation of 'One mind less, one world less'.

However, if Orwell, paradoxically, learnt some of his humanism in the colony, it appears that he also acquired, in a more direct fashion, an acquaintance with the 'totalitarian' state of mind. Interestingly enough, in view of his own insight into the Fascist mentality, Orwell suggested that Jack London 'could foresee Fascism because he had a Fascist streak in himself' (IV, 25). But in the broadcast talk on which the article (IV:7) is based, Orwell said something more which suggests that the colonial experience might have provided him too with some foreknowledge:

Socialist thought has suffered greatly from having grown up almost entirely in urban industrialised societies and leaving some of the more primitive sides of human nature out of account. It was Jack London's understanding of the primitive that made him a better prophet than many better-informed and more logical thinkers.[40]

Orwell believed that since he himself had experience of something other than a 'liberal' society, he could imagine a 'totalitarian' society more easily than his contemporaries who had breathed only the free and foggy air of England. His complaint against 'the soft-boiled emancipated middle-class' was precisely that 'they can swallow totalitarianism *because* they have no experience of anything except liberalism' (I, 516). Orwell, of course, did.

The idea of using the colonies as laboratories where social and political theories might be tested was suggested, ironically enough, by the father of Utilitarianism, Jeremy Bentham, busily pursuing the greatest good of the greatest number.[41] Hannah Arendt, working out a theoretical response (albeit without adequate historical controls) to the enormity of the twentieth-century European experience, located the origins of 'totalitarianism' in the colonies;[42] but I think it might be nearer the truth to say that the relative 'freedom' of the colonial situation, rather than actual design, facilitated the emergence of social and administrative practices – and the distillation of these practices into principles – in a manner which might, initially, have been unthinkable in the metropolitan countries themselves. The history of our century demonstrates, of course, that the customs-barriers of the mind are not, after all, very dependable, and practices and principles which were engendered in colonial situations *did* flow back into the metropolitan countries. This process was recognised by Bernard Semmel in his book *The Governor Eyre Controversy* (1962):

The War of 1939 brought the technique into operation once more against non-colonial peoples. It is dreadful to think that the forces at play in 1865 may have helped to set into motion our own greater calamities. Race prejudice – the view that what might be considered an outrage if committed against a white people could go unnoticed if committed against an 'inferior' coloured people – was the principle underlying the acceptance of the deeds of Governor Eyre and of Colonel Nelson by the British public. As we now see, it was a principle capable of infinite extension in all directions.[43]

However, Semmel's insight into the pernicious nature of the lies whereby colonial barbarities were ratified is not, apparently, as obvious as it seems. Alan Sandison, for example, writing on the literature of colonialism, notes, but fails to see the significance of, the fact that Kipling is unable to 'glamorise' the South African War or the

First World War, in both which whites fought whites; 'when war can no longer be reconciled', Sandison writes:

with heroic personal combat and heroic ideals, glorification of fighting is heard no more; in fact, it never survives translation from its Indian context. Neither the South African War nor, later, the European, allowed him to write as he had done before, they only revealed to him that an ideal of action conceived in India had no place in *A Sahib's War*.[44]

It apparently does not occur to Sandison to ask why Kipling should have felt inhibited in this fashion in 'white' contexts. Orwell, of course, knew all about the 'ideal of action' to which Sandison alludes:

When a subject population rises in revolt you have got to suppress it, and you can only do so by methods which make nonsense of any claim for the superiority of Western civilisation. In order to rule over barbarians, you have got to become a barbarian yourself.

(I, 235)

Orwell's Burmese experience is relevant in the context of his insight into 'totalitarianism' precisely because he had lived the realities which were only implied, and disguised, in Sandison's 'ideal of action'.

I suppose policemen everywhere, confronted by crime and sedition, by the sheer inefficiency of human systems, the stubborn and infinite fallibility of the human animal, have always yearned (and no doubt still yearn) for the simplicities of absolute power. Again and again, the Burmese Police Reports voice the desire for:

some unassailable theory of authority, a conception in which the large majority of the country can believe with single trust

so that the police might be able:

to enforce . . . with vigour and thereby instruction, the discipline of the new age.[45]

The date of this 'Note' is 1927, and explicit references to Mussolini and Stalin remove any residual ambiguities as to what the District Commissioner of Sandoway had in mind when he referred to 'the discipline of the new age'. There is, of course, no reason other than hero-worship to assume that Orwell remained entirely and scrupulously unaffected by the situations which engendered such yearnings in his fellow-policemen.

The signature of Orwell's colonial experience, however, is not to be found merely in identifiable and apparently detachable attitudes: it

shows itself in surprising and secret places. A critic has argued that
the Burmese experience 'strengthened' the contradictory elements in
Orwell's make-up.[46] One might even speculate that the Burmese
experience might have, by its very excess, *induced* a contradictoriness
which might otherwise have remained latent, an unopened 'fault' in
the mind. However, this much at least is certain: there appears to be a
kind of fit between the intrinsic contradictoriness of the circumstances
in which Orwell acquired his colonial experience – the reluctant
imperialist, the conscience-stricken policemen, the keeper of the law
with a secret sympathy for anarchism – and the strenuously divided
and tense, polemical form of his political attitudes, in respect of
colonialism of course, but also more generally.[47]

It is of critical importance to realise that Orwell's radical attitudes
took shape, as it were, *against* the grain of the life which he had himself
lived for five years, against its necessary responses and against its
necessary consciousness. Consider, by way of illustration, the tensions in the following brief extract from *The Road to Wigan Pier*:

I hated the imperialism I was serving with a bitterness which I probably
cannot make clear. In the free air of England that kind of thing is not fully
intelligible. In order to hate imperialism you have got to be a part of it. Seen
from the outside the British rule appears – indeed, it *is* – benevolent and even
necessary.

(*The Road to Wigan Pier*, 145)

At an obvious level, Orwell's political radicalism is an act of
rebellion against capitalist society, glimpsed naked at the periphery.
From what we know of the history of his family, that rebellion, tense
with anti-imperialism, is also an act of rebellion against family
tradition, particularly against his father. But, most important of all, it
is an act of rebellion against aspects of himself, and it is this fact which
I believe determines the form which his development takes: a restless
and extended argument with himself, an interior colloquy which is, in
one respect, Orwell's career itself.

The Road to Wigan Pier was one of the most successful books ever put
out by the Left Book Club and sold over 40,000 copies.[48] Thus, when
the miners of Harworth, who could not afford many books because
they were out on strike, had to choose only a few, they requested
copies of two books in particular, John Strachey's *The Theory and
Practice of Socialism* and *The Road to Wigan Pier*.[49] It is an important
work from my point of view because of the fact that it reproduces, in
microcosm, the problem which Orwell's writings considered as a

whole present – it has an elusive 'importance', a value which it is notoriously difficult to specify. Considered simply as social observation it is competent, but not much more. Moreover, as Richard Wollheim has pointed out.[50] Orwell suffered from the journalistic fault of seeking out unrepresentatively unpleasant details in quest of the sensational. My own suspicion is that Orwell's motivation in this regard might have emerged from something profounder within him than a mere quasi-journalistic desire to be striking; but irrespective of whether Orwell's motive was superficial or profound, determined by the nature of the market or having its roots deep in his psychological make-up, the fact remains that his reportage, considered simply as reportage, is vitiated by a kind of subjective 'dishonesty'. The Brookers, for instance, with their squalid lodging-house-cum-tripe-shop are an essential part of Orwell's Wigan. Their memorable amalgam of filth and futility acquires, for Orwell, something of an emblematic significance:

For they exist in tens and hundreds of thousands; they are one of the characteristic by-products of the modern world. You cannot disregard them if you accept the civilisation that produced them.

(*The Road to Wigan Pier*, 16, Penguin edition)

However, Orwell didn't simply happen to find himself *chez* Brooker. Bernard Crick has recounted how Orwell deliberately sought out those fetid lodgings:

he found the shop on his own.

'We found him, professor, ' said an old communist miners' leader to me, 'perfectly clean and decent lodgings. Most people had more time to clean when out of work and had prided themselves on it. He left them after a while for no good reason and went to that hole. Did he think it made better propaganda? Did he have a bit of a taste for that sort of thing: I don't know. Can you tell me? But that wasn't what unemployment did to the miners.' I couldn't tell him.[51]

As a discussion of socialist, or even social, issues, *The Road to Wigan Pier* is admittedly, unarguably, naive and even irresponsible: 'This, then, is the case against the machine', Orwell writes, and 'whether it is a sound or unsound case hardly matters' (*The Road to Wigan Pier*, 206–7), In his breezy, freewheeling, Don Quixote-on-a-typewriter manner,[52] Orwell takes on, in an apparently random sequence, unspecified and unspecific opponents and then proponents of socialism, laying it about him in an eloquent frenzy which is exhilarating but not, alas, very illuminating about the matters which are his ostensible subject. Orwell's theoretical ineptitude was brilliantly and aptly castigated by Harold Laski:

having first very ably depicted a picture, Mr Orwell does what so many well-meaning people do: needing a remedy (he knows it to be socialism) he offers an incantation instead. He thinks that an appeal to 'liberty' and 'justice' will, on the basis of facts such as he has described, bring people tumbling over one another into the Socialist Party. People, he seems to say, who have seen ugliness such as he has seen it will become socialist if only they can be made to understand that socialists are not 'cranks' but people like themselves. The walls of Jericho, as it were, will tumble down if only the trumpeter has the right kind of accent and the right kind of clothes when he blows the trumpet.[53]

Yet, in spite of these limitations, or perhaps because of them, *The Road to Wigan Pier* remains important both in the history of 1930s radicalism and, more particularly, in Orwell's own development.

It is important to realise that *The Road to Wigan Pier* is not a relapse into the radical but somewhat callow phrase-mongering of the early 'socialist' articles. Orwell is not, in *The Road to Wigan Pier*, rediscovering an early socialism which had got lost or otherwise been in abeyance for the intervening years, and neither is he embracing a socialism which others – Gollancz or Murry of the *Adelphi* or the Independent Labour Party – have made available to him. In a manner which is curiously impressive but also, admittedly, somewhat absurd, in 1936 Orwell sets about almost reinventing socialism. The ultimate success or failure of the attempt is, at least, arguable, but the attempt itself – an act of both innocence and staggering arrogance – has, in a time too beset by orthodoxy, a certain freshness. Ironically enough, Orwell's theoretical 'innocence' is his biggest asset. He approaches the afflicted areas with all the clear-eyed ignorance of, in current metaphor, a Martian, recording with meticulous zeal the dimensions of rooms, itemised grocery bills, the rubber stamps in a mines office ('death stoppage') – the legal niceties of an inhuman system. Richard Hoggart suggested[54] that the value of *The Road to Wigan Pier* results from the fact that Orwell rejects the stock, 'the expected, the social class response', the dismissive reflex of 'the fat-bellied bourgeoisie' (*The Road to Wigan Pier*, 71). However, I believe that a significant part of the continuing interest of *The Road to Wigan Pier* results from the fact that Orwell rejects also the stock responses of the Left. Indeed, he makes a patient attempt to understand for himself – are the slums dirty and degrading, or are they friendly and home-like? Are the new council estates clean but prison-like, or are they 'decent'? (There appears to be some connection in Orwell's mind between 'home' and 'dirt', as, for example, in this description of the bug-infested Hôtel des Trois Moineaux in *Down and Out in Paris and London*: 'a dirty place, but homelike' p. 6.) The answer he arrives at suggests the difficulty of the process, 'On balance the Corporation Estates are better than the slums; but only by a small margin' (*The Road to Wigan Pier*, 74). Programmatically, this is ambiguous – should one aim for better housing estates, or improved slums? – but the uncertainty at any rate bears witness to the complexity of the considerations involved. The internally argumentative form of *The Road to Wigan Pier*, for all its limitations, re-enacts the dissident gesture of socialism, the secular non-conformism which is *one* of its enabling conditions.

The theoretical inadequacies and inconsistencies of Orwell's 'invention' are evident enough. However, I suggest that to try and understand Orwell's socialism thus, in the abstract, as a logical/ ideological system, is quite simply to miss the point. Only by focussing once again on the vanishing middle term, Orwell himself, will we be able to identify the secret of its vitality. Perhaps the best way in which I can illustrate what I mean is by analysing Orwell's repeated and obsessive reference to the issue of 'class' in *The Road to Wigan Pier*.

Orwell himself was of the opinion that 'before you can be sure of whether you are genuinely in favour of socialism . . . you have got to take up a definite attitude on the terribly difficult issue of class' (*The Road to Wigan Pier*, 123). The issue of 'class' has, historically, been an important one for the Left. 'Class' is important as a category of explanation and consequently also as a principle of organisation and action. Orwell shares this mental set in a general sort of way – in other words, he is more inclined to see social process in terms of class-exploitation rather than in terms of, say, geography, or racial origin. However, upon looking closely, it becomes apparent that Orwell's *difficulties* with the issue of class do not belong in this set at all. Orwell has a powerful, if somewhat blurred, sense of economic injustice, but the organisational principles which flow from this understanding reflect the blurring of 'class' as an economic category. Thus, Orwell writes:

It has got to be brought home to the clerk, the engineer, the commercial traveller, the middle-class man who has 'come down in the world', the village grocer, the lower-grade civil servant, and all other doubtful cases that they *are* the proletariat.

(The Road to Wigan Pier, 226)

However, although class becomes practically negligible as an economic category, it remains crucially important as a social category, as a way of describing manners and accents, 'tastes and prejudices' (*The Road to Wigan Pier*, 162) – and it is here that the difficulties arise.

Orwell's extreme sensitivity to the class issue – in his sense of manners, etc. – clearly indicates that it touches on some radical and deep-seated insecurity. This insecurity is suggested by Orwell's remark, in a review of Cyril Connolly's *The Rock Pool* which he wrote while he was at work on the manuscript of *The Road to Wigan Pier*:

The fact to which we have got to cling, as to a life-belt, is that it *is* possible to be a normal decent person and yet to be fully alive.

(1, 226)

This carries the obvious implication that the attempt to become 'fully alive' to one's society tends to take one away from 'normal decent' people – though it is still possible, and crucially important, to be both 'alive' and 'decent'. It is noteworthy that this is hardly a secure belief, and has to be 'clung' to 'as to a life-belt'. When, for instance, Orwell writes that a person who doesn't noisily slurp his soup fails to do so only 'because in his heart he feels that proletarian manners are disgusting', and that from the manner in which he drinks his soup it can be inferred that he 'hates, fears and despises the working class' (*The Road to Wigan Pier*, 138), the violence of his assertion is clearly disproportionate, and deeply suspect. The ponderous, and slightly comical, intensity with which he bears down upon the awful truth in that famous passage: 'another and more serious difficulty . . . the real secret . . . the real reason why . . . *The lower classes smell*' (*The Road to Wigan Pier*, 129) seems really to betray a secret about himself. As Philip Toynbee pointed out, 'There were many radicals then, just as there are many today, who neither believe that all virtue resides in the proletariat, nor that proletarian manners are disgusting. It was Orwell who believed both.'[55] It seems apparent that Orwell experiences the emotions which he imputes vehemently to others, and even as he resents the fact that he experiences them, he is also aware that his own sense of his identity is dependent upon experiencing them. Thus, he recognises that 'it *is* necessary to wish class-distinctions away', but realises also that 'to abolish class-distinctions means abolishing a part of yourself' (*The Road to Wigan Pier*, 162). Moreover, as he expands on the theme, it becomes apparent that the 'part' thus threatened is no mere snobbish appendage, but consists rather of things more deeply constitutive and valuable:

All my notions – notions of good and evil, of pleasant and unpleasant, of funny and serious, of ugly and beautiful – are essentially *middle-class* notions; my taste in books and food and clothes, my sense of honour, my table manners, my turns of speech, my accent, even the characteristic movements of my body, are the products of a special kind of upbringing and a special niche about half-way up the social hierarchy.

(*The Road to Wigan Pier*, 162)

It is evident from all this that Orwell's commitment, even to his own kind of socialism, can only be deeply ambivalent.

Orwell's attitude to class is, by his own account, bound up with his experience of imperialism:

The thing that changed my attitude to the class-issue was something only indirectly connected with it – something almost irrelevant. I was in the Indian Police five years.

(*The Road to Wigan Pier*, 145)

However, although Orwell's rejection of imperialism is sincere – 'I felt that I had got to escape not merely from imperialism but from every form of man's dominion over man. I wanted to submerge myself, to get right down among the oppressed, to be one of them and on their side against the tyrants' – its articulation with his attitudes on the class-question is rather complex. 'At that time', Orwell writes, describing his state of mind after resigning from the Indian Police:

failure seemed to me the only virtue. Every suspicion of self-advancement, even to 'succeed' in life to the extent of making a few hundreds a year, seemed to me spiritually ugly, a species of bullying.

It was in this way that my thoughts turned towards the English working class. It was the first time that I had ever been really aware of the working class, and to begin with *it was only because they supplied an analogy*. They were the *symbolic victims* of injustice, *playing the same part* in England as the Burmese played in Burma.

(*The Road to Wigan Pier*, 150; italics added)

It is only too easy to be seduced and swept along by the moral passion, the strenuously urged virtue, the high-mindedness of a passage such as the one above and so miss significant detail. Thus, what are we to make of the word 'symbolic' in the quotation? It is implausible that Orwell wishes to suggest that the Burmese in British-held Burma, and the working class in England, are not *real* victims of injustice. Yet, it appears that these real victims are also, simultaneously, *symbols* in some other private drama that is here only fleetingly implied.

The italicised portions in the quotation above make it apparent that the processes being described are considerably more complex than simply a rejection of the economic aspects of capitalism and imperialism. The 'victims' of economic processes 'supply' an 'analogy', they 'play' 'parts' in a 'symbolic' drama! Strictly speaking, and the difficulty is similar to that which we encountered in our attempt to characterise the development of Orwell's anti-imperialism, it is impossible to say whether the 'adversarial' mental and emotional set so characteristic of him, the split within his own consciousness between 'victimisers' and symbolic 'victims', was *produced* by the situations to which Orwell was exposed, both as an anti-imperialist policeman and as a bourgeois socialist, or whether it was merely *precipitated* by them. There is the further possibility that the author's mind, taut with its symbolic tensions, actually *sought out* situations, real as well as imaginary, which reproduced or reflected or in some obscure sense 'confirmed' its own 'adversarial' structure. It seems clear to me, however, that this dialectical tension, between mind and reality, is relevant to a consideration of Orwell's socialism, irrespective of however 'natural' a response it may seem, in its various forms, to particular historical situations. To say this is not, on my part, to belittle Orwell's socialism. On the contrary, I believe this socialism derives its strength and durability, as well as its complexity, from the fact that it is, in some such way, psychologically 'underwritten'.

When the adversarial cast of Orwell's mind meets with an appropriate reality, then his mental energies work in harmony with his materials, producing an effect of both fluency and power. In situations wherein, so to speak, 'mind' and 'reality' confirm each other's structures so that the adversarial cast of one does not do violence to the complexity of the other or, to put it simply, in situations where the 'victims' and 'victimisers' are clearly such, the paranoia is 'justified' in persecution. Catalonia is a real-life example of what I mean, the world of *Nineteen Eighty-Four* an imaginary one. However, this happy coincidence is not always the case, and the same mental energies, ruthlessly splitting reality into 'adversarial' forms – 'victims' and 'victimisers', bourgeois proletarians and proletarian bourgeois, St

George and the dragons – also lead him into vulgar simplifications and confusions. In fairness to Orwell, it should be said that, still fresh (and perhaps raw) from the experience of *two* socialist summer schools – that conducted by the Independent Labour Party at Letchworth and the *Adelphi*'s at Langham in Essex – he was perhaps justifiably critical of middle-class socialists, the 'right Left people', earnestly imagining that revolution was merely their shedding of bourgeois ideology, which in turn was as easy as the shedding of bourgeois manners; or even that the shedding of bourgeois manners, or 'declassing', was as easy as merely intending to shed them. Q. D. Leavis referred to Orwell himself as one of the 'right Left people',[56] a term which probably alludes to an advertisement that appeared periodically in *Left Review*:

ARE YOU LEFT? Then try Rockshill (Guest House and Rest Home), Limpsfield, Surrey, and you will become right Left. Picturesque, comfortable house in beautiful country. Recommended by doctors. Psychological attention if necessary. Victoria under one hour.[57]

However, irrespective of the justifiability (or otherwise) of a particular polemic against his fellow-socialists, it appears that Orwell's sense of his own identity as a 'socialist' is constituted by the tensions between the two terms of the symbolic conflict discussed above, between 'victims' and 'victimisers', and so is, crucially, dependent upon their *continued, antagonistic, coexistence.*

Let us return briefly to consider, in the light of the above argument, Orwell's fervent confusion with respect to the question of the relationship between class and ideology in *The Road to Wigan Pier*. Thus, Orwell believes that it is politically *unnecessary* to abandon or abjure the tastes and preferences of one's class: this is why, he suggests, people from different social classes – navvies and school-masters – can unite in the socialist cause. Further, he suggests that it is in any case *impossible* for middle-class socialists to lose the cultural characteristics of their class, and those who pretend otherwise are liable to be unpleasantly surprised when they come up against the Orwell Test for Ideological Purity:

force them into any real contact with a proletarian – let them get into a fight with a drunken fish-porter on Saturday night, for instance – and they are capable of swinging back into the most ordinary middle-class snobbishness.

(*The Road to Wigan Pier*, 164)

However, although it is unnecessary and anyway impossible to shed one's bourgeois characteristics in order to join the socialist cause, to join without doing so is, again, the direst hypocrisy, in that one is evading the cultural implications of one's choice (*The Road to Wigan Pier*, 160). Thus, the only thing one can do, apparently, is to cling to cultural characteristics of one's class – its prejudices and predilections – as a kind of destiny which one may try to reverse, rhetorically, but to which one must in the end, ineluctably, submit. Orwell seems to acknowledge something similar towards the end of *The Road to Wigan Pier*: 'It is in fact very difficult to escape, culturally, from the class into which you have been born' (*The Road to Wigan Pier*, 223).

The classic counterpoint to this kind of pessimism is, of course, Orwell's own example – his life. It is, in every significant way, a persistent refusal to be submerged in the class into which he was born. But for all the impressive energy of his rejection, it is difficult to miss the fact that Orwell also felt a deep sense of complicity with that class. Thus, although he rebelled against the patterns and expectations of the middle class, he judged his rebellion, and perhaps revolutionary possibilities in general, in the light of precisely those patterns and expectations. Perhaps the saddest example of Orwell's bizarre sense of complicity with the very people he spent his life fighting against comes from the manuscript notebook which Orwell kept during his last invalid months. As he lay dying in the sanatorium at Cranham in Gloucestershire, Orwell noted, on 17 April 1949, the 'curious effect . . . of hearing large numbers of upper-class English voices' on Easter Sunday:

It is as though I were hearing these voices for the first time. And what voices! A sort of over-fedness, a fatuous self-confidence, a constant bah-bahing of laughter about nothing, above all a sort of heaviness and richness combined with a fundamental ill-will – people who, one instinctively feels, without even being able to see them, are the enemies of anything intelligent or sensitive or beautiful. No wonder everyone hates *us* so.

(IV, 515; italics added)

That 'us' is both unexpected and wrenching – but it is also deeply significant.

Given Orwell's rather pessimistic (if also confused) view of the relations between class and culture and political ideology, it is hardly surprising to find that the judgement on working-class socialists is also harsh. In 'The Road to Wigan Pier Diary', Orwell notes:

I am struck again by the fact that as soon as a working man gets an official post in the Trade Union or goes into Labour politics, he becomes bourgeois. The fact is that you *cannot* help living in the manner appropriate and developing the ideology appropriate to your income.

(I, 173)

This contains, it will be noticed, the disturbing implication that the only way a worker can preserve his virtue is by *not* fighting the bourgeoisie, and also asserts the vulgar idea, which Orwell attacked in others, that ideology is a simple function of income.[58] However, of even greater significance is the insistence, even in the case of the working class, that class, in the sense of cultural characteristics, is a sort of destiny which must be undergone. Thus, the possibility of working-class socialists is flatly denied: 'no genuine working man grasps the deeper implications of Socialism' (The Road to Wigan Pier, 176). It is significant that 'The Road to Wigan Pier Diary' contains no such observation. It would appear, therefore, that it is only the relative distance from the observed reality which enables Orwell to make it, and also that the roots of the observation lie in the economy of his mind rather than in the characteristics of the reality he is describing. Orwell's somewhat simple-minded identification of political ideology with manners and accents only too obviously leads him into absurdity and error. Thus, Wal Hannington of the NUWM (National Unemployed Workers Movement), who was, by all accounts, a Cockney of authentic pedigree, is decreed by Orwell to be 'though a Communist entirely a bourgeois' because, Orwell believes, he speaks with 'the wrong kind of Cockney accent' (I, 176). However, this error and absurdity is not without significance. It appears that Orwell finds socialist workers as disturbing to his sense of 'rightness' as he finds bourgeois socialists. Thus, Philip Toynbee wrote in 1959 about the 'particular loathing' with which Orwell wrote about 'working-class intellectuals'.[59] Despite the endorsement of socialism to which his (consciously sought) experience as well as his identification with 'symbolic' victims compels him, the mental complex out of which the identification springs condemns that endorsement to being crucially limited as well. Identifying with 'victims', Orwell becomes a socialist: yet being a 'victim' (his own, for he is also the 'victimiser'), Orwell must cling to his own cultural characteristics (as well as requiring others to cling to theirs) for it is on those characteristics that the precarious equilibrium of his own identity rests. This is, admittedly, tortuous, but not, I suggest, more tortuous than Orwell's 'socialism'.

Orwell has himself described, unwittingly, the nature of the threat that his own socialism carries for him:

All such deliberate, conscious efforts at class-breaking are, I am convinced, a very serious mistake. Sometimes they are merely futile, but where they do show a definite result it is usually to *intensify* class-prejudice . . . You have forced the pace and set up *an uneasy, unnatural equality* between class and class: the resultant friction brings to the surface all kinds of feelings that might have otherwise remained buried, perhaps for ever.

(*The Road to Wigan Pier*, 163; second set of italics added)

It is perhaps some sense of having come too close to the heart of his own political attitudes which prompts Orwell, towards the end of chapter 10, to provide himself with an escape clause:

I have been looking at this from the point of view of the bourgeois who finds his secret beliefs challenged and is driven back to a frightened conservatism.

(*The Road to Wigan Pier*, 166)

Orwell then tries to represent the 'difficulty' of the class issue as it might appear to a 'proletarian intellectual'. However, it is interesting to note that the perspective keeps slipping and Orwell gets sucked back by degrees to a dismissive bourgeois perspective. Thus, Orwell starts with: 'All he [the 'proletarian intellectual'] finds . . . is a sort of hollowness, a deadness', but soon deflates this assertion: 'this at any rate is what he *says*.' The representation degenerates by sentence-end to 'spin you this line of talk' and in the next sentence we are back to 'the "proletarian" cant from which we now suffer' (*The Road to Wigan Pier*, 167). I am not, I must insist, expressing an opinion as to the issues involved – indeed, I suspect that they have been incorrectly framed – but I find it significant that, despite trying, Orwell finds it impossible to be even-handed, and ends up sounding as if he is himself 'the bourgeois who finds his secret beliefs challenged' – paradoxically enough, by his *own* 'socialism'.

In a thoughtful essay – 'Orwell reconsidered' – written ten years after Orwell's death, Richard Wollheim suggested that Orwell's 'socialism' was analogous to the 'anti-imperialism' which prompted his resignation from the Indian Police – both were ways of seceding from corrupt systems.[60] It would appear to follow from this that *becoming* a socialist would be almost more important than *being* one since in the former the tension of the act of secession, of resistance, could be repeatedly re-enacted. This ties in, it will be noticed, with the account I proposed above – of a psychological or internal struggle between 'symbolic victims' and their 'victimisers'. When the 'victims' cease to be victims they have no further relevance to the drama which needs to be re-enacted. What is common between Wollheim's explanation and my own is precisely the element of continuity, of ongoing process as being significant in itself – whether as a continuing act of rebellion against a pervasive capitalism, or a protracted act of resistance against the victory of the 'victimisers' in the mind. Indeed, I would suggest that my explanation is more apt because, as we know from Orwell's writings, the 'victimisers' who must be resisted can switch their ideological colour and appearance with relative suddenness. Considered purely on the grounds of political feasibility, of course, such a strategy of secession is fraught with problems because, as Wollheim has argued, one cannot really 'leave' capitalism in the way that one can the Indian Police, but becoming a socialist, in significant continuous tense, is a way of trying to do so.

It is possible, on the basis of an explanation such as the one advanced above, to make sense of the fact which has been widely remarked: that Orwell, in his political journey, was recurrently and no doubt with important consequences, drawn to the most isolated, unorganised, vulnerable and marginal of groups.[61] Expiating colonial guilt after Burma, Orwell plunged to the bottom of the social ladder, consorting with tramps and other derelicts. And, seeking a political orientation in that crucial year, 1936, Orwell was drawn to what was fast becoming the most vulnerable and marginal of parties, the Independent Labour Party.[62] Thus, in 1936, the Independent Labour Party's great rival on the Left, the Communist Party, declared, no doubt with biassed glee but nevertheless with some accuracy: 'No matter how long the shadow may linger on, for all practical purposes the Independent Labour Party is dead.'[63] Typically, this was the party with which Orwell chose to align himself. (He took up formal membership only later, and for a short while, in 1938.)

Not less typically, Orwell also attacked the Independent Labour Party, just before going to Spain with their credentials. Thus, a significant part of the polemic of *The Road to Wigan Pier* is directed specifically against the Independent Labour Party. The famously maligned 'Socialists' in pistachio-coloured shirts and tight-fitting shorts – 'you could study every dimple' (*The Road to Wigan Pier*, 174) – are specifically identified as heading for the Independent Labour Party summer school, which Orwell also attended, at Letchworth. Indeed, the attack was as good as acknowledged in the review of *The Road to Wigan Pier* published in the Independent Labour Party journal *New Leader*:

[Orwell] has curious fixed ideas that Socialists are 'bearded fruit-juice drinkers', 'sandal-wearers', nudists, sex-maniacs, and heaven knows what . . . There is a great deal in this book which the informed Socialist will find irritating, and even infuriating; sheerly silly and a tilting at windmills.[64]

But, the reviewer went on to assure readers, despite these curious ideas Mr Orwell was really a good socialist. This was confirmed by the fact that he was at that moment fighting with the POUM (Partido Obrero de Unificacion Marxista) militia in Spain – an experience which drove him deep into the embrace of the Independent Labour Party.

The way Orwell tells it, it might almost be accidental that he joined the POUM militia: 'I had joined the POUM militia rather than any other because I happened to arrive in Barcelona with Independent Labour Party papers' (*Homage to Catalonia*, 48). He wrote in a similar vein to Victor Gollancz: 'Owing partly to an accident I joined the POUM militia instead of the International Brigade' (I, 267). (It appears, incidentally, that there might have been some mysterious affinity between English literary intellectuals and POUM since John Cornford, a Communist, also fought in the POUM militia.[65]) However, we can hardly fail to notice that Orwell's joining this relatively marginal and ultimately persecuted minority fits into an underlying pattern which recurs throughout his life. It appears that the persecution of POUM by the Communist-influenced government of Catalonia even strengthened Orwell's commitment to the group, despite his reservations about their political programme: 'I myself never joined the party – for which afterwards, when POUM was suppressed, I was rather sorry' (*Homage to Catalonia*, 74). In a diary entry of 28 July 1942 there is, indeed, an almost bizarre avowal of this tendency to be drawn towards minorities which he perceived as being persecuted or vulnerable:

Looking back I see that I was anti-Russian (or more exactly anti-Stalin) during the years when Russia appeared to be powerful, militarily and politically, i.e. 1933 to 1941. Before and after those dates I was pro-Russian. One could interpret this in several different ways.

(II, 439)

Orwell's 'socialism' is, in a precise sense, existential: a matter of personal integrity, a way of preserving oneself in a deeply corrupt and corrupting world. There is, I suggest, a further way in which Orwell's socialism, understood thus, is organically related to his later 'anti-totalitarianism'. It is the possibility of endless, endlessly defeated rebellion – a state of permanent 'victimhood' – which accounts, at least in part, for the grip of the theory of totalitarianism, with its implicit idea of an entity which is simultaneously absolutely evil and absolutely powerful, upon Orwell's imagination. This is, however, to anticipate – because in order to understand the apparently discontinuous development from the euphoric *Homage to Catalonia* (1939) to the gloom of *Nineteen Eighty-Four* (1949) we need first to take a close look also at Orwell's wartime writings. The realignments and revaluations which Orwell made, under the stress of war, have not been given the critical recognition they deserve. They were far-reaching and comprehensive, and so should be of intrinsic interest. They also provide, I hope to show, an oddly neglected perspective on the manner in which Orwell viewed the post-war world.

5

WAR AND REVOLUTION

On 8 June 1937, while he was recovering from his bullet wound in the Sanatori Maurin, Orwell wrote to Cyril Connolly:

I have seen wonderful things and at last really believe in Socialism, which I never did before.

(1, 269)

Taken literally, this casts a curious light on Orwell's numerous 'socialist' professions of the past – not excluding those in *The Road to Wigan Pier*, which was published by the Left Book Club while Orwell was in Spain. However, it seems merely graceless to quibble in the face of an experience which was clearly special, deeply moving and profoundly significant, both for Orwell and for those who seek to understand him.

The Italian militiaman who gripped Orwell by the hand, 'bridging the gulf of language and tradition and meeting in utter intimacy' (*Homage to Catalonia*, 1), is well known. It is important to remember that this famous meeting was not an isolated incident – 'One was always making contacts of that kind in Spain' (*Homage to Catalonia*, 1). It is clear that revolutionary Barcelona, 'a town where the working class was in the saddle' (*Homage to Catalonia*, 2), touched off some powerful and powerfully denied longing in Orwell – for fraternity, for comradeship (though, in fastidious bourgeois reflex, he flinched at the word – 1, 233), for a humane and egalitarian society in which the curse of class difference, ratified by institutions, recognised and reinforced and even celebrated in cultural practice, did not poison the 'natural' relations between man and man. It is worth noting, incidentally, that Orwell was able to experience this feeling of release, of liberation, outside his native context, away from situations which could activate his ingrained reflexes. The words in which Orwell

describes the experience indicate that he himself was not quite aware
or even in control of the longings which had been aroused:

Practically everyone wore rough working-class clothes, or blue overalls, or
some variant of the militia uniform. All this was queer and moving. There was
much in it that I did not understand, in some ways I did not even like it, but I
recognised it immediately as a state of affairs worth fighting for.

(*Homage to Catalonia*, 3)

Orwell remarked, somewhat self-consciously, that 'to anyone from
the hard-boiled, sneering civilisation of the English-speaking races
there was something rather pathetic' in the ardour which the
idealistic Latins brought to 'the hackneyed phrases of revolution'
(*Homage to Catalonia*, 4). But Orwell himself was touched by that
ardour, and in this, I believe, lay his salvation from the arid destiny of
the bourgeois mockers. Indeed, writing about the Spanish wife of
Williams, 'the other English militiaman', 'a gentle, dark-eyed, in-
tensely feminine creature', Orwell is reduced (or elevated) to a state of
babbling and uncharacteristic alliteration. She was, Orwell tells us:

at this time . . . carrying a baby which had been born just ten months after the
outbreak of war and had perhaps been begotten behind a barricade.

(*Homage to Catalonia*, 12)

Naturally, Orwell was not alone in being moved by the Barcelona of
the heroic period. It inspired political ardour in the most unlikely
people, and Cyril Connolly expressed the thoughts of many when he
wrote about Barcelona:

The pervading sense of freedom, of intelligence, justice and companionship,
the enormous upthrust in backward and penniless people, of the desire for
liberty and education, are things that have to be seen to be understood. It is as
if the masses, the mob, in fact, credited usually only with instincts of stupidity
and persecution, should blossom into what is really a kind of flowering of
humanity . . . Anyone who could see this could see that here was something
which it would be an unimaginable piece of human malignity to destroy,
which it would indeed be impossible to destroy.[1]

It is chastening to recall, in this context, Hugh Thomas's parody of
such Spanish rhapsodies:

Hemingway, Ilya Ehrenburg, Claud Cockburn and I drove up to the front in a
taxi painted in anarchist colours. The olive trees stood motionless like sentries
against the grey of the sierra. We gave the password – *dignidad* – to a bronzed
and smiling militiaman, and were shown to Major Martinez' command post.
Martinez, peasant son of a long line of peasants, was of the stuff of Goya,

Pissarro, Lope de Vega, Cortes. Pointing overhead to where Mussolini's Capronis were beginning once more to circle in a blue sky reminiscent of the background of Velasquez' portraits, Martinez remarked: 'We are, I fancy, the only European nation who have committed suicide at the hands of others.'[2]

However, Thomas himself is careful to distinguish Orwell's Spanish experience from such picturesque travelogue. Orwell's afflatus survived even the horrors of his last days in Spain, the bitterness of the 'squalid brawl' in sad, heroic Barcelona, and was no doubt a source of sustenance to him when he had returned to the 'money-tainted atmosphere' of capitalist England:

No one who was in Spain during the months when people still believed in the revolution will ever forget that strange and moving experience. It has left something behind that no dictatorship, not even Franco's, will be able to efface.

(I, 287)

There was a marked increase in the level of Orwell's political militancy after his return from Spain. This could have been due to one (or more) of a variety of reasons. It could possibly have been a consequence of the 'wonderful things' Orwell wrote about to Connolly – the actual experience of a society, fragile but defiant, which was founded on socialist principles. On this account, Orwell's militancy would appear to be a spin-off, as it were, of 'the most deliberate attempt he ever made to become part of a believing community'.[3] Or it might have been a response to the rapidly worsening international situation. It might even, conceivably, have been an effect of Orwell's bitter discovery of a force which, within the terms of Orwell's mental economy, could 'sanction' his radicalism by appearing to threaten it – to wit, the Communists. Whatever the reasons for it might have been, the fact of this increased, uncompromising militancy is amply borne out by Orwell's writings of this time. It appears morbidly symbolic that, as a consequence of his Spanish wound, Orwell not only lost his voice briefly, he soon found another that was subtly, identifiably different.

The crucial issue on which this militancy was expressed was that of the coming war, and of the proper political attitude towards it. Declaring his reasons for having joined the Independent Labour Party in June 1938, Orwell stated his firm opposition to any preparations for the forthcoming war, although he did so in terms which seem to indicate the possibility of the sudden reversal which did in fact occur:

we know the terrible temptation of the present moment – the temptation to fling every principle overboard in order to prepare for an imperialist war. It is vitally necessary that there should be in existence some body of people who can be depended upon, even in the face of persecution, not to compromise their Socialist principles.

(I, 338)

Still, though he acknowledged the 'temptation', Orwell also stated his unwillingness to 'be led up the garden path in the name of capitalist democracy' (I, 338). In September 1937 Orwell wrote to Geoffrey Gorer about the Communists who were 'aiming . . . to get British capitalist-imperialism into an alliance with the USSR and thence into a war with Germany'. Orwell, on the other hand, having seen what he had seen in Spain, had 'come to the conclusion that it is futile to be "anti-Fascist" while attempting to preserve capitalism. Fascism after all is only a development of capitalism, and the mildest democracy, so called, is liable to turn into Fascism when the pinch comes' (I, 284). 'Rubber truncheons and castor oil', Orwell wrote, 'have scared people of the most diverse kinds into forgetting that Fascism and capitalism are at bottom the same thing' (I, 305). Arguing from such a position, Orwell was implacably opposed to the Popular Front strategy which the Communists were pursuing – 'an unholy alliance between the robbers and the robbed' (I, 305) he called it. However, it appears also that Orwell at any rate was not quite happy being out on a purist, sectarian limb along with his Independent Labour Party colleagues, and needed to believe simultaneously in some kind of 'popular' sanction. Thus, although he polemicised against the idea of the working class 'collaborating' with bourgeois–capitalist elements in a Popular Front to resist Fascism, he complained also that the counter-strategy of the 'Workers' Front' proposed by the Independent Labour Party used too narrow a definition of the working class:

too much dominated by the concept of a 'proletarian' as a manual labourer. In all western countries there now exists a huge middle class whose interests are identical with those of the proletariat.

(I, 305)

There are two points to be made about this: one, that, functionally, the strategy as modified by Orwell is not greatly dissimilar to the Popular Front strategy of the dreaded Communists; two, that on the other side of his own 'patriotic' transformation, this 'populist' element was to become relatively stronger.

It is worth noting, and perhaps indicative of the delicately poised, paradoxical economy of Orwell's mind, that, during this period of hectic, upbeat militancy, he was also at work on his mellow, despairing narrative *Coming Up for Air* (1939). Orwell did some work on *Coming Up for Air* while he was convalescing in Morocco, and it is possible that homesickness is, in some measure, responsible for the warmth of his evocation of his boyhood in the Thames Valley. But one can also see that for Orwell, on the rebound from the internecine and present bitterness of his Spanish experience, Edwardian England, 'the golden age before 1914' (III, 48), was an obvious recourse. Deploying that fertile myth, the innocence of his own childhood could be transferred to the social order. In that 'golden country' of the imagination, Orwell could escape from the raucousness of his immediate environment.

Cyril Connolly said of Orwell that he was a revolutionary in love with 1910.[4] However, it is important to see that Orwell was revolutionary *in* his love for '1910' – to see, in effect, the radical thrust of his nostalgia. (The American critic Fredric Jameson is explicit about the radical potential of nostalgia: 'if nostalgia as a political emotion is most frequently associated with Fascism, there is no reason why a nostalgia conscious of itself, a lucid and remorseless dissatisfaction with the present on the grounds of some remembered plenitude cannot furnish as adequate a revolutionary stimulus as any other'.[5])

For Orwell the thrust is, as it happens, doomed – George Bowling's pilgrimage to the 'golden country' is a disaster. Orwell helps his protagonist to the discovery that 'There's no way back to Lower Binfield' (*Coming Up for Air*, 227); the prelapsarian world of which it is a symbol is irretrievably lost. Deep in his totalitarian nightmare, in *Nineteen Eighty-Four*, Orwell again made use of Edwardian nostalgia: 'a sort of ancestral memory' (*Nineteen Eighty-Four*, 81, Penguin edition) which enables the subversive perception that the 'present' of the novel is 'intolerable . . . things had once been different' (*Nineteen Eighty-Four*, 51, Penguin edition). However, between these two contrasting uses of Edwardian nostalgia, there lies Orwell's wartime communitarian affirmation, that curious process whereby the energies which were directed towards a socialist vision of an 'alternative' community, subversive of the status quo, were appropriated by what appeared, for a time, to be immediate, present, 'available'.

On 4 January 1939 Orwell wrote to Herbert Read from Marrakech:

I believe it is vitally necessary for those of us who intend to oppose the coming war to start organising for illegal anti-war activities.

(I, 377–8)

He went on to make specific suggestions about 'the things we should need for the production of pamphlets, stickybacks, etc.' Finally, mindful of security, Orwell asked Read:

Would you drop me a line and let me know whether you are interested in the idea? But even if you are not, don't speak of it to anyone, will you?

(ibid.)

It appears likely that Read reacted with some scepticism to Orwell's suggestion because, writing to Read again on 5 March 1939, Orwell agreed:

it's in a way absurd to start preparing for an underground campaign unless you know who is going to campaign and what for.

(I, 386)

A little later in the year, on 12 August 1939, Orwell noted in his Political Diary: 'It appears that the P.O. authorities are now able to read a letter, sufficient to determine nature of contents, without opening it.' Two days later, he noted: 'It appears that the opening of letters to persons connected with leftwing parties is now so usual as to excite no remark.'[6]

The implicit 'absurdity' was to become only too evident in just under one year when Orwell, throwing such energies as he was allowed to into the war effort, and hurriedly dissociating himself from his Independent Labour Party colleagues, who were still opposing the war,[7] wrote to Victor Gollancz:

The intellectuals who are at present pointing out that democracy and fascism are the same thing depress me horribly.

(I, 409)

It is reasonable to suppose that the depression was exacerbated by the fact that, until recently, Orwell had himself argued that 'Fascism and bourgeois "democracy" are Tweedledum and Tweedledee' (I, 274), and that, consequently, the only course for serious radicals was to reject the spurious appeal of Allied 'democratic' propaganda and oppose the process of mobilisation for war. Orwell also, it appears, wrote an anti-war pamphlet which is believed to have been published in a mimeographed form but is now lost.[8]

In Deceeber 1938 Orwell voiced opposition to the war effort, on behalf of the silent majority:

The mass of people are normally silent. They do not sign manifestoes, attend demonstrations, answer questionnaires or even join political parties. As a result, it is very easy to mistake a handful of slogan-shouters for the entire nation.[9]

Soon, as we shall see, Orwell would *support* the war effort, deriving his sanction from the unthinking patriotism of the same ordinary 'mass of people'. The silence of the silent majority allows for a certain diversity of interpretation.

By Orwell's own account of this transformation, he discovered his patriotism in a dream on the night of 22 August 1939:

For several years the coming war was a nightmare to me, and at times I even made speeches and wrote pamphlets against it. But the night before the Russo-German pact was announced I dreamed that the war had started. It was one of those dreams which, whatever Freudian inner meaning they may have, do sometimes reveal to you the real state of your feelings. It taught me two things, first, that I should be simply relieved when the long-dreaded war started, secondly, that I was patriotic at heart, would not sabotage or act against my own side, would support the war, would fight in it if possible . . . what I knew in my dream that night was that the long drilling in patriotism which the middle classes go through had done its work.

(1, 538–9)

It must have been a difficult avowal for Orwell to make, and it is significant that in the essay from which the above quotation has been taken, Orwell is describing the process of his patriotic awakening over a year after it happened. In an essay entitled 'Democracy in the British Army' which was published in *Left Forum* in *September* 1939 – after the 'dream', that is – Orwell is still using his ultra-radical rhetoric, criticising the 'left-wing jingoes' (1, 405) for obscuring the class struggle with talk about the 'defence of democracy'. However, by January 1940, as the letter to Gollancz I have already quoted from indicates, Orwell had mentally dissociated himself from the 'intellectuals who are at present pointing out that democracy and fascism are the same thing'. Still, it is perhaps significant that in a person who, to quote from the blurb of the Penguin *Collected Essays, Journalism and Letters*, 'forged a unique literary manner from the process of thinking aloud', the discovery of his patriotism took so much time working itself through into his public writings.

It is worth remarking, however, that the Political Diary which Orwell maintained during this period contains *no* hint of any sudden conversion to patriotism. On 24 August 1939, Orwell notes coolly that the Russo-German Pact has been signed, and, closing the diary on 3 September 1939 with the British declaration of war on Germany, remarks that 'controversy about the Russo-German pact continues to some extent'. However, a letter to Orwell from Ethel Mannin, dated 30 October 1939, makes it clear that certainly by that time the switch was complete. Ms Mannin confesses to being 'staggered' by Orwell's statement that he wishes he 'were fit enough to get into uniform and help smash Hitler and Fascism . . . It leaves me bitched, buggered and bewildered. I can't think of any reason why you should want to fight unless to get into the army and do anti-war propaganda there.' Orwell's evidently disconcerting avowal was made in response to an earlier letter from Ethel Mannin, dated 20 September 1939.[10] However, the crucial conclusion to be drawn from all this is that Orwell's account of his discovering his patriotism in a dream 'the night before the Russo-German pact was announced' is another instance of aesthetic heightening, a piece of self-conscious self-dramatisation.

There is a kind of oblique indication of the reversal in Orwell's essay 'Boys' weeklies', published in *Horizon* in March 1940. Here, Orwell writes approvingly of the patriotism of ordinary people which 'has nothing whatever to do with power politics or "ideological" warfare. It is more akin to family loyalty' (1, 472). Writing in a similar vein in *Time and Tide* on 2 March 1940, Orwell chided the 'Mass-Observers' Tom Harrisson and Charles Madge, which had merely based their conclusions on opinion surveys, for underestimating the strength of popular patriotism:

The volume of discontent, apathy, bewilderment and, in general, war-weariness is probably far smaller than the Mass-Observers seem to imply. The fact is that inquiry of this type is bound to be coloured to some extent by preconceived opinions . . . The one thing the compilers do not seem to have encountered is the sentiment of patriotism. If one may make a guess at the reason, it is that people capable even of imagining a thing like Mass Observation are necessarily exceptional people – exceptional enough not to share the rather unthinking patriotism of the ordinary man.[11]

Orwell's objections are hardly serious enough to cast doubt on the evidence which Harrisson and Madge were gathering with increasing professionalism, but they do indicate the populist direction in which Orwell's own views are tending. Thus, one can observe Orwell manoeuvring himself into becoming the authentic voice of the 'ordinary man'. In April 1940, in a review of Malcolm Muggeridge's *The Thirties*, Orwell seems on the edge of a confession:

It is all very well to . . . proclaim your emancipation from all traditional loyalties, but a time comes when the sand of the desert is sodden red and what have I done for thee, England, my England? As I was brought up in this tradition myself I can recognise it under strange disguises, and also sympathise with it.

(I, 535)

The full public avowal of his patriotic transformation – 'My country right or left' (I, 168) – had to wait a little longer. But we know from the 'Autobiographical note' (II:7) which Orwell wrote on 17 April 1940 that, at the beginning of the war in August 1939, he left the Independent Labour Party, which had continued to argue that the proclaimed conflict between Fascism and 'democracy' was an unreal one, and which Orwell had joined with a public endorsement of its policies in 1938.

Orwell's somewhat unlikely though not unexpected companions in the opposition to the war had been, of course, the pacifists. The pacifists were opposed to the war on moral rather than on political grounds. Still, Orwell had a kind of common cause with them and even defended them, on one occasion, against the attacks of one Romney Green (see I:129). It should, however, be emphasised that Orwell was careful to distinguish his position from that of the pacifists. Thus, he wrote to Rayner Heppenstall in 1937: 'I don't, however, agree with the pacifist attitude, as I believe you do. I still think one must fight for Socialism, and against Fascism, I mean fight physically with weapons' (I, 280). Writing in the *New Statesman* of 28 August 1937, Orwell went straight to the heart of the matter:

The test for any pacifist is, does he differentiate between foreign war and civil war? If he does not, he is simply saying in effect that violence may be used by the rich against the poor but not by the poor against the rich.

(I, 283)

Thus, to Orwell in this mood, civil war for socialism, as in Spain, is justified, but foreign war is not. Still, the fact is that Orwell was sufficiently identified with the pacifist opposition to the war for the fact to be remarked with some acerbity by George Woodcock during the course of a controversy in 1942:

Comrade Orwell, former fellow-traveller of the pacifists and regular contributor to the pacifist *Adelphi* – which he now attacks!

(II, 224)

For, of course, on the other side of his patriotic transformation Orwell discovered, and gave frequent and vehement utterance to, the opinion that 'pacifism is objectively pro-Fascist' (II, 180).

Another set of ironic dislocations precipitated by Orwell's sudden emergence into patriotism concerns his relations with the Communists. I have already remarked earlier that Orwell sometimes endorsed Communist Party theses from anti-Communist locations. However, in the rapidly changing alignments of the pre-war period, this irony was compounded. The Communists, it is well known, opposed Hitler and Fascism by working for a Popular Front – until the Russo-German Non-Aggression Pact of August 1939. After that, they discovered that the conflict between Hitler and the West was an internecine imperialist one, and they maintained this perception until Hitler sent his armies marching into Russia in June 1941 – then, once again, Fascism became the enemy. This is comic enough, but Orwell's own development is hardly less so. Until the night *before* the Russo-German Pact was announced, Orwell denounced the imminent war and preparations therefor as relating to a conflict between imperialists; then, at the very moment in which the Communists started to see the situation in these terms, Orwell discovered that Fascism was the enemy after all. After 22 June 1941 – that is, after Hitler attacked Russia – Orwell and the Communists found themselves on the same side – 'allies', in a manner of speaking – but this did not make for any greater warmth in their relationship. Thus, when Orwell's essay 'Patriots and revolutionaries', first published in *Left News* in January 1941, was republished as chapter 10 of Gollancz's *The Betrayal of the Left* (1941), Orwell deleted a reference to Priestley having been 'shoved off the air' by right-wing elements in the government which were alarmed at the tone and success of Priestley's Sunday evening broadcasts.[12] Priestley was believed to have Communist sympathies.

The full depth of Orwell's 'patriotic' transformation, the fundamental nature of the shifts that it necessarily entailed, is not always apparent at a casual reading and has not, in my opinion, been accorded due critical recognition. One possible explanation for this neglect could be that right across this process of realignment, Orwell continued to employ a consistently radical rhetoric. It is only when we look closely at the reality to which this rhetoric is supposed to correspond – at the *specific* interplay of the themes of war and revolution – that the differences become apparent.

Orwell's refusal to be drawn into the war effort in any form, like that of his Independent Labour Party colleagues, was predicated on the assumption that there was a contradiction between the war and the possibility, however distant and abstract, of revolution. Indeed, in his controversy with Romney Green over the pacifist opposition to the war (I:129), and in other writings of the immediate pre-war period, Orwell frequently expressed the view that the war was being promoted to obstruct and inhibit the revolution:

The real enemies of the working class – are those who try to trick them into identifying their interests with those of their exploiters, and into forgetting what every manual worker inwardly knows – that modern war is a racket.

(I, 332)

The Communists, working for a Popular Front at the time this was written, were of course part of the devilish conspiracy. We have seen how this hyper-radicalism, at least in the case of Orwell, derived from the impulse provided by his Spanish experiences. Spain had revealed to Orwell, as he has memorably recorded, the socialist possibilities of the working class. However, Spain had also shown how the working class could be conned and bludgeoned into ceding the fruits of its victory. What is particularly significant in the present context is that one of the ways in which 'the ragged, weaponless armies of the Republic' (II, 263) were deprived of what 'they knew to be their birthright' (II, 264) was by the insistence on the primacy of the war. The implicit assumption was that the revolution would come later, but also that, in the immediate context, there was a contradiction between the needs of war and those of revolution. Orwell had some initial sympathy with this point of view: 'the war was worth winning even if the revolution was lost' (*Homage to Catalonia*, 71). Opposed to this was the POUM view of the matter, wherein there was no contradiction between the war and the revolution, in fact the way to win the war was precisely to make and consolidate the revolution. It is a matter of record that by the time Orwell left Spain, he was more sympathetic to this view of the fundamental identity of war and revolution. Digesting the lesson of the communist-inspired compromise with liberal-bourgeois elements in Catalonia, and the related suppression of 'extremist' groupings such as POUM, Orwell wrote that:

perhaps the POUM and Anarchist slogan: 'The war and the revolution are inseparable', was less visionary than it sounds.

(*Homage to Catalonia*, 73)

In his hyper-radical post-Catalonia phase, in the context of a very different war, Orwell reverted to the notion of a contradiction between war and the possibility of revolution. However, when Orwell moved – suddenly, as we have observed – from a radical opposition to the war to patriotic support of it, he did so precisely by dissolving the contradiction on which the anti-Popular Front radicalism of his Independent Labour Party phase had rested, and reverting to the POUM-inspired conflation of war and revolution. Thus, Orwell's 'patriotic' writings of the early war years have a sort of similarity to his Spanish writings in their imagery of a popular revolution in which the people will get their birthright – and their victory. However, it is important to see that, despite the apparent similarity, the 'revolutionary' affirmation of Orwell's 'patriotic' wartime writings is sharply distinguished from the radicalism of his brief, militant Independent Labour Party days as also from the revolutionary fervour of *Homage to Catalonia*. The fundamental nature of the transformation involved is obscured by the fact that while Orwell's pre-war Independent Labour Party radicalism derives, in one way and another, from his Spanish experience, the conflation of war and revolution through which the patriotic transformation of that radicalism is achieved also derives from the Spanish experience. It is therefore easy to miss the substantive transformation that is masked by the rhetorical continuity.[13]

The emergence of the wartime community, markedly in and after the disaster of Dunkirk, was, not only for Orwell, a moving and inspiring experience. The historian Angus Calder has noted the appearance, 'during the first weeks of war', of 'a bizarre phenomenon', a stereotypically British and understated adumbration of the 'alternative' socialist community of radical aspiration:

In the buses, the trains and pubs of Britain, strangers were speaking to one another.[14]

The change, the apparent disappearance of class society was not, after all, as durable or consequential as some hoped – and no doubt others feared – it might be. However, for those who were, whether for personal or for ideological reasons, susceptible to its blandishments, the wartime community must have been a remarkable experience. Orwell's friend Julian Symons is eloquent on the subject:

A wretched time, people say, I recall it as one of the happiest periods of my life. I have always desired a society in which everything should be impermanent and in which the possession of property and the inheritance of money should be eliminated. I know now that I shall never see such a Utopia, but life in London at the time gave us a hint of it as life in Russia must have done in the months after the Revolution . . . Living became a matter of the next meal, the next drink. The way in which people behaved to each other relaxed strangely. Barriers of class and circumstances disappeared, so that London was more nearly an equalitarian city than it has ever been in the last quarter of a century. Was it mere romanticism that discovered 'new styles of architecture, a change of heart' in the bombed places? For a few months we lived in the possibility of a different kind of history.[15]

J. B. Priestley accurately expressed the popular feeling of the time when he wrote:

It so happens that this war, whether those at present in authority like it or not, has to be fought as a citizen's war . . . The new ordeals blast away the old shams. Britain, which in the years immediately before this war was rapidly losing such democratic virtues as it possessed, is now being bombed and burned into democracy.[16]

Ralph Miliband specifically declines the suggestion that 'the popular radicalism of wartime Britain was, for the most part, a formed socialist ideology, let alone a revolutionary one. But', he writes:

in its mixture of bitter memories and positive hopes, in its antagonism to a mean past, in its recoil from Conservative rule, in its impatience of a traditional class structure, in its hostility to the claims of property and privilege, in its determination not to be robbed again of the fruits of victory, in its expectations of social justice, it was a radicalism eager for major, even fundamental changes in British society after the war.[17]

In an obvious way, it was part of official propaganda to foster the illusions of community – but these illusions should not therefore be dismissed. Priestley's rhapsodic evocation of the 'English' community is clearly romantic:

I felt too up there [an LDV (Local Defence Volunteers) post on a hill] a powerful and rewarding sense of community. There we were, ploughman and parson, shepherd and clerk, turning out at night, as our forefathers had often done before us, to keep watch and ward over the sleeping English hills and fields and homesteads.[18]

But it was also perceived to be dangerous. These 'illusions', these myths of community, could, as Orwell recognised, have become powerful social forces in themselves – and there is some possibility that this might have eased for Orwell some of the pain of his separation from his former political colleagues.

He wrote with infectious zest about the possibilities for peaceful social transformation which, paradoxically, the war had opened up. In his wartime diaries – published in *The Collected Essays, Journalism and Letters* (hereafter, *CEJL*) – and in his journalistic writings – most notably *The Lion and the Unicorn* – as well as in the broadcasts which he wrote for the BBC, Orwell developed the theme of war-induced socialism: 'the equalisation in the standard of living and the wiping out of class distinctions which is happening in Britain as a result of the war'.[19] The fact that these broadcasts were closely monitored by the same A. H. Joyce, Principal Information Officer, and C. H. Silver, Political Intelligence Officer at the India Office, who had, discreetly, sabotaged the appointment which had been offered to Orwell on the Lucknow *Pioneer* in 1938, was probably not known to Orwell.[20]

To him, there was 'no question that the spirit and structure of British life are infinitely more democratic and wealth is far more evenly distributed than was the case two years ago'.[21] Orwell welcomed the austerities imposed by the necessities of war:

The British people are disciplining themselves yet harder for the demands of total war . . . No one complains against these restrictions – on the contrary, the general public are demanding that the restrictions shall be made even stricter, so that the selfish minority who behave as though Britain were not at war can be dealt with once and for all.[22]

In his script 'Money and guns', Orwell unambiguously contrasted the new, spartan, hardworking wartime society with the bad old one which was, he thought, finished:

Before the war there was every incentive for the general public to be wasteful . . . [Now] . . . we have had to simplify our lives and fall back more and more on the resources of our own minds instead of on synthetic pleasures manufactured for us in Hollywood or by the makers of silk stockings, alcohol and chocolates. And under the pressure of that necessity we are rediscovering the simple pleasures – reading, walking, gardening, swimming, dancing, singing – which we had half forgotten in the wasteful years before the war.[23]

Orwell was not, as we have seen, alone in perceiving the possibility of a social transformation under duress of war: the perception/ expectation was widely shared. But, finally, it must be said that a mood is still not a movement, and while Orwell responded with zest to the afflatus of the early phase, he was also left vulnerable to its eventual deflation. As the utopian possibilities got modified and distorted in the realities of the real political world, in which precise social and political groups interacted within the limits of particular institutional arrangements, Orwell could do little more than lament, bitterly, the passing away of an opportunity. Thus, in his 'Letter from England' of 3 January 1943, Orwell wrote:

so long as things went badly Britain was driven part of the way towards a revolutionary strategy. There was always the possibility, therefore, of democratizing the war without losing it in the process. Now, however, the tide begins to turn and immediately the dreary world which the American millionaires and their British hangers-on intend to impose upon us begins to take shape.

(II, 282)

The perception of an opportunity undoubtedly derived in significant measure from the real transformations wrought by the necessity of mobilising for war. But I suggest that it owed something also to Orwell's *need* to believe in some such possibility – the need, that is, to mask the sudden incursion of his patriotic loyalties into the field of his political opinions.[24]

The major document of Orwell's wartime communitarian affirmation is *The Lion and the Unicorn: Socialism and the English Genius* (1941). In fairness to Orwell, it should be recognised that *The Lion and the Unicorn* is no mere patriotic panegyric: the 'Socialist' component is genuine enough. Along with the celebration of things English – 'Smoky towns and winding roads, green fields and red pillar boxes' (II, 57) – there is also, echoing Auden's 'Song for the New Year', a rejection of other things English: 'It is goodbye to the *Tatler* and the *Bystander*, and farewell to the lady in the Rolls-Royce' (II, 109). (There is a little-realised irony here in Orwell's breezy dismissal of the *Tatler*: I was informed by one of the directors of the firm of Secker and Warburg, Orwell's publishers, that the commercial success, and specific recognition, of Orwell's most influential book, *Nineteen Eighty-Four*, was sparked off by a review by Elizabeth Bowen in precisely, surprisingly, the *Tatler* of 6 July 1949).

Orwell is impatient with 'the rat-trap faces of bankers and the brassy laughter of stockbrokers' (II, 83), and Hitler is applauded for having 'made the City of London laugh on the wrong side of its face'. There is verbal violence – 'A generation of the unteachable is hanging upon us like a necklace of corpses' (II, 84) – and more, a recognition that 'at some point or other it may be necessary to use violence . . . It is no use imagining that one can make fundamental changes without causing a split in the nation' (II, 95). Finally, Orwell's proposed political programme (II, 96), particularly in its domestic aspects, is rather more radical than the Labour Party is happy to countenance even at this date – after all, it is aimed at 'turning England into a Socialist democracy'.

However, that said, it must also be said that the double affirmation of Orwell's sub-title, necessitated by his avowal of his 'patriotism', does not really work as well as he supposes. Still, before criticising Orwell, I wish to draw attention to his own criticism of Wyndham Lewis's celebration of *The Mysterious Mr. Bull* in a review which was published in June 1939:

He makes the usual claim for the English – they are peace-loving, kindly, unassuming, etc. etc. The closing paragraph of the book would do almost as it stands for a leader in the 'Daily Telegraph'. And yet the fact remains that for a hundred years these kind-hearted English have exploited their fellow-creatures with a callous selfishness unparalleled in history . . . at any moment when the Empire is actually menaced, the anti-imperialist of yesterday is always found to be in hysterics about the safety of Gibraltar.[25]

This was, of course, before the 'break' which I am trying to establish – after the 'break', a large part of Orwell's charge against Wyndham Lewis of patriotic self-love would, *mutatis mutandis*, appear applicable to Orwell himself.

The basic argument of *The Lion and the Unicorn* is simple enough – that 'war is the greatest of all agents of change. It speeds up all processes' (II, 94), and that the strength of English patriotism, roused by war, provides the English people with a unique opportunity to bring about socialism more or less painlessly. The theme of war precipitating revolution had been available to the political imagination at least since 1917, and there is an intriguing hint of precisely that historical context in the entry in Orwell's wartime diary for 17 September 1940:

When you see how the wealthy are *still* behaving, in what is manifestly developing into a revolutionary war, you think of St Petersburg in 1916.

(II, 374)

The possibility of war 'leading to' revolution was fleetingly acknowledged by Orwell even in a letter written during the time that he was still opposing participation in the war effort (see I, 387). Then, the suggested strategy was for the real leftists to preserve their anti-war identity so that they could avail themselves of the 'revolutionary situation' which the war would, mysteriously, produce. The conjunction of war and revolution was also, as we have seen, one of the staples of POUM rhetoric. Now, in 1940, it appears that the conflation of the two in Orwell's mind was reinforced by the authority of someone whose influence on Orwell was, regrettably, to grow stronger – Franz Borkenau. The historian Walter Laqueur records that 'Borkenau, a Communist until 1929, had worked for the Comintern',[26] but eventually became an anti-communist, specialising in 'predictions'. Writing in *Horizon* in November 1947, Borkenau made a more or less explicit call for pre-emptive nuclear war against the Soviet Union: 'In times such as these there is only one upright attitude: *Amor fati.*' Borkenau was also one of the figures at the centre of the horrific hate-orgy of hysterical anti-communists, reported by Hugh Trevor-Roper from the First Congress for Cultural Freedom held at Berlin in June 1950: it reminded him of Hitler's Nuremberg rallies.[27] Borkenau came to England as a refugee at the beginning of the war and Orwell got to know him then.

Bernard Crick (*Life*, pp. 227–8) describes Borkenau's influence on Orwell. On 30 May 1940, Orwell wrote in his diary: 'Borkenau says England is now definitely in the first stage of revolution.' (II, 341); and in the same month he reviewed appreciatively (see II: 8) Borkenau's book *The Totalitarian Enemy* (1940), in which he would have read the following statement: 'War . . . is one of the strongest mechanisms of rapid change, a change which, within the community concerned, is generally much more peaceful than it would have been in time of peace . . . war, by forcing through overdue changes in the structure of this country, may spare us serious social upheaval' (p. 252).

However, irrespective of what the historical sanctions and the reinforcing influences for Orwell's enthusiastic rediscovery of the unity of war and revolution might have been, it seems clear to me that the conflation, drawing as it did upon rich Spanish associations, and resulting in a sort of mysticism of war, enabled Orwell to effect a fundamental transformation of his ideological position while disguising the fact from himself – and apparently from many of his readers as well. The mysticism of war – 'greatest of all agents of social change' – is for Orwell the necessary means of accommodating his newly discovered patriotism in his intellectual position while preserving a radical continuity. With an alacrity which makes instant sense when seen in this way, Orwell made the theme of war and revolution his own and proceeded to expound it with the characteristic vehemence of the convert:

The war and the revolution are inseparable. We cannot establish anything that a western nation would regard as Socialism without defeating Hitler; on the other hand we cannot defeat Hitler while we remain economically and socially in the nineteenth century . . . We cannot win the war without introducing Socialism, nor establish Socialism without winning the war. At such a time, it is possible, *as it was not in the peaceful years*, to be both revolutionary and realistic.

(II, 90, 94; italics added)

He saw here a possibility of escape from the sterilities of the 1930s:

we can turn it into a revolutionary war if we can bring into being a revolutionary movement capable of appealing to a majority of the people, a movement, therefore, not sectarian, not defeatist, not 'anti-British', not resembling in any way the petty fractions of the extreme left, with their heresy-hunting and their Graeco-Latin jargon.[28]

The possibility of the war-induced revolution is, for Orwell, dependent upon a particular scenario for the war. While his patriotism, unalloyed, might have predisposed him to desire an easy triumph for Britain, Orwell is deeply committed to the idea that the very difficulty of winning the war will precipitate the revolution. Thus, his diary entry for 7 June 1942 affords us an amusing glimpse of an earnest Orwell trying to explain to Sir Stafford Cripps that he would regard an easy victory over Germany as 'a disaster pure and simple (because if the war were won as easily as that there would have been no real upheaval here and the American millionaires would still be *in situ*)'. Cripps, hardly surprisingly, 'appeared not to understand' (II, 429; it might be worthwhile recalling this when we try and understand Orwell's mood after 1945, in Attlee's Britain, nominally 'socialist' but increasingly under the influence of the 'American millionaires'). Orwell wrote in a similar strain in a letter of 16 July 1940:

Personally I am much more afraid of Hitler mopping up north Africa and the Near East and then making a peace offer. I actually rather hope that the invasion will happen . . . if we are invaded we shall at any rate get rid once and for all of the gang who had got us into this mess.

(II, 34)

On another occasion, Orwell ventured the even more extreme opinion that it was just as well that the Popular Front strategy had not worked and also that France had fallen so easily, because the consequent *difficulty* of defeating Hitler single-handedly (this was before Hitler attacked Russia and moved the brunt of the war to the East, and before the US entered the war) would result in a revolution as well in valiant, beleaguered England.[29] I hope one is not overstating the case in saying that these intellectual contortions are indicative of strains in Orwell's own attempt to reconcile the two possibilities – war and revolution – which he had, in the period leading up to the war, regarded as antithetical.

It does not require much acquaintance with Orwell's writings to see, somewhere near the core of his political attitudes, from first to last, a yearning for a humane, human community – a community of free and equal beings. Even if we look at Orwell's writings about the derelicts of Paris and London, we notice that, underlying the harrowing details of degradation and destitution, there is a tendency that runs counter to the polemical purpose. There is, even in these writings, a positively affirmed sense of a community based on shared experiences, a relish of the unanxious social relations which Orwell, fresh from the ossified, sclerotic society of the colonies, found at the bottom of the social pyramid. Describing the tramps scattering in the morning after the spike-gates are opened, Orwell wrote in his first article on tramps:

Lugubrious and sordid caravanserai these workhouses where the sad pilgrims of England assemble for a few houses before wandering away again in all directions.[30]

Despite the melancholy adjectives and, indeed, the melancholy phenomena themselves, the ironic 'pilgrims' and 'caravanserai' combine to convey something of a sense of warmth, togetherness, and even of purpose, drawing as they do upon traditional images of this world as being but a brief, convivial occasion. Flory, in *Burmese Days*, yearns to 'live with the stream of life, not against it. It would be better to be the thickest-skulled pukka sahib . . . than to live silent, alone, consoling oneself in secret, sterile worlds' (*Burmese Days*, 70). The 'hop-picking' chapters of *A Clergyman's Daughter*, despite the rigours of the work, tell of 'those long, laborious hours in the strong sunlight, in the sound of forty voices singing' (*A Clergyman's Daughter*, 126). Comstock in *Keep the Aspidistra Flying*, mired in the world of the down-at-heel bourgeoisie, suffers from:

the coldness, the anonymity, the aloofness. Seven million people, sliding to and fro, avoiding contact, barely aware of one another's existence, like fish in an aquarium tank.

(*Keep the Aspidistra Flying*, 89)

Finally, Winston's cry, from the depths of his despair, seeking relief in an insecure privacy from the enforced community of the telescreen and the Hate Week, is still, significantly, 'from the age of solitude' (*Nineteen Eighty-Four*, 31). However, metaphors apart, the quest for 'the stream of life' is inevitably enmeshed in the complexity of real historical situations.

There is a delicately observed incident in *Burmese Days* which embodies for me, in microcosm as it were, the complexity as well as the ironic history of Orwell's quest for community. Early in the novel, before Elizabeth has appeared, Flory is shown as escaping from the suicidal tedium of his everyday existence to the forest outside Kyauktada. In this forest there is a pool which prefigures the fish- and significance-laden pools of Orwell's later fiction:

The roots of the tree made a natural cavern, under which the clear, greenish water bubbled. Above and all around dense foliage shut out the light, turning the place into a green grotto walled with leaves.

(*Burmese Days*, 57)

Here, unsuspecting Flory's presence, a single green pigeon flutters down and perches on a lower branch, where it can be seen clearly. It is a beautiful bird, and the intensity of his feeling for it evokes in Flory a realisation of the solitariness of his existence: 'Beauty is meaningless until it is shared. If he had one person, just one, to halve his loneliness' (*Burmese Days*, 57). As we know from the novel, Flory seeks to find an escape from this solitariness into community through the unlikely person of Elizabeth Lackersteen. The climax of their relationship is the hunting episode, when their brief romance attains its all too few moments of happiness. Flory shoots a tiger and Elizabeth is sufficiently affected by the exoticism of the *shikar* to imagine herself in love with him (*Burmese Days*, 161). It is during this episode that we encounter the green pigeon again:

Flory took one of the little green corpses to show to Elizabeth. 'Look at it. Aren't they lovely things? The most beautiful bird in Asia.'

(*Burmese Days*, 165)

A little later we have an image of Flory and Elizabeth:

kneeling face to face with the dead bird between them. With a shock they discovered that their hands . . . were clasped tightly together.

(*Burmese Days*, 168)

Elizabeth becomes 'conscious of an extraordinary desire to fling her arms around Flory's neck and kiss him; and in some way it was the killing of the pigeon that made her feel this' (*Burmese Days*, 167). There is an obvious irony here, because it was precisely in the context of sharing the experience of the bird's beauty that Flory had desired that relief from solitariness which is now offered to him over its 'little green corpse'. The desire which had been born in a situation in which Flory was seeking escape from the coercive colonial community is thus ironically fulfilled through an episode in which Flory's own conduct – the conduct of the great white *shikari* with his beaters and his servants – betokens membership of that community.

Returning to *The Lion and the Unicorn*, we can see that the asserted compatibility between 'socialism and the English genius' enables Orwell to manoeuvre himself out of a difficult ideological position – reconciling, as I suggested earlier, his socialist commitment to an alternative society with his patriotic commitment to the one that is given, 'available'. By taking a particular view of English society, not merely of its historical character but, crucially, of that character as it is expressed in a moment of national emergency – 'Dunkirk' – Orwell transfers the feeling that properly belongs to the *alternative* community of socialist aspiration towards the *available* community of patriotic Englishmen. This is not to suggest that there is any duplicity or mendacity in Orwell's taking such a view of English society – moving by the force of its inherent dynamic towards socialism. Orwell's view was, I am convinced, 'sincere'. However, it is possible to see, past the sincerity, the fact that Orwell's 'patriotic' transformation compels him towards *a formula of accommodation* with his 'given' society. Thus, Orwell's writing, under the stress of his patriotic affirmation, inevitably becomes enmeshed in:

the strange mixture of reality and illusion, democracy and privilege, humbug and decency, the subtle network of compromises, by which *a nation keeps itself in its familiar shape.*

(II, 63; italics added)

Abstracting from the specificities of the identifications urged in the two cases, one may note the ironic, formal similarity between Orwell's evocation of an atavistic English community – 'an everlasting animal stretching into the future and the past' – and the contemporaneous and sinister evocation of *Volksgemeinschaft* across the water, in Nazi Germany. Both work to suppress the fact of significant social differences: the former in the naive expectation that those differences are disappearing under the stress of war, the latter to generate oppressive majorities and persecuted minorities excluded from the range of social compassion.[31]

It is this 'formula of accommodation' which, I believe, lies at the root of some of Orwell's most notable achievements. The writings on popular culture, for instance, are almost certainly a by-product of his new ideological location. In 1936, Orwell had written to his anthropologist friend, Geoffrey Gorer:

What you say about trying to study our own customs from an anthropological point of view opens up a lot of fields of thought, but one thing to notice about ourselves is that people's habits etc. are formed not only by their upbringing and so forth but also very largely by books. I have often thought it would be very interesting to study the conventions etc. of *books* from an anthropological point of view.

(I,222)

However, it wasn't until he had discovered the wartime community that Orwell was able to make something of this insight.

Watching Max Miller perform in a variety show called *Applesauce* in September 1940 – 'Anyone wanting to see something really vulgar should visit the Holborn Empire' – Orwell was reminded of:

how closely knit the civilization of England is, and how much it resembles a family, in spite of its *out of date* class distinctions. The startling obscenities which occur in Applesauce are only possible because they are expressed in *doubles entendres* which imply a common background in the audience.

(II, 162; italics added)

A similar affection for the popular community warms the essays 'The moon under water' and 'A nice cup of tea', and tempts him, as it does in the quotation above, into what seems like excess – 'In defence of English cooking'. It is, again, the same complex of inspiration and affection which motivates the analyses of comic postcards, of boys' weeklies and of pulp crime fiction.

Swimming at last with the mainstream, Orwell's writing acquires a new ease and assurance. His 'As I please' column, which Orwell wrote for the *Tribune* from 1943 to 1945, is a vehicle for his new-found 'popular' identity. In its relaxed, unbuttoned quality, the characteristic tone and form of 'As I please' seems, in retrospect, to be the consummation of that aesthetic of ambivalence which I have described in chapter 3. In 'As I please', as the collective title indicates, Orwell frees himself from the need to hammer out some kind of consonance, some stabilisation, however temporary, between the contending elements of his personality. I had suggested earlier that the formal recognition of their contention had been the crucial step in Orwell's aesthetic breakthrough. In the tolerant ambiance of 'As I please', this contention is itself transcended, dissolved in a kind of lax pluralism. Freed from the necessity of evolving a unity, however fragile or temporary, Orwell declines into eccentricity, becoming a sort of licensed *enfant terrible*, his socialism merely another aspect of his inexhaustible personality. The world which Orwell affirms in his wartime writings is, it is important to note, still the world in which, as he had recorded, tramps froze out of doors. It is true that he sincerely believes that this world, 'English' society, is undergoing a fundamental transformation, but it is also true that by now Orwell is celebrating the virtues of the householders.[32] It is worth noting, for instance, that the lower middle class, which is seen, in *Coming Up for Air*, as potentially Fascist, becomes, in *The Lion and the Unicorn*, the repository of fine, proto-socialist virtues.

I believe that in affirming or endorsing, albeit in a perceived moment of transformation, the given English community, Orwell is drawn, despite the qualifications with which that affirmation is hedged, into endorsing also some of the hypocrisies and prejudices of that affirmed community. To some extent, Orwell did not need to *acquire* those prejudices (see the remarks about Catholics and women's rights activists in the early letters to Brenda Salkeld, and the diatribe against vegetarians and other 'deviants' in *The Road to Wigan*

Pier).[33] However, now he could give vent to these relatively inhibited aspects of his character with a new assurance. There is an amusing but minor affair which illustrates what I mean. In his weekly *Tribune* column, on 9 February 1945, Orwell aired certain ideas about 'rationalising the interiors of our houses', and about communal washing up:

Every morning a municipal van will stop at your door and carry off a box of dirty crocks, handing you a box of clean ones (marked with your initial of course) in return.

(III, 330)

(If we read 'number' instead of the mocking 'initial' suggested by Orwell, we are quite near *Nineteen Eighty-Four*-land.) One Betty Miller of Abbots Langley reacted angrily to Orwell's suggestions, and wrote an irate letter which deserves quotation, not only because of a delicious hint of self-parody but also because it sounds like a parody of Orwell himself, one year later. This is Mrs Miller:

Mr Orwell advocates 'rationalising the interiors' of our homes as we have 'rationalised' . . . transport and communications. No quisling could suggest a more cunning method of human self-sabotage . . . Home life, that last resort of self-expression, of spontaneity, home life, too is to be mechanised . . . Let Mr Orwell think twice before he advocates the communal washing-up centre; the empty sink is as dangerous to the stability of national life as the empty cradle.[34]

It appears that Mr Orwell did 'think twice', because one year later, reviewing Lawrence Wolfe's book *The Reilly Plan*, Orwell as good as defended the kitchen sink and the whitened doorstep as the last threatened bastions of humanity (see IV:22). Lawrence Wolfe, hardly surprisingly, found it 'disturbing that George Orwell . . . being George Orwell . . . should have responded to the impact of real planning ideas with the cataleptic conservatism of a Corporal Blimp'.[35] However, we should find Orwell's emergent populist conservatism, at any rate, comprehensible in the light of the communitarian development I have tried to describe above.

Perhaps the most far-reaching effect of this development, and one that best illustrates what has happened to Orwell's 'socialism' on this side of my suggested 'break', is his growing impatience with logic and rationality. Consider the thought process of 'an ordinary Englishman' as admiringly evaluated by George Orwell:

An ordinary Englishman, Conservative, Socialist, Catholic, Communist, or what-not, almost never grasps the full logical implications of the creed he professes: almost always he utters heresies without knowing it. Orthodoxies, whether of the Right or the Left, flourish chiefly among the literary intelligentsia, the people who ought in theory to be the guardians of freedom of thought.

(III, 12)

It is interesting to note that slippage from 'logical implications' to 'orthodoxies', and from there to the deeply significant antithesis with 'freedom of thought'. Thus, 'freedom of thought' is, albeit roughly and indirectly, equated with illogicality. It is with obvious admiration, again, that Orwell writes:

a profound, almost unconscious patriotism and an inability to think logically are the abiding features of the English character.

(III, 7)

It is true that even in *The Road to Wigan Pier* Orwell had written with apparent approval of the alleged inability of the working class to think in a 'logically consistent' way (*The Road to Wigan Pier*, 176). But in his populist phase Orwell provides himself with a licence to indulge in that higher mental process, irrationality. C. E. M. Joad is patronised by Orwell for being a 'helpless anachronism' because he is merely 'sensible' whereas 'the future is with the fanatics' who can, in turn, only be comprehended by people, like Orwell, who have not lost touch with popular emotions.[36] Similarly, H. G. Wells is reprimanded:

The energy that actually shapes the world springs from emotions – racial pride, leader-worship, religious belief, love of war – which liberal intellectuals mechanically write off as anachronisms, and which they have usually destroyed so completely in themselves as to have lost all power of action.

(II, 141)

This sudden awareness of the strengths of irrationalism will be of obvious relevance when we consider the roads by which Orwell arrives at the nightmare world of *Nineteen Eighty-Four*.

I do not intend to suggest that Orwell lapsed into a simple-minded, Podsnappian conservatism, nor even the muted sort which he identified in Galsworthy: 'his discontent healed itself, and he reverted to type' (I:119). The wartime writings affirm a society that is, emphatically, in the throes of a transformation that is simultaneously desirable, inevitable, and superfluous. The agency of this paradoxical transformation – or certainly one of the agencies, since Orwell did not formulate his ideas on the operational aspects – was to have been the Home Guard. Orwell had high hopes of the Home Guard, the original Dad's Army, officered by superannuated military fossils from the Home Counties and composed of enthusiastic but, by definition, largely unfit, patriotic recruits. The Home Guard was critically short of weapons and even uniforms, but Orwell's revolutionary fervour was unabated. He wrote warmly of the school – Osterley Park – in which Tom Wintringham and Hugh Slater briefly taught the elements of guerilla warfare (before they were edged out by the War Office).[37] Orwell even went so far as to make the somewhat ambitious proposal that the Government should 'arm the people', but it appears that this proposal was rather coldly received (II:9; II, 351). In one of his wilder fancies, Orwell even imagined the bomb shelters which the Government had 'thoughtlessly' provided being used as machinegun nests by an aroused populace (III, 73). Orwell's rhetoric is, I hope to show, *deceptively* violent, but violent it undoubtedly is:

now the revolution has started . . . I daresay the London gutters will have to run with blood. All right, let them, if it is necessary. But when the red militias are billeted in the Ritz . . .

(I, 539, 540)

If, however, we look closely at the writings of this period – even at the Home Guard writings – it becomes clear that the image of revolution which Orwell espoused around this time was rather gentler than is suggested by these sanguinary fantasies. Although the change envisaged was fundamental, it was expected to happen more or less painlessly, the trauma masked by the anaesthetic of war. The relatively cosy nature of the fantasy is apparent in the sociological conception which underlies the writings of this period. This is the famous conception of the nation as a family:

a rather stuffy Victorian family, with not many black sheep in it, but with all its cupboards bursting with skeletons . . . It is a family in which the young are generally thwarted and most of the power is in the hands of irresponsible uncles and bedridden aunts. Still, it is a family. It has its private language and its common memories, and at the approach of an enemy it closes its ranks. A family with the wrong members in control.

(II, 68)

It is surprising to find revolutionary rhetoric flowing from this metaphor, because the concept of the nation-as-family implies a wholly different kind of politics.[38] However, if we examine the implied image of revolution it becomes apparent that the rhetoric is misleading, or at least critically ambiguous:

It is only by revolution that the native genius of the English people can be set free. Revolution does not mean red flags and street fighting, it means a fundamental shift of power . . . What is wanted is a conscious open revolt by ordinary people against inefficiency, class privilege and the rule of the old.

(II, 86)

It is not even, it turns out, 'primarily a question of change of government', for the desired results will come about if, and the vagueness here is deeply significant, 'we alter our structure from below' (II, 86). A little later in the same essay Orwell writes: 'even without an election we can get the government we want, provided that we want it urgently enough. A real shove from below will accomplish it' (II, 101). At the head of the red militias which will be billeted in the Ritz after the London gutters have run with blood, Orwell would not be surprised to see, a diary entry tells us, Churchill or Lloyd George (II, 352). For a while, in some of the writings it appears as if the Home Guard, trembling uncertainly between being 'a real People's Army or a not-very-good imitation of the pre-war Territorials',[39] waiting for the influx of ardent leftists who will 'diffuse political consciousness' among its ranks, may provide the armed might of the revolution. However, on closer inspection, it appears that what is envisaged is something altogether gentler – a strategy of 'obtaining influence . . . by being as good a soldier as possible, by being conspicuously obedient, efficient and self-sacrificing', because 'the influence of even a few thousand men who were known to be good comrades *and* to hold Left-Wing views could be enormous'.[40] The revolution, it appears, will almost be a revolution by consent, a sort of superfluous revolution. It is hardly surprising therefore that, despite the dithering and sense of futility of which Orwell complained bitterly in his wartime diary (see II, 432–4), he is forced, towards the end of the war, to conclude that the Home Guard, far from being the army of the revolution, had been valuable rather as a 'symptom' that the revolution was not really necessary: 'No authoritarian State would have dared to distribute weapons so freely.'[41] A diary entry for 12 April 1941 contains the observation that, although the specific predictions have been falsified, 'the revolutionary changes that I expected *are* happening, but in slow motion' (II, 394).

One cannot, admittedly, *disprove* what is after all only a metaphor – the nation-as-family – appropriate or inappropriate according to the analogies it brings into focus. However, it is clear that there is no politics, no *doing* that flows from this metaphor, unless we accept the 'shoves' (ii, 101) and 'tugs' (ii, 68) which must suffice in familial politics. Thus, and this is the nub of my argument, in accommodating himself under the stress of war and a reflexive 'patriotism' with the 'available' community, Orwell has, in a political sense, manoeuvred himself into a position of *tactical apathy*. All is well as long as 'socialism' and 'the English genius' as interpreted by Orwell run parallel to each other. It is when the two divide, when, as in the post-war period, there appears to be but little socialist zeal in the English people, that the negative effects of Orwell's reliance on the agency of 'the English genius' begin to show: *the radical commitment to things as they ought to be and might be is unavoidably shackled by a conservative commitment to things as they are.*

One last, little-known example of the immediate but camouflaged ideological consequence of Orwell's 'patriotic' affirmation must suffice. Orwell had been, and in many senses was to remain, a critic of imperialism. However, when in 1943 one Robert Duval published a proposal that Burma be granted a certain measure of independence as a way of countering the appeal of Japanese propaganda, Orwell reacted sharply. Perhaps by virtue of the years that he had spent in Burma, Orwell was regarded as something of an expert on that country, and he was asked by *Tribune* to write a 'Background note' to Duval's 'Plan'. Orwell wrote:

Burma is a small, backward agricultural country, and to talk about making it independent is nonsense in the sense that it can never be independent. There is no more reason for turning Asia into a patchwork of comic-opera states than there is with Europe ... I suggest that even from the short-term propaganda point of view it is dangerous to transfer European slogans and habits of thought to Asiatic countries where, for example, there are no trade unions and the name of Marx has barely been heard.[42]

Not surprisingly, *Tribune* readers were shocked, and one E. A. Richards wrote to the Editor thus:

When I read George Orwell's 'footnote' to Robert Duval's 'Whitehall's Road to Mandalay', I began to wonder whether I had stumbled on the *Daily Telegraph* instead of *Tribune* ... Orwell's suggestion that it is 'dangerous to transfer European slogans and habits of thought' to countries like Burma is an echo (whether or not intended as such) of what the Tories are always saying . . . Does Orwell think that the British Raj, under Amery's care, is going to develop the trade unionism and Socialism whose absence in Burma he makes the excuse for the retention of empire?[43]

The tone of Orwell's reply is slightly huffy:

The plain fact is that small nations *cannot* be independent, because they cannot defend themselves.

He proposes, instead, a plan which he suggests has the merit of being 'realisable':

I would place the whole mainland of south-east Asia, together with Formosa, under the guidance of China, while leaving the islands under an Anglo-American-Dutch condominium.[44]

The proposal runs, with characteristic if naive generosity, to loans of experts, technical guidance, etc. – in a word, imperialism as welfare. Interestingly enough, Orwell had made a similar proposal in respect of the French colony of Morocco in November 1942:

A country like Morocco cannot be genuinely independent because it cannot defend itself; it must be under some kind of tutelage and it must have the loan of European technical experts; but to free the Arabs from economic exploitation would be very simple, and would hurt nobody except a few wealthy men in Paris and Casablanca . . . It would be very easy for us and the Americans to do this, our own interests not being directly involved.

However, he concluded, 'But when one tries to imagine it actually happening, and then looks at the faces of the people who rule us, one remembers rather sadly that the age of miracles is over.'[45]

We cannot help seeing, in retrospect, that we are here very close to the imaginative universe of *Nineteen Eighty-Four* – and, indeed, that Orwell is himself proposing solutions which, after the idealism has been deleted from them, are strikingly similar to the fantasies of multinational conglomerates and condominiums which James Burnham was developing: fantasies which, be it said, Orwell himself polemicised against, and of which the paralysed world of *Nineteen Eighty-Four* with its three superstates – no 'patchwork comic-opera states' there – is a fictional condemnation. In *The Lion and the Unicorn*, Orwell actually chided the left-wing intelligentsia for 'the general weakening of imperialism, and to some extent of the whole British morale' (II, 74). In the same essay, Orwell is also toughly dismissive of the prospects of anti-imperialism:

In the age of the tank and the bombing plane, backward agricultural countries like India and the African colonies can no more be independent than can a cat or dog.

(II, 91)

At one level, clearly, Orwell is being merely realistic, drawing out the lesson from the experience of the smaller European nations in the years leading up to the Second World War:

The whole story of Czechoslovakia . . . brings out in its most painful form the problems of self-determination. When small nations are independent they are unable to protect themselves; when they are not independent they are invariably misgoverned.[46]

However, it is not difficult to see that such 'realism' could, under the circumstances of post-war Europe, mutate into the nightmare vision of *Nineteen Eighty-Four*, divided into the three monster states of Eurasia, Eastasia and Oceania.

One might recall, in this context, Orwell's confident distinction between 'patriotism' and 'nationalism'. 'By "patriotism"', Orwell writes:

I mean devotion to a particular place and a particular way of life, which one believes to be the best in the world but has no wish to force upon other people. Patriotism is of its nature defensive, both militarily and culturally. Nationalism, on the other hand, is inseparable from the desire for power.

(II, 362)

'Patriotism', for Orwell, appears to be a sort of contented, unaggressive nationalism. However, it is surely not that difficult to see that the patriotism of violated peoples must inevitably be aggressive, as they seek to recapture their sense of their identity from the perceptions and distortions of others.[47] Although he is unwilling to condone the 'centuries of English tyranny and oppression' (IV, 32) in Ireland, Orwell still finds it possible from his 'English' location to jeer at Sean O'Casey's evocation of Cathleen ni Houlinan, the symbol of Irish nationalism:

why is it that the worst extremes of jingoism and racialism have to be tolerated when they come from an Irishman?

(IV, 14)

With such awareness of the real history of the world, and more particularly of British imperialism, as Orwell demonstrably has, such innocence ill becomes him.

It is, indeed, something more than innocence which prompts Orwell in 1941 to write:

It is a fact that many of the events which the jingo history books make the most noise about are things to be proud of.[48]

Orwell was sternly dismissive of Celtic nationalisms (see III, 373) even while he praised the underrated strengths and virtues of his own 'patriotism'. The contradiction was pointed out by a correspondent in *Tribune*:

Is George Orwell being merely provocative when he talks of 'comic-opera' states, 'petty nationalism' and the absurdity of giving small nations their freedom? . . . Some time ago he told me that intellectuals had underrated the depth of national feeling everywhere. Apparently he has now changed his views.[49]

Orwell replied:

In a world of power politics and intolerant nationalism . . . there are only five or at most six countries capable of holding their own, and each of these would, of necessity, be quite ruthless in crushing any minor national group that got in its way.[50]

It appears that, at the time Orwell wrote this, he was still secure in the afflatus which comes from the feeling of being/believing that one is on the side of history, from riding the swell of a real, if confused, popular arousal. More cynically, Orwell was perhaps shielded from the gloom which envelops the imaginative world of *Nineteen Eighty-Four* by the feeling that Britain, not yet Airstrip One, would itself be one of the 'five or at most six countries' which, Orwell believed, were capable of 'holding their own'. Still, it is quite easy to see that, with little shifts of mood and perspective, we are quite near the world of *Nineteen Eighty-Four*.

Writing in late 1943 or early 1944 of the Marxist parties, 'all of them claiming to be the true and uncorrupted successors of Lenin' (this must include the Independent Labour Party to which Orwell had latterly belonged), it is significant that Orwell uses the third-person form:

The average Englishman is unable to grasp *their* doctrines and uninterested in *their* grievances.

(III, 16; italics added)

Where, one asks, is Orwell himself located? Obviously, with 'the average Englishman' in the 'available' community of which *The Lion and the Unicorn* is both a recognition and, in a moment of imagined fundamental transformation, a celebration. But, and this is my argument, the afflatus is deceptive and shortlived, and in time Orwell comes down with a bump, the euphoria is followed by suffocation, the revolutionary 'red militias' of the superfluous revolution giving way to equally melodramatic nightmares about the impossibility of social transformation. And one miraculous and brilliantly ironic fable about its foredoomed futility.

listeners 'among the wealthier classes all over Europe'.[2] In his broad-cast of 13 June 1942, Orwell welcomed the recently signed Anglo-Russian Treaty about wartime coordination and post-war colla-boration: 'the two regimes are now in far greater political and economic agreement than would have been possible or even think-able five years ago. It means, in fact, that the ancient ghost of Bolshevism and "bloody revolution" has been laid for ever.'[3] This new-found respectability of the Soviet Union – as also the popularity – could support several different conclusions. It might, for instance, be seen as an index or factor of the processes that conduced towards the Labour victory of 1945. Orwell however had for several years been of the opinion that the interests of the Soviet Union were antithetical to those of socialism, and the endorsement of the Soviet regime by His Majesty's Government was hardly likely to make him change his mind. He was, thus, surprised by the 'Upper Crust' delight at the dissolution of the Comintern in 1943: 'a fact which I record but cannot readily explain', because, of course, in Orwell's eyes, 'the Comintern has been one of the worst enemies the working class has had' (II:46). From his somewhat eccentric location, therefore, raising the 'ancient ghost of Bolshevism' once again, albeit in a left-wing version, could well appear to be a sacred and lonely *socialist* duty.

When first offered for publication in early 1944, *Animal Farm* was so far out of line with prevalent opinion, and official policy, that it nearly ended up not being published at all. Or published, in despair, as a broadsheet by Orwell's impecunious friend, the poet Paul Potts – which might have been very nearly the same thing. The story of the rejections of the *Animal Farm* ms is well known. Cape rejected it on advice from the Ministry of Information, and relayed, in its rejection letter, the 'imbecile' (III, 207) advice that the ms might become more acceptable if the *Animal Farm* elite were depicted not as pigs but as other, less offensive beasts. T. S. Eliot rejected it on behalf of Faber, and Orwell reports an American publisher turning it down on the grounds that 'animal stories did not sell well in the U.S.A.'. Stung by the rejections, Orwell wrote an angry 'preface' to the projected broadsheet which, in the event, was not used because Warburg, finally, decided to publish the unwanted ms. The rest is history. *Animal Farm* became one of the publishing sensations of our time, and Orwell's 'provocation' achieved apotheosis as a universal school text. 'If liberty means anything at all'. Orwell wrote in the 'lost' preface, 'The freedom of the press', in early 1944 when the popularity of the

Soviet Union was at its height, 'it means the right to tell people what they do not want to hear.'[4] Ironically enough, it was written in defence of a fable that people never seem to tire of.

However, Orwell's achievement in *Animal Farm* is ironic not only in respect of the disjunction between its anticipated unpopularity and its popular success, it is ironic also in respect of the gap between what Orwell had first intended to write, and the fable he actually wrote. Explaining the genesis of *Animal Farm* in the 'Author's preface to the Ukrainian edition of *Animal Farm*' (III:110), Orwell said:

if only animals became aware of their strength we should have no power over them . . . I proceeded to analyse Marx's theory from the animals' point of view. To them it was clear that the concept of a class struggle between humans was pure illusion . . . the true struggle is between animals and humans. From this point of departure, it was not difficult to elaborate the story.

It is evident from this that *Animal Farm* had been intended as an allegory of the common people, awaking to a realisation of their strength and overthrowing their oppressors – a sort of farmyard version of *The Lion and the Unicorn*. In working out the fable, however, in the winter of 1943–4, the euphoria has collapsed. In 1954 a critic suggested that *Animal Farm* was not really about the Russian Revolution but rather about the English 'revolution' which had seemed imminent in *The Lion and the Unicorn*.[5] At a superficial level, this is clearly wrong. The tragic course of the Russian Revolution was very much in Orwell's mind in *Animal Farm*, to the extent that he made a correction, at proof stage, in recognition of Stalin's bravery, in the face of the German advance on Moscow: when the windmill was blown up, 'all the animals except Napoleon', he insisted, 'flung themselves on their faces' (III, 359). In an unpublished letter to his agent, now in the Berg collection in New York, Orwell wrote: 'If they question you again, please say that *Animal Farm* is intended as a satire on dictatorship in general but *of course* the Russian Revolution is the chief target. It is humbug to pretend anything else.'[6] However, at a deeper level, it is still possible to see that the disappointment of his wartime hopes – his feeling that 'the political advance we seemed to make in 1940 has been gradually filched away from us' (III, 226) – lent its specific accent of anguish and despair to Orwell's critique of the Russian Revolution. In this mood, the grotesque transformation of the Russian Revolution, of which Orwell had been openly critical for some time, became a paradigmatic instance of *all* attempts at revolutionary social transformation.

One unintended effect of Orwell's avowedly leftist critique of the violence and tyranny of the pigs – the post-revolutionary elite – is that the regime of Jones, softened by nostalgia, begins to appear almost prelapsarian. This was *not* an avowal that Orwell could make explicitly. Thus, as the pigs become more ruthless and tyrannical they become, Orwell insists, more like men – like Pilkington and Frederick, like Jones. However, between the men who act like pigs and the pigs who become like men, there is precious little room for the animals who dreamt of revolution – or for the imagination that dreamt that dream. Thus, it is precisely my argument that with his wartime affirmation, the infectious euphoria that ended in disappointment, Orwell has boxed himself in. In this state, Orwell's intended allegory of the spontaneous revolution becomes an allegory of the revolution endlessly betrayed, a perverse and brilliant distillation of the worst features of the Russian Revolution into a sort of supra-temporal fatality, an iron destiny of treachery, and despair, and endless anguish, an exuberant and flamboyantly sarcastic prelude to Orwell's final, gloomy masterpiece, *Nineteen Eighty-Four*.

Nineteen Eighty-Four is, as an object of critical attention, constantly on the point of vanishing; it lives perilously on the borderline beyond which lies its own impossibility. Thus, the novel would be inconceivable without Winston, a recalcitrant protagonist who, through his exiguous resistance, shows up the tyranny of the State. However, for the tyranny to appear truly horrific, that recalcitrance must itself appear pathetic and shabby – ultimately, just delusory. Thus, the 'manhood' of 'the last man in Europe' is essential as a fundamental premise for the novel to become possible; but it is also negated by the larger intention which informs the novel, the depiction of a tyranny that is absolute, total, 'totalitarian'. If Winston is 'the last man', *Nineteen Eighty-Four* must be, necessarily, 'the last novel'. The Goldstein interpolations illustrate the same difficulty. They are essential in order to say what the novel, bereft of this device, cannot say; in other words, the interpolations are necessary in order to say what the novelist wishes his novel to say but cannot, by the same token, allow it to say. The necessity of the criticism of the State of Big Brother which the interpolations offer is directly proportional to the novel's impossibility without these formally awkward interpolations. Ultimately, however, the impossibility consumes the criticism, when it is discovered that the Goldstein interpolations are also an invention of the State. The tyranny is rendered absolute, but the novel leads, for that very reason, a highly endangered existence, constantly on the point of becoming invisible, consumed in the effulgence of its perfection in its meticulous rendering of the absolute tyranny of Big Brother.

Nineteen Eighty-Four tends towards invisibility also because its ostensible subject matter is one with which practically every literate person is familiar. Oceania is, at superficial and deeper levels, a known country. The novel's dominant images, of Big Brother and the endlessly suspicious State, have been endlessly drawn upon, until they have become blurred. Its daringly innovative concepts, of Newspeak and 'doublethink', have become the common currency of the intellectual marketplace, and their connotative universes are inevitably cacophonous with the clamour of the marketplace, the special pleading of the vociferous sellers.

The novel itself stands in a peculiar, complex and slippery relationship to a recognisable historical world. Nineteen Eighty-Four might be seen to be a product of an arguable but specifiable historical experience – 'the product', according to one account, 'not of a mind but of a culture'.[7] More arguably, it might be seen as being, itself, a historical agent, a significant propaganda weapon – 'a key work in the international literature of resignation'.[8] One critic has gone so far as to call Nineteen Eighty-Four 'one of the most influential books of the modern period, even for those who have never read it'.[9] It might thus be said to relate to the world of history at the level of cause as well as that of consequence. One cannot say about Nineteen Eighty-Four, any more than Orwell suggested one could about Koestler's Darkness at Noon, that it is:

simply a story dealing with the adventures of an imaginary individual. Clearly, it is a political book, founded on history and offering an interpretation of disputed events.

(III, 240)

However, one can hardly discuss the novel as history, for Nineteen Eighty-Four has, after all, a residual and almost impregnable formal defence in that it is a fantasy set in the future. As such, it is not vulnerable to criticisms emanating from outside its universe, from the world of real time. If one reaches for the novel with historical tools, it retreats into fictionality; if, on the other hand, one approaches it as fiction, and reproaches it as such for, say, the meagreness of its characterisation, it escapes into history, in pleading the well-publicised, character-crushing nature of 'totalitarianism'.[10]

It is, however, *because* of the novel's imbrication with a known and controversial historical world that it is essential to gain a certain critical distance from it. Otherwise, I believe, it is fatally easy to bypass the book altogether, and land directly in the thickets of political controversy, irrespective of whether one approaches it from the Right or the Left. Jennifer McDowell read *Nineteen Eighty-Four* as a quasi-documentary account of life in the Soviet Union[11] and Matthew Hodgart 'interpreted' *Nineteen Eighty-Four* as a portrait of life in Russia *and* China.[12] Arthur Calder-Marshall, reviewing *Nineteen Eighty-Four* in 1949, no doubt *also* read *Nineteen Eighty-Four* as an attack on the Soviet Union, and dismissed it therefore as 'a jejune affair'.[13] James Walsh's famous 'Communist' attack on *Nineteen Eighty-Four*[14] shares with the above an inability to focus on the fictionality of the novel. The Soviet commentator who wrote that *Nineteen Eighty-Four* was an account of life in the USA[15] might well have been unusually obtuse, but, purely from a critical point of view, his contribution was about equal to that of Jennifer McDowell, who plumped for the Soviet Union as the site of Orwell's field-study.

As the above brief survey, mere appetiser to the whole grotesque banquet that awaits the diligent scholar, will have made clear, Orwell's *Nineteen Eighty-Four* has been subjected to a great deal of partisan interpretation. But it would be wrong to allow ourselves to be misled by the obvious and frequently highlighted presence of one set of Cold War stereotypes in Orwell's novel into missing the fact that Orwell's targets are chosen eclectically, with a fine disregard for intellectual caste barriers – the polemic of the book is directed against 'the barren world of monopoly industry and centralised government' (*Nineteen Eighty-Four*, 211), against 'totalitarianism' as well as monopoly capitalism. Although Orwell had little love for Soviet Communism, he also had few illusions about 'the dreary world which the American millionaires and their hangers-on intend to impose on us' (II, 282). There are incorporated in the imaginative world of *Nineteen Eighty-Four* distinct elements from that late-capitalist reality which Orwell spent an enormous number of words polemicising against. Elements of his own ambient reality merge with the assembly-line propaganda put out by the USSR to produce in *Nineteen Eighty-Four* the:

whole chains of separate departments dealing with proletarian literature, music, drama, and entertainment generally. Here were produced rubbishy newspapers containing almost nothing except sport, crime, and astrology, sensational five-cent novelettes, films oozing with sex, and sentimental songs which were composed entirely by mechanical means on a special kind of kaleidoscope known as a versificator.

(*Nineteen Eighty-Four*, 46–7)

What George Steiner argued in 1967 is evident enough, though it is frequently lost sight of in the Cold War view of Orwell:

The polemic of the fable is not unilinear. Orwell's critique bears simultaneously on the police state and the capitalist consumer society, with its illiteracy of values and its conformities. 'Newspeak', the language of Orwell's nightmare, is both the jargon of dialectical materialism and the verbiage of commercial advertisement and mass media . . . To make of *Nineteen Eighty-Four* a pamphlet in the intellectual cold war is to misread and diminish the book.[16]

Similarly, and unsurprisingly, elements of post-war London, of the reality of the England of Attlee and the first Labour Government, also enter the fantasy. This Labour Government inherited the extensive apparatus of economic direction and control which had been set up during the war – apparatus which, hindsight suggests, might have mitigated some of the possible harshness of the post-war situation.[17] However, the administrative machinery could hardly substitute for the widespread shortages of capital as well as of materials, and came, in time and in certain quarters, to be identified with those shortages and their effects.[18] The 'remote committees which', in *Nineteen Eighty-Four*, 'were liable to hold up even the mending of a window-pane for two years' (*Nineteen Eighty-Four*, 24) owe as much to post-war Britain as they do to the burgeoning bureaucracy of 'totalitarianism'.[19] The physical landscape of *Nineteen Eighty-Four* is, as has been remarked, pure post-war London:

these vistas of rotting nineteenth-century houses, their sides shored up with baulks of timber, their windows patched with cardboard and their roofs with corrugated iron, their crazy garden walls sagging in all directions . . . the bombed sites where the plaster dust swirled in the air and the willow herb straggled over the heaps of rubble; and the places where the bombs had cleared a larger patch and there had sprung up sordid colonies of wooden dwellings like chicken-houses . . .

(*Nineteen Eighty-Four*, 7)

The last, but by no means either least or inadequately remarked, source of ideas and images for Orwell's nightmare is, of course, the reality of the 'totalitarian' societies themselves – Hitler's Germany and Stalin's Russia. The falsifications of history, the leader-worship, the palpably framed-up trials, the purges and the deportations, the intolerance of dissent, the brutal insensitivity, the deaths – these derive equally from Nazi Germany and from Stalinist Russia. But rather more remarkable than the awareness of the scale of the tyranny is Orwell's insight into the psychology of the perpetually hunted, haunted citizens of 'totalitarian' societies. It was this which evoked the admiration of Czeslaw Milosz: 'Even those who know Orwell only by hearsay are amazed that a writer who never lived in Russia should have so keen a perception into its life.'[20] However, it is also true that Orwell had been concerned with the obscenities, not only of Nazism but also of Stalinism, long before the majority of his contemporaries, particularly those who saw themselves as belonging on the political Left. While this redounds, somewhat monotonously, to his credit, this concern is, by the same token, insufficient to account for the specificity of the mood of anxiety and despair in which *Nineteen Eighty-Four* is cast. Orwell was never 'illusioned' enough to be made part of the great disillusionment which is associated with *The God That Failed*.[21]

Orwell scholars have noted the continuity between *Nineteen Eighty-Four* and Orwell's earlier writings, at the level of images as well as of themes.[22] As Julian Symons remarked in his 1949 review of the novel, *Nineteen Eighty-Four* is the culmination of a development whose roots can be traced through all the phases of Orwell's career: 'It is a queer route that Mr Orwell has taken from Burma to the Oceania of *Nineteen Eighty-Four*, by way of Catalonia and Wigan Pier.'[23] Flory's isolation in his colonial outpost, his sense of confinement in the tightly controlled, taboo-ridden colonial situation, is clearly related to Winston's sense of suffocation, of close and unbearable confinement in a 'community' he cannot accept, and from which he recoils into an equally unbearable solitude. Similarly, Orwell's reminiscence in *The Road to Wigan Pier* of a night of ordinary candour with a person on the train to Mandalay, followed by their parting 'guiltily' in 'the haggard morning light' (p. 147), as if in acknowledgment of the inescapability of the tyranny which they both detest, is paralleled in the air of surreptitiousness and avidity which surrounds the most ordinary human contacts, between Winston and Julia, or between Winston and the old 'prole' in the pub, in *Nineteen Eighty-Four*. In the formidable apparatus of historical revision through censorship which Orwell deploys in *Nineteen Eighty-Four*, one can clearly hear echoes of his Spanish experience, and its aftermath. At the level of images also, the rats of Room 101 are foreshadowed in the rats that crawl over Republican militiamen in the trenches of Catalonia (*Homage to Catalonia*, 87). The boot stamping on a human face which O'Brien offers Winston as a picture of the future – 'for ever' (*Nineteen Eighty-Four*, 274) – is anticipated in Bowling's vision, at the anti-fascist meeting, of the speaker 'smashing people's faces in with a spanner' (*Coming Up for Air*, 151). Even the green pigeon of *Burmese Days*, whose beauty strengthens Flory's desire to escape from his loneliness, reappears as the thrush whose singing complements the fear-stricken communion of Winston and Julia (*Nineteen Eighty-Four*, 127). The famous young woman of *The Road to Wigan Pier* who, 'kneeling there in the bitter cold, on the slimy stones of a slum backyard, poking a stick up a foul drainpipe' (*The Road to Wigan Pier*, 20), becomes a symbol of the degradation of ordinary human beings in man-made systems, reappears in *Nineteen Eighty-Four*:

He seemed to see a vision of London, vast and ruinous, city of a million dustbins, and mixed up with it was a picture of Mrs Parsons, a woman with a lined face and wispy hair, fiddling helplessly with a blocked waste-pipe.

(*Nineteen Eighty-Four*, 78)

Indeed, themes and images from his entire career bear down with such concentrated force on *Nineteen Eighty-Four* that Orwell could with justification have said, in the manner of Whistler when he was charged with having dashed off his portrait of his mother, that he had, in effect, been writing it all his life.[24]

A concern with the threat of 'totalitarianism', too, is common to all the stages of Orwell's career, at least from the mid-1930s. Thus, by 1948, Orwell had coexisted with the idea of 'totalitarianism' for a considerable period of time. He had inveighed against its Russian 'incarnation' and, as it happens, somewhat less so against the German one. However, in 1941, Orwell described the process of war-mobilisation in Britain also as 'totalitarianisation' . . . (II:19) – and was, indeed, far from averse to its social consequences, which he, somewhat confusingly, described as 'democratic':

I would not mind seeing the whole nation in dyed battledress for five years if by that means one of the main breeding points of snobbery and envy could be eliminated. Clothes rationing was not conceived in a democratic spirit, but all the same it has had a democratising effect.

(III, 89)

During the war, while working for the BBC, Orwell experienced at first hand the official manipulation of the flow of information, ironically, in the service of 'democracy' against 'totalitarianism'. (I cannot resist the temptation of quoting from a letter written by Eric Blair, Talks Producer, Indian Section, on 29 September 1942: 'I am returning the enclosed script because I am afraid we cannot use it. Much as it interested me, it is politically quite impossible from our point of view. I don't mean that there is not a great deal to be said for the views that you express, but we cannot of course broadcast anything that is not in line with official policy.'[25]) In various writings of the time, Orwell noted the 'totalitarian' possibilities of the BBC and other big corporations, of radio and of cinema in 'the monopoly stage of capitalism' (II, 335). In early 1944, Orwell even identified something which he called 'The world tendency . . . towards nationalism and totalitarianism' (III, 147). However, while these somewhat blurred tendencies were noted, and castigated, they were not felt to overwhelm and wholly usurp the areas and institutions in which they were found, nor did they overwhelm and wholly usurp Orwell's imagination in the way that the possibility of an eternal, unbreachable 'totalitarian' tyranny does in *Nineteen Eighty-Four*. Thus, while we note the continuities, it is the specific discontinuity that we must seek to comprehend.

The matter of language – 'Newspeak' – is central to Orwell's conception of the suffocating tyranny of *Nineteen Eighty-Four*. Language is one of the key instruments of political domination, the necessary and insidious means of the 'totalitarian' control of reality. As Syme explains to Winston:

The Revolution will be complete when the language is perfect. Newspeak is Ingsoc and Ingsoc is Newspeak.

(*Nineteen Eighty-Four*, 56)

Winston's struggle in the novel is, to a large extent, a struggle to find an adequate language or, what is nearly the same thing, an adequate critical location from which he can regard the world whose language holds him in bondage. The struggle is, we know, a failure – Goldstein's language, which Winston needs as much as Orwell himself does to describe the tyranny of Big Brother, is revealed to be another manifestation of that same, enveloping tyranny. Thus, Winston's rebellion is quenched in an involuntary, unconscious complicity. The suffocation is total. The idea of Newspeak, thus, is crucial to Orwell's conception of *Nineteen Eighty-Four*. The development of this idea, considered along with two earlier essays on language by Orwell, offers a dramatic illustration of that larger collapse of hope, that perverse deflation which, it is my argument, lies at the root of Orwell's terminal despair.

The first piece of evidence that I wish to consider is an essay, 'New words', first published in 1958 in *CEJL* II, which has been estimated by the editors of *CEJL* to date from 1940.

The suggested project of 'New words' is, quite simply:

to invent a vocabulary, perhaps amounting to several thousand words, which would deal with parts of our experience now practically unamenable to language.

(II, 3)

This inadequacy of language – 'practically useless for describing anything that goes on inside the brain' – was also pointed out by Orwell in a review he wrote in 1942:

our language is so crude compared with our mental processes that communication between human beings is chancy at best.[26]

There is a fleeting suggestion that Orwell might be extending the perception of inadequacy to external material reality and its relation with language as well: 'we find that words are no liker to the reality than chessmen to living beings' (II, 3). However, it soon becomes apparent from the context that Orwell is dealing exclusively with the relation between language and consciousness. (The significance of this omission will become apparent later.) Orwell suggests that there is a pre-lingual content of consciousness – 'The disordered, unverbal world . . . a stream of nameless things' (II, 4) – and that this might be 'the most important part' of our minds since 'it is the source of nearly all motives. All likes and dislikes, all aesthetic feeling, all notions of right and wrong.' Since words cannot adequately describe this 'inner life', all human beings are condemned to living in 'star-like isolation' (II, 5) and 'nearly all literature is an attempt to escape from this isolation by roundabout means'. However, although words are inadequate to describe consciousness accurately, they are nevertheless possessed of 'accidental qualities' which 'constantly tempt and frighten' the artist away from his 'true meaning' (II, 6). Thus, what is expressed is often a distorted version of what was intended, and this distortion is compounded in the act of communication by the 'further falsifications' which result because the 'reader or hearer . . . sees meanings which are not there' (II, 6). This is, it will be seen, a rather extreme relativistic position: language and therefore communication is beset by an apparently inescapable subjective falsification.

Orwell's proposed answer, in 'New words', is to invent a new vocabulary to articulate and thus objectify this elusive subjective content. There is, of course, still the difficulty of agreeing about 'what we are naming' (II, 8) since, by definition, words are not available. Somewhat oddly, Orwell suggests that 'the film is one possible medium for conveying mental processes . . . there is very little in the mind that could not *somehow* be represented by the strange distorting powers of the film' (II, 10). Orwell recognised that there might be difficulties: 'putting thoughts into visible shape would not always be easy – in fact, at first it might be as difficult as any other art' (II, 11). Still, once it is accomplished, when we have 'show[n] a meaning in some unmistakable form', and 'when various people have identified it in their own minds and recognised it as worth naming', then we have a word, and a solution to the problem – we have found 'a way in which one can give thought an objective existence'.

All this is amazingly naive as well as being logically unsound. As it happens, however, Orwell also sensed this (II, 12) and even if he had not, there would have been little point in dredging up an old essay – not even published by Orwell – merely in order to gloat over its shortcomings. What makes it valuable is the ironic light it sheds on Orwell's subsequent thinking on the question of language, as represented in his famous essay 'Politics and the English language', and in the conception of 'Newspeak'. Thus, in order to get around the problem of the verification of the non-verbalisable, Orwell has recourse to something that he calls 'unmistakable common knowledge' (II, 9). However, a little later it appears that this 'common' stock, in addition to being the basis of linguistic reform, is also its object: 'What is wanted is to discover the now nameless feelings that men have *in common*' (II, 11). Once again, the important point to notice is not the obvious circularity of the reasoning, but rather the important part which the notion of a durable, secure stock of common language plays in Orwell's thinking about language. By the time we get to *Nineteen Eighty-Four* and the world of 'Newspeak', this assurance is gone, and Winston's recourse is not to the vulnerable certitudes of human experience and memory but rather to the abstract certainties of mathematics: '$2+2=4$'. In 'New words', Orwell writes that after the new vocabulary has been invented, 'expressing one's meaning' would become 'simply a matter of taking the right words and putting them in place, like working out an equation in algebra'. 'I think', Orwell writes, 'the advantages of this would be obvious' (II, 7). The ironic reappearance of this idea in the prefabricated phrases, the neatly slotting mendacities of Newspeak is only too evident.

To be fair to him. Orwell was never *very* enthusiastic about invented, 'made-up' (II, 7), languages – not even, in the 1930s, about the Basic English of C. K. Ogden *et al.*, as has been suggested by Hodge and Fowler.[27] Orwell did, while at the BBC, produce a radio programme on the subject of Basic English by Leonora Lockhart which was broadcast on 2 October 1942. Writing to Miss Lockhart in connection with this programme, Orwell said that he was 'particularly anxious to have the subject put on the map with a view to dealing with it more elaborately later'. He also had some correspondence with C. K. Ogden on the subject around this time.[28] In 1944, apropos Basic, Orwell wrote with mild approval of 'the need for an international language' (III, 86), and later that same year commented on the fact that Basic tended to deflate high-sounding phrases, and also that, Orwell believed, in Basic 'you cannot make a meaningless statement without its being apparent that it is meaningless' (III, 210). This idea reappears in 'Politics and the English language': in it Orwell writes that one of the advantages of 'simplifying' one's language in the ways suggested by him is that 'when you make a stupid statement Its stupidity will be obvious, even to yourself' (IV, 139). Intercut with this desire for a more or less self-correcting language, however, we notice also a suggestion of anxiety with respect to the idea of an invented, functional language – 'an instrument which we shape for our own purposes' (IV, 127). However, this suggestion is not really developed until we come to Newspeak, which may be derived simply by exaggerating some aspects of Ogden's Basic and Hogben's Interglossa.[29] Orwell had, as it happens, approved, though mildly, of the two 'languages' which do appear as plausible sources of Newspeak – the crucial difference of course being that in Newspeak the 'purposes' realised are those of the dreaded and reviled State of Big Brother. (It appears unlikely that Orwell would ever have gone all the way with Basic. As Leonora Lockhart notes, 'The words for which

Basic has no need come roughly into three groups: first, there are complex fictions such as *liberty* and *civilisation*, which may be covered, and are in some ways better covered, by putting together simpler units. Second, there are words such as *picturesque* and *sublime*, which are chiefly an outlet for the feelings . . .')[30] But it is important precisely in order to understand the meaning of that revulsion to see that Newspeak reproduces in ironic distortion many of the qualities which Orwell had once described as being desirable. Thus, the quality of self-correction referred to above reappears as the intrinsic inability, in Newspeak, to think a heretical thought. The glorious rhetoric of the American Declaration of Independence is deflated, in Newspeak, to obtuse platitudes – as Orwell had suggested high-sounding phrases would be in Basic. Precise, controlled reference, which is a desideratum in 'New words', is a potent means of oppression in the world of *Nineteen Eighty-Four* and Newspeak. The latter, Orwell writes, is a language in which 'a heretical thought [is] literally unthinkable . . . This was done partly by the invention of new words and by stripping such words as remained of unorthodox meanings, and so far as possible of all secondary meanings whatever' (*Nineteen Eighty-Four*, 305–6). Syme, the technician of language in *Nineteen Eighty-Four*, informs Winston that when Newspeak is fully developed:

Every concept that can ever be needed, will be expressed by exactly *one* word, with its meaning rigidly defined and all its subsidiary meanings rubbed out and forgotten.

(*Nineteen Eighty-Four*, 56)

Writing in 1944 for *Persuasion*, a periodical devoted to advertising and related arts, Orwell recommended effective propaganda as essential to the fulfilment of democracy (III:35). Yet in *Nineteen Eighty-Four* it is precisely the effectiveness of the propaganda which is feared. An important step in understanding this development is Orwell's essay 'Politics and the English language' (PEL).

From August 1941 to November 1943 – that is, between the time of the writing of 'New words', and that of PEL – Orwell worked for the Eastern Service of the BBC, broadcasting Allied propaganda. It is possible that the exigencies of wartime propaganda, in addition to the normal 'coordinating' tendencies (see III, 97) of a large organisation such as the BBC, might have provided Orwell with some insight into the neglected term of his first essay on language – the relation between language and external, material reality. Whatever the origins of the insight, PEL marks a clear advance on 'New words' in that whereas the latter concerned itself almost exclusively with the 'inner life', in PEL Orwell is able to see that language is not only an inadequate mirror of the contents of consciousness, it is also vulnerable to the needs of ideology, or, to alter the metaphor, language is the terrain on which conflicting perceptions of reality do battle, a field which bears the scars of the conflicts that rage over it. Thus, George Steiner writes of Orwell's 'view of language as the essential, the threatened locale of truth and political freedom'.[31] It should be pointed out that this insight is only present in a rudimentary and largely implicit form in PEL. Its potential is not really developed until we come to the world of *Nineteen Eighty-Four*, wherein language, Newspeak, is one of the key instruments of political domination, the necessary means for the 'totalitarian' control of reality. Translating itself into the very form of reality, until it is transparent and coextensive with 'reality', language, following Orwell's insight, becomes, precisely because of its 'invisibility' and its insidious, irresistible power, the focus also of a terrible vulnerability. A particular language, such as Newspeak, after its establishment as the sole mode of discourse within a society (which, incidentally, I believe to be possible only in paranoid fantasies), affords the possibility of a corruption which is irredeemable because it is unknowable.[32]

In his insight into the politics of language Orwell is a pioneer and has been acknowledged as such by people who have built on his insight.[33] Fowler and Kress, writing in 1979 about the imbrication of political power (as well as other kinds) and language, are clear, and self-confessed, inheritors of Orwell:

Language serves to confirm and consolidate the organisations which shape it, being used to manipulate people, to establish and maintain them in economically convenient roles and statuses, to maintain the power of state agencies, corporations and other institutions.[34]

Similarly, those people, writers, scholars and journalists, who seek to uncover the ways in which societies are encouraged to perceive themselves and others, also derive their original inspiration from Orwell's linguistic insight. However, if we ask what Orwell himself made of his insight – how he himself applied and developed it – we notice something curious and significant within the present context, which is that of Orwell's reconciliation or accommodation, under stress of war, with his ambient society. Orwell's critical insight into language is acquired, paradoxically, at a time when he is losing his critical perspective on his own society.

Orwell's most powerful insight is into the political/ideological sensitivity of language, and into the areas of use and misuse which that opens up – into how language can be a subtle and insidious instrument for the enforcement of particular, desired perceptions of 'reality'. This insight is, obviously, relativistic in tendency, suggesting as it does the necessary mediation of 'reality' through different linguistic 'systems', and the implicit impossibility of bringing supra-lingual criteria to bear upon inter-lingual comparisons. Clearly, there is a limit beyond which such relativism slips into absurdity – that is, we cannot function as human beings except in terms of a historically variable 'positivist' consensus. Thus, Orwell's relativism has, perhaps inevitably, a positive core, which derives its substance from his everyday world, and from the commonsensical consensus on which it rests. This world is the world of ordinary, 'decent' human beings, who instinctively *know* what is right and what is wrong, what is true and what is not. It seems to me, however, that on the rebound from excessive relativism, Orwell is led into adopting an excessively uncritical attitude to the ambient world of common sense, to its language and to the forms of its understanding. I would suggest that the conservative tendency in Orwell's temperament is evident not so much directly in his language itself as in the limits which it sets to Orwell's thinking about language. Typically, again, his radicalism is subverted by his own conservatism.

Few people, I believe, would fail to accept Orwell's criticisms of the samples of prevalent political styles which he selected for castigation in 'Politics and the English language', or disagree with his view that 'in our time, political speech and writing are largely the defence of the indefensible'; and that, therefore, 'political language has to consist largely of euphemism, question-begging, and sheer cloudy vagueness' (IV, 136). This observation, it should be noticed, cuts right across political systems. It applies not only to grey-faced *apparatchiks* doling out implausible fictions about Soviet reality but also to the US State Department's blond whiz-kids pontificating about defending freedom and democracy with napalm and Agent Orange in the Indo-Chinese peninsula and at sundry locations around the globe; to South African politicians defending systematic inhumanity as 'separate develop-ment'; and, of course, to Her Majesty's urbane officers lying smoothly about the brutalization of Northern Ireland. Orwell's strictures apply equally to the 'totalitarian' rhetoric which he inveighs against and the 'anti-totalitarian' rhetoric to which he is himself prone. However, the point of immediate interest to me is the interaction between the relativism of Orwell's conception of language and the residual (or emergent, or threatened) positivism of his temperament.

In a famous sentence in 'Politics and the English language', after listing all the things one ought not to do, Orwell synthesised, as it were, the wisdom he had gleaned:

What is above all needed is to let the meaning choose the word, and not the other way about.

(IV, 138)

This sounds unobjectionable enough, until one reflects that that is, more or less, the manner in which Newspeak, that ultimate horror, is to be constructed – by shedding the words that do not correspond to predetermined meanings. My contention is that Orwell is here evading or bypassing his insight into the inevitable interdependence between words and meanings. He is tempted, compelled, or merely permitted by the positivism of his temperament, into thinking that the meaning, or more precisely *his* meaning, is pre-verbal and pre-conceptual, and thus unsullied by the particularity of perception which, unacknowledged, manifests itself as dishonesty in political language, as awkwardness and a lack of facility in 'choosing words'. It is immaterial at this point whether or not the conceptions and meanings which Orwell wished to put across are preferable to those urged by the persons whose language he holds up for ridicule in 'Politics and the English language'. What is crucial is the fact that Orwell fails to extend his insight into the interweaving of political conceptions and language to the dialects favoured by ordinary 'decent' people like himself. Orwell, it is important to note, resists the obvious inference that, to use his own terms, Newspeak is only a refinement, especially malign but also especially unsubtle, of Oldspeak.[35] After all, even 'ordinary' language restricts the range of expressible meanings, as every bilingual person knows – in other words, there is no open, unconstraining Oldspeak, there are only variations, at different levels of complexity, of Newspeak. Still, one should note also that Orwell is, at this stage, secure enough in his affirmation of the ordinary 'decent' world, its language and its durability, to be *able* to resist the implications of his own linguistic insight.

In his 1946 essay 'Why I write', Orwell wrote what appears, in the context, to be a non sequitur:

I am not able, and I do not want, completely to abandon the world-view that I acquired in childhood. So long as I remain alive and well I shall continue to feel strongly about prose style . . .

(I, 6)

However, in the light of the foregoing discussion, it is perhaps not a non sequitur after all, in other words, there may well be an integral connection between a particular conception of 'prose style' – unstrained, fluid, limpid – and a particular 'world-view'. If we return now to 'Politics and the English language' we find that whereas the demolition work is done with gusto, Orwell is curiously weak and negative about what needs to be done to promote the right kind of political language. He offers six rules (IV, 139), of which five are negatives, and the sixth is an admonition to break all the rules 'rather than say anything outright barbarous'. In the same essay. Orwell also writes: 'The great enemy of clear language is insincerity' (IV, 137), the implication being that sincerity will of itself produce clarity and that lack of clarity reflects back on the credibility of the belief that is sought to be articulated. The thrust of all this – clarity, fluency, the banishment of all that is rough and 'barbarous' – is obvious enough, and implies a kind of cultural centrality which the 1930s Orwell did not feel.

Orwell's first novel, *Burmese Days*, also touches on the problem of language within an oppressive social order. It is a crucial part of that oppression that the thoughts one can think are, in this case, prescribed by 'the pukka sahib's code' (*Burmese Days*, 69). Orwell's novel as a whole is an attempt, in fact, to think about the colonial situation without submitting to the constraints of that code. Yet the novel is also, as I have argued in an earlier chapter, a significant record of the difficulty of thinking subversively with any consistency, let alone fluency or clarity. Flory's distinctive quality is precisely that he is endowed, by Orwell, with 'secret thoughts that could not be uttered' (*Burmese Days*, 70). Flory could only attain to ease of utterance, to an uncluttered, unself-conscious flow, like the 'louts' at the Club, by sacrificing that which makes him worthy of attention.

Given Orwell's sensitivity to language, his insight into its nature, he should have been able to see, what in his conception of Winston he was able to sense, that the ruling, 'hegemonic' conceptions and perceptions of a given social order, and the language in which they are articulated, are bound to appear 'natural' and unforced – but also that they are no more 'natural' than those others, gauche and awkward, clumsy and cumbersome, which seek to criticise that order. Unfortunately, however, Orwell acquired his linguistic insight during the time that he was, as I have argued, making his peace with his 'given' society. But for that, he might have had a little more sympathy with his victims, all left-wing in 'Politics and the English language'; he might have felt for them a little of the sympathy which he himself evokes for Winston in *Nineteen Eighty-Four*, struggling for speech against an oppressive order.

In the context of wartime democracy, in the flush of that 'patriotic' sentiment which the Government had skilfully manufactured out of the disaster of Dunkirk, Orwell had written:

> to *preserve* is always to *extend*. The choice before us is not so much between victory and defeat as between revolution and apathy.
>
> (II, 108; italics in original)

If we apply this to Orwell's activity in the area of language we find that while he is admirable in the protective aspect, he is rather less certain about the radical extensions of which his critique of language is capable. There is, of course, an absolute sense in which an overriding concern with language represents a narrowing of the generous political (and literary) conceptions which Orwell had entertained earlier. However, even apart from that, I believe that the specific form of that concern with language is marked by the conservative tendency which becomes dominant during this phase, whether the theme be language or, in a beautiful essay, the common toad.

The positivism in Orwell's linguistic conceptions – the sense which he conveys that while other people's language distorts reality, his own offers unmediated access to it – is not, I believe, accidental. This positivism is, I suggest, the form in which the process of reconciliation or accommodation manifests itself in language. In defending language against the 'barbarous' critics of the social order at a time when his own faith in his alternative conceptions was under stress, Orwell is led into accepting uncritically the ordinary language, the self-conceptions, of his ambient society, and so, following his insight, the implicit attitudes as well. It is perhaps some renewed awareness of his radical critique of that society which accounts for the fact that in

Nineteen Eighty-Four, as I have pointed out above, the crucial 'positivist' assertion with which Winston attempts to resist the 'insanity' of Newspeak takes an arithmetical rather than a verbal form.

For the linguistic insight into relativism, which is merely adumbrated in 'Politics and the English language', to grow into the nightmare of Newspeak in *Nineteen Eighty-Four*, certain changes must take place: changes not only in the external, public circumstances of the time – the sense of purpose generated by the war being dissipated and distorted by the deepening tensions of the Cold War – but also, and relatedly, in Orwell's own thinking.[36] 'Politics and the English language' is written on the explicit assumption (IV, 137) that the decay of language is corrigible, that if language can be corrupted through malign intent or through sheer inattention, it can also be cleansed. There is also the related assumption, implicit in the interpenetration of language and politics, that such a process of linguistic cleansing can react back on politics, that hope is not lost. One half of the insight Orwell came upon in 'Politics and the English language' – into the ideological sensitivity of language and the consequent possibilities of ideological bondage – is, as we have seen, preserved in *Nineteen Eighty-Four*, in the conception of Newspeak. But 'Politics and the English language', as we have seen, not only confronts the threat, and emergent reality, of the political degeneration of language, it also carries the promise of its regeneration in conjunction with a higher politics. Of this aspect of 'Politics and the English language' little survives in the bleak world of *Nineteen Eighty-Four*. Again, the attenuation of Orwell's faith in ordinary 'decency' and common sense (that which had, so to speak, provided a limit to the depredation of *his own relativism*), this too is essential for the possibility of Newspeak, implicit in 'Politics and the English language', to be realised. Orwell's despairing, unconvinced and unconvincing affirmation of decency in *Nineteen Eighty-Four* illustrates the general argument which these last chapters are intended to advance – that in the wartime phase of reconciliation or accommodation with his ambient society, Orwell is lulled into making a 'conservative' commitment which he can later neither live with nor reject. That is to say, the roots of Orwell's terminal despair are to be found in the hope of his wartime writings.[37] He is his own prisoner, imprisoned in conceptions and forms of understanding which he can neither relinquish nor use without guilt. Consider, for instance,

Winston's dilemma in *Nineteen Eighty-Four*: Orwell invents the language of Goldstein – different alike from Newspeak and from the language of the novel – as a means of characterising the State of which Newspeak is the impenetrable armour; as a means whereby Winston (and we) can gain a critical perspective on the oppressive society. However, as we know, Orwell's imagination subverts itself: Goldstein's language also turns out to be an invention of the rulers of Oceania, and offers no escape from the nightmare. Winston Smith, therefore, is imprisoned not only in Newspeak but also in the language in which he seeks to criticise the world of Newspeak.

In her famous study *The Origins of Totalitarianism* (1951), Hannah Arendt referred to the 'paranoid coherence' of the socio-political systems which were her subject. She described them as:

logical systems in which, as in the system of paranoiacs, everything follows comprehensibly and even compulsorily once the first premise is accepted. The insanity of such systems lies not only in their first premise but in the very logicality with which they are constructed.[38]

This notion of a 'paranoid coherence', apprehensive and intolerant of anything outside its control, has an obvious application to the world of *Nineteen Eighty-Four* as well. This intense, manic coherence, this tight and unrelenting dialectic – between victims and victimisers, between the objective of thought control and its realisation through an artificial language of rigidly controlled reference, between the fact of absolute power and its necessarily perverse demonstration in manifest illogicality (after all, if two plus two equals simply four then Winston's assent is not simultaneously an affirmation of Big Brother's unlimited power) – this brutal and suffocating consistency is an essential part of the universe which Orwell invents. We might remember the analyst of *The Paranoid Style in American Politics* (1966), Richard Hofstadter: 'the paranoid mentality is far more coherent than the real world, since it leaves no room for mistakes, failures, or ambiguities . . . it believes that it is up against an enemy who is as infallibly rational as he is fatally evil, and it seeks to match his imputed total competence with its own, leaving nothing unexplained and comprehending all of reality in one overreaching, consistent theory' (pp. 36–7).

It is this coherence which accounts in a great measure for *Nineteen Eighty-Four*'s obsessive, hypnotic power, its claustral intensity – there are no obvious fissures, no crevices in the confining walls of the paranoid imagination. Goldstein offers at least the notional possibility of release, but he is revealed to be a fiction of the political police, invented precisely to trap dissidence, or, more comprehensively, reluctance of assent. The framed engraving of St Clement Danes which adorns the walls of Winston's refuge and love nest is merely camouflage for a telescreen. The children's nursery rhyme which symbolises for Winston an earlier, happy time of innocence (presumably his own and the world's) turns out to be a code in which Winston is enmeshed, and the sinister significance of its last line becomes fully apparent only in the cellars of the Ministry of Love: 'Here comes a chopper to chop off your head!' Julia should, appropriately, have been a member of the secret police, an undercover agent, party to the elaborate conspiracy whereby the State of Oceania, with more than a hint of disproportionate interest, sets out to trap the miserable Winston:

There was no physical act, no word spoken aloud, that they had not noticed, no train of thought that they had not been able to infer. Even the speck of whitish dust on the cover of his diary they had carefully replaced.

(*Nineteen Eighty-Four*, 283)

In fact, Julia's blamelessness enables Orwell to add one further twist of humiliation and horror to Winston's betrayal of her. Julia enables Orwell, or rather, Orwell enables himself through Julia, to intensify the paranoia by suggesting still deeper abysses of inhumanity, still further reaches of persecution and anxiety. The sense of the author's imagination turning upon itself, as it were, *trapping* itself, is reinforced when one studies, for instance, the evolution of O'Brien in the facsimile edition of *Nineteen Eighty-Four*. O'Brien starts out as a sympathetic character, a man of conscience and irony, 'large enough to have remained human, to enjoy the process of life',[39] who collaborates with the unlikely Winston towards the overthrow of the regime. He ends up as the sadistic and wordy bureaucrat of the novel we know.

I believe, moreover, that this coherence also constitutes part of the critical difficulty in dealing with *Nineteen Eighty-Four*. One can assert one's agreement with its presumed theses, or argue against them; one may identify its presumed historical referents, or qualify those identifications, or reject them – but the book, quite simply, resists opening itself up to critical scrutiny. It isn't only secure in its formal stance of being a futuristic fantasy, it is whole and self-sufficient and dauntingly formidable in its internal coherence. However, this very coherence, which Arendt characterised as 'paranoid', and which so baulks critical investigation, might be our clue. If this coherence were simply a reflection of historical realities, one could do little more than applaud the artistic skill with which those realities had been rendered. However, if this paranoia is not simply a reflection of public history, if the roots of this paranoid universe do not lie simply in public events, then one has a point at which to start. It is clear that Arendt's (and Orwell's) 'paranoid' theory of 'totalitarian' societies rested on a plausible account of certain historical societies, but that plausibility has now begun to appear rather vulnerable. Thus, in a recent essay, the historian Arthur Schlesinger Jr, himself an early proponent of the theory of totalitarianism, wrote almost casually:

now . . . we see that the theory of absolute totalitarian power expounded so memorably by George Orwell in *Nineteen Eighty-Four* (1949) and Hannah Arendt in *The Origins of Totalitarianism* (1951) was, after all, an illusion.[40]

However, the matter doesn't simply end there. The further question, particularly for students of Orwell (and, presumably, Arendt), is: whence does this intense paranoid coherence, this *logical* tyranny which Arendt 'describes', and Orwell invents in *Nineteen Eighty-Four*, derive? I suggest that, as elsewhere with Orwell, one must be particularly wary of 'plausibility', and struggle to become aware of the mediating consciousness, the disappearing middle term that is both the person/persona Orwell and his 'windowpane prose'. What appeared to be the world out there, the empirical sanction of the fantastic universe, turns out to be 'after all, an illusion' – and the windowpane becomes, sometimes, a mirror.

I believe that the key to the stagnant, locked universe of *Nineteen Eighty-Four*, static and logical, with its superstates frozen in eternal, indecisive hostility; its monotonous tyranny whose viciousness feeds not off rebellion but rather off subservience and is therefore inexhaustible; its sterile unproductive anxiety which is itself produced by a State which serves little purpose other than the production of anxiety – the key to all this, the State and the tyranny, lies, I believe, in the blocked, hemmed-in, impotent but undefeated state of mind of Orwell's protagonist. The anxiety which, within the novel, appears as the product of tyranny is also part of the casual matrix out of which that vision of absolute tyranny springs. There are, unquestionably, historical parallels to be found for various aspects of this tyranny, but my contention is that these historical features are present in a mediated form, mediated through a state of mind, in both the author and his protagonist, which they help to produce, but of which they are also, simultaneously, rationalisations. Isaac Deutscher criticised Orwell for having, in *Nineteen Eighty-Four*, declined into a mysticism of cruelty, for having abdicated comprehension of an undeniably complex reality in favour of a metaphysic of sadism.[41] I would, however, suggest that the origins of *Nineteen Eighty-Four* are not to be found in a mysticism of cruelty but rather in a metaphysic of impotence. The meaningless and therefore unlimited cruelty of the State of Big Brother is, in my opinion, secondary, and merely reinforces – or, more subtly, rationalises and thus ratifies – the condition of impotence with which it is locked in a dialectical harmony. It is interesting to note, in this connection, that Orwell described Burnham's political prophecies as 'the rationalisation of a wish' (IV, 179). I am inclined, following Orwell, to think of Orwell's own nightmare of the future as the rationalisation of a specific state of paranoid anxiety, of a fear rather than of a wish.[42]

For reasons which have, ultimately, to do with the exigencies of international politics, Big Brother and the tyranny of which he is author, instrument and symbol have been taken to be the primary elements out of which the world of the novel is constructed. Yet the strongest impression which I, at any rate, derive from *Nineteen Eighty-Four* is that of the helplessness and sense of suffocation of the protagonist, Winston Smith. It is true that these states of being are believed, by Winston and perhaps by Orwell also, to be caused by the aforementioned tyranny, but it is remarkable that this tyranny is seen almost entirely through Winston's eyes. It would be stretching the evidence to say that the tyranny which finally claims Winston is a mere neurotic hallucination, but the vehement helplessness which characterises Winston is, unquestionably, a necessary complement of the tyranny and without it the perverse universe of *Nineteen Eighty-Four* would be incomplete. This helplessness is, deliberately, foregrounded. At the very beginning of the novel, Winston starts writing his diary – an act of deep symbolic significance within the terms of the novel. 'To mark the paper', Orwell informs us, slowing down the action, defamiliarising the commonplace in order to emphasise the strangeness of the context which renders that commonplace action heroic, 'was the decisive act.' And yet it is interesting to note that the act itself produces the exact opposite of a feeling of liberation: 'A sense of complete helplessness had descended upon him' (*Nineteen Eighty-Four*, 11). It is from the depths of this helplessness that Winston regards the tyranny which he presumes to challenge. The sheer ineffectuality of Winston's refusal to be finally 'incorporated', the very weakness of the rebellion, is essential: without the rebellion the tyranny would be undemonstrable, but without the helplessness of that rebellion, the tyranny of the State would be limited in a manner which the underlying intention of the novel cannot permit. In an obvious sense, it might be said that Winston's condition is caused by the State of Big Brother, that his anguish and anxiety are effects which the tyranny produces. However, in an equally real though less obvious sense, at least within the economy of the novel, the State of Big Brother is 'caused' by Winston's anxious, guilt-ridden condition. The author provides us little perspective on Winston himself. The critic Ellen Douglass Leyburn has made an acute critical point which deserves attention in this context. She writes:

Orwell manages a highly effective double consciousness for the reader: while we participate with Winston in his efforts to escape detection, to stay alive exactly because he realises that he is a dead man, we see with a greater clairvoyance than he achieves, the futility of his present precautions. Big Brother is watching.[43]

We, as readers, both feel with, and observe Winston – in other words, we are, simultaneously, Winston *and* Big Brother. This is acute, and probably accounts in some measure for the sadistic element in the pleasure which the novel gives. However, since Winston's own mind contains the sense, obsessively, of being observed by Big Brother and his minions, the ability to observe Winston from that perspective, as Leyburn suggests, still offers no escape from the sense of being imprisoned in the mind of the paranoid protagonist. Indeed, this impression of paranoia is further reinforced by the fact that the State itself seems to have little purpose other than to make Winston suffer. The helpless anxiety and the perverse opaque tyranny produce each other, and depend upon each other – and the very coherence of the two inhibits the possibility of inserting a thin wedge of primacy between them.

Winston's passionate sense of insecurity is, in fact, the major means by which the horror of the world of *Nineteen Eighty-Four* is rendered – rather than, for instance, the sub-science-fiction machinery of the third part, the dials and levers of Room 101 which Julian Symons, in the course of his important and sympathetic review of the novel, dismissed as 'schoolboyish sensationalism'.[44] Writing his diary, against time, against the present time, 'To the future or to the past, to a time when thought is free' (*Nineteen Eighty-Four*, 31), Winston is unable to shake off his sense of fundamental futility:

> The diary would be reduced to ashes and himself to vapour. Only the Thought Police would read what he had written, before they wiped it out of existence and out of memory. How could you make appeal to the future when not a trace of you, not even an anonymous word scribbled on a piece of paper, could physically survive?
>
> (*Nineteen Eighty-Four*, 31)

When, in the company of O'Brien, Winston drinks to the past (*Nineteen Eighty-Four*, 181), or when he addresses his diary 'to the future or to the past', it is not merely nostalgia he is expressing. More importantly, it is the finished, immutable and therefore secure nature of the past that is being evoked. But of course, in the world of *Nineteen Eighty-Four*, the past is *not* immutable, indeed, it is wholly malleable:

> All history was a palimpsest, scraped clean and reinscribed exactly as often as was necessary.
>
> (*Nineteen Eighty-Four*, 43–4)

That is part of its special horror.

The very insecurity of Winston's resistance, his sense of suffocation, even of involuntary complicity with the hated tyranny, is crucial to the horror of *Nineteen Eighty-Four*:

> The horrible thing about the Two Minutes Hate was not that one was obliged to act a part, but, on the contrary, that it was impossible to avoid joining in. A hideous ecstasy of fear and vindictiveness, a desire to kill, to torture, to smash faces in with a sledgehammer, seemed to flow through the whole group of people like an electric current, turning one even against one's will into a grimacing, screaming lunatic.
>
> (*Nineteen Eighty-Four*, 18)

This insecurity is made explicit during the description of the extraordinary and, on any realistic level, implausible Socratic exchange between O'Brien and Winston in the torture chambers of the Ministry of Love:

> What most oppressed him was the consciousness of his own intellectual inferiority . . . O'Brien was a being in all ways larger than himself. There was

no idea that he had ever had, or could have, that O'Brien had not long ago known, examined, and rejected. His mind *contained* Winston's mind.

(*Nineteen Eighty-Four*, 262)

There are hints of this critical insecurity all along the course of the novel:

His heart sank at the thought of the enormous power ranged against him, the ease with which any Party intellectual would overthrow him in debate, the subtle arguments which he would not be able to understand, much less answer. And yet he was right! . . . The obvious, the silly, and the true had got to be defended. Truisms are true, hold on to that! The solid world exists, its laws do not change. Stones are hard, water is wet, objects unsupported fall towards the earth's centre.

(*Nineteen Eighty-Four*, 84–5)

This last-ditch, bedrock 'positivism' is itself, it need hardly be pointed out, an index of desperation.

Winston's fundamental, and fictionally necessary, lack of confidence in his own radical challenge – his 'horror that he might also be wrong' (*Nineteen Eighty-Four*, 83) – his crucial awe in the face of that which he is aiming to subvert, bears, I would suggest, a certain analogy with Orwell's own ambivalent radicalism. This loss of nerve, so to speak, is particularly relevant in the bitter aftermath of the euphoria that produced *The Lion and the Unicorn*. In *Nineteen Eighty-Four*, this awe expresses itself not only in Winston's sense of his own 'inferiority' but also in other, subtler ways. There is, for instance, Winston's strange desire to know and fantasise about Julia's sexual promiscuity. The idea of sexual liberation as revolution has, of course, a remarkable and continuing pedigree.[45] However, the curious thing is that Winston characterises his liaison, his frolicking with the promiscuous Julia, as 'breaking down that wall of virtue' (p. 72), within which the grossly immoral State of *Nineteen Eighty-Four* keeps its citizens. Somewhat later, Winston says to Julia:

I hate purity, I hate goodness, I want everyone to be corrupt to the bone.

(p. 129)

However, immediately after this, the lover of corruption reveals a residual prudishness: as they fall apart after making love, 'he reached out for the discarded overalls and pulled them partly over her'. Winston's inability to refuse the right of the State to define 'virtue' is immediately reminiscent of Orwell's statement, recorded around the

time of the writing of *Nineteen Eighty-Four*, about the value system of
St Cyprian's:

Virtue consisted in winning: it consisted in being bigger, stronger, hand-
somer, richer . . . I was aware of the impossibility of any subjective conformity
. . . I could not invert the existing scale of values.

(IV, 359–61)

What is remarkable, though rather more excusable in the timorous
schoolboy than in the adult rebel, is the involuntary subscription to
the official definition of 'virtue', the insecurity or absence of its radical
redefinition. Despite the apparent rationalism of Winston's assertion
in his diary that 'Freedom is the freedom to say that two plus two
make four' (*Nineteen Eighty-Four*, 85), there is a significant admixture
of irrationalism in Winston's rejection of the State's tyranny, a sort of
desperate claim, whether in the name of decency or in that of the
instincts of ordinary people, which already implies a surrender of
territory which Winston himself no longer believes to be rationally
defensible.[46] This critical weakness in Winston's resistance is, as we
have remarked, integral to the novel as it stands, and is repeatedly
made evident by the unconvincing quality of the positives which he
counterposes to the monstrous tyranny – make-up, a fragment of
coral embedded in 'rainwatery' glass, a nursery rhyme, pint pots
instead of litre jugs. 'You are a flaw in the pattern', O'Brien says to
Winston. But we realise that Winston is not that much of a flaw after
all. Not only are the positive values in the name of which he seeks to
challenge Big Brother weak and insecure but, as the taped exchange
which O'Brien plays back to him in the torture chamber makes clear,
Winston has progressed a considerable distance towards acquiring
the self-protective inhumanity by virtue of which he may rightfully
belong to the 'pattern':

'If for example, it would somehow serve our interests to throw sulphuric acid
in a child's face – are you prepared to do that?'
    'Yes.'

(p. 140, Penguin edition)[47]

Perhaps the sharpest illustration of what I mean is provided by the
manner in which, during the course of the novel, 'darkness' is
transformed from something that must be transcended – Winston and
O'Brien agree to meet in the place where there is no darkness – into
the significantly negative form of desire itself, the necessary relief from
the inescapable glare in the cells of the Ministry of Love. But, for an

intellectual to cede rationality is an important concession, and it is hardly surprising if the outcome is despair. Consider, by way of contrast, Barthes's Voltaire: 'It was, then, a singular happiness to have to do battle in a world where force and stupidity were continually on the same tack: a privileged situation for the mind. The writer was on history's side.'[48] For the Orwell who writes *Nineteen Eighty-Four* history, in more ways than one, appears threatening.

To some extent, no doubt, the tremendous propagandist pressures generated by the Cold War were responsible for the magnification of the *threat* of 'totalitarianism' in Orwell's imagination. In actual fact, hardly any serious historian now believes that this post-war 'threat' from Russian 'totalitarianism' was a real one.[49] 'The detailed records', writes A. J. P. Taylor, 'destroy the accepted legend completely. They show, almost too emphatically, that the Cold War was deliberately started by Truman and his advisers.'[50] George Kennan, who was the American Ambassador in Moscow at the time that the Cold War started, said in 1956: 'The image of a Stalinist Russia, poised and yearning to attack the West, and deterred only by our possession of nuclear weapons, was largely a creation of Western imagination.'[51] Other historians suggest that hard economic factors, rather than mere imagination, might have determined the genesis of the Cold War.[52] Finally, this is Arthur Schlesinger Jr, the American 'liberal' historian and one of the proponents of the original 'melodramatic'[53] interpretation of the Cold War: 'Post-revisionist historiography accepts that the Soviet Union acted less out of some master plan for world domination and more for local and defensive reasons than the official West admitted or, probably, understood at the time.'[54] I suggest that Professor Schlesinger is being disingenuous here because the records suggest that people in the know, as opposed to the manipulated multitudes of the 'Free World', *knew* that the central myths of the Cold War were, precisely, lies.[55]

This, however, is not the place to go into the sordid history of the genesis of the Cold War – and, in any case, Orwell was not someone who had access to the official information which, becoming available now, has completely destroyed the authorised Western version of that genesis. He had been writing against 'totalitarianism' long before the propaganda which fostered such a version became the major Western ideological export. As such, however, he was in a poor position to resist the anti-Soviet hysteria, to regard with the scepticism they deserved the official myths about the aggressive post-war intentions of 'totalitarianism'. Still, one can hardly maintain that Orwell became a victim of Cold War hysteria about expansionist, engulfing 'totalitarianism'. But one can say that he was, because of the forms of his own political understanding and imagination, especially vulnerable to that hysteria.

Moreover, I suggest, the fortunes of the idea of 'totalitarianism' in Orwell's mind are bound up with his faith in the possibility of a 'democratic' transcendence of a capitalist present which he assumes flatly 'has manifestly no future' (IV, 375). Thus, it is not to the real, or even the mythical, history of post-war Europe, but rather to the dialectic of the ideas of 'totalitarianism' and 'democratic Socialism' in Orwell's mind that we must look for our clue to the way in which the former overwhelms Orwell's imagination in Nineteen Eighty-Four. During his wartime populist phase, when the possibility of a peaceful passage to democratic socialism appeared, naively or otherwise, real, the idea of 'totalitarianism' hardly appeared so threatening. However, in Attlee's Britain, beset by shortages and by anti-Soviet hysteria, Orwell's vision of democratic socialism, of happy, harmonious communities developing in freedom and equality, must have seemed rather distant. Gradually, as the Cold War confrontation became starker, the 'socialist' component in 'democratic Socialism' got attenuated – but it was not an adjustment which Orwell could make without far-reaching ideological consequences. The attenuation of the 'socialism' was bound to be reflected in changes in the economy of the mind. This ideological balance, this mental dialectic, was affected not only by the strength (or relative weakness) of 'totalitarianism'; it was affected also by the weakness (or relative strength) of 'democratic Socialism'. And affecting the latter were not only the specific difficulties of Attlee's Britain, but also the emotional and ideological capital which Orwell had invested in the thwarted possibility of socialist transformation under just such a government – a Labour government with a massive popular mandate – during his populist phase. The fear of 'totalitarianism', which Orwell claimed in 1946 he had been gripped with for the past decade (I, 5), is not by itself sufficient to account for the specificity of Nineteen Eighty-Four. Crucial to any explanation is the dwindling of his wartime hope, the dimunition of Orwell's 'socialism', through the wartime celebration of the 'English genius', to a suffocating complicity with his 'given' society.[56]

The inertial pressure of his own political language, his commitment to the theory of totalitarianism, is such that he cannot resist being swept up to some extent in the hysteria, the rituals of the anti-communist Hate Week. One remarks, for instance, the disjunction between Orwell's rejection of Burnham's projections at a polemical level (see IV:46, 'James Burnham and the managerial revolution') and the conceptual undertow which, dragging against the grain of Orwell's conscious political preferences, produces the horrified vision of *Nineteen Eighty-Four*. I would suggest further that Orwell might even have been, in the post-war period when the populist euphoria had, inevitably, faded, *bound* to the conception of 'totalitarianism' because it offered a kind of justification for the earlier affirmations – in other words, if 'totalitarianism' was as bad as it was, then the naiveté of *The Lion and the Unicorn* was proportionately exonerated. However, although the conception of 'totalitarianism' might have offered him such partial exoneration, it also, and progressively, deprived him of a political location from which to criticise his own 'democratic' society. It is true that, at the level of explicit political assertion, Orwell retained his belief that the only alternative to Russian-style 'socialism' and American capitalism, *both* of which merge in the imaginative vision of *Nineteen Eighty-Four*, was 'democratic Socialism'. However, the stronger 'totalitarianism' became, in fact as in 'anti-totalitarian' imagination, the more constricted became the space that 'democratic Socialism' could occupy.

There is, thus, a history of ideological surrender concealed in Orwell's reluctant affirmation, in 1945, of the 'semi-anaesthesia' of the common people, whom he had only recently celebrated as the bearers of a unique destiny:

I don't know whether this semi-anaesthesia in which the British people contrive to live is a sign of decadence, as many observers believe, or whether on the other hand it is a kind of instinctive wisdom.

(III, 385)

The 'anaesthetised' masses reappear, of course, as the 'proles' of *Nineteen Eighty-Four*, drugged and apathetic, the *necessarily unlikely* locus of hope in that world to which hope is alien. From a purely formal point of view, the 'proles' disturb the monomaniacal unity of the novel, the intimate harmony between the persecutors and the persecuted, the fit between the tyranny and the tyrannised. However, the 'proles' are a necessary part of the fantasy, particularly if we see *Nineteen Eighty-Four* as being a perverse development from the wartime populism in which the 'proles' – then, the 'people' – had been the chosen bearers of hope.

In the first instance, the presence of the 'proles' in the fantasy, and the explicit assertion that if there was hope it lay in the 'proles' (*Nineteen Eighty-Four*, 73), is a clear index of Orwell's continued socialist loyalties, a radical memory in the midst of the despair. However, the representation of the 'proles' as drugged, stupid and apathetic – as well as having untold and uncomprehended reserves of strength – indicates the complexity of the mood in which *Nineteen Eighty-Four* is conceived. At one level, I think, the apathy of the 'proles' is a reflection of Orwell's disappointment with the process of the realisation of 'democratic Socialism' under the Attlee Government (see IV:48, Orwell's last 'London letter' to the *Partisan Review*). At another level, this representation of the common people as 'proles' is an index of Orwell's persistent proneness to middle-class perceptions, and for this he has been sharply criticised:

It needs to be said, however, bitterly, that if the tyranny of 1984 ever finally comes, one of the major elements of the ideological preparation will have been just this way of seeing 'the masses', 'the human beings passing you on the pavement', the eighty-five percent who are *proles*. And nobody who belongs to this majority or who knows them as people will give a damn whether the figure on the other side of the street sees them as animals or as unthinking creatures out of whose mighty loins the future will come.[57]

If Orwell (or Winston) could see the 'proles' as people, living, working and thinking, whole human beings, rather than merely an obtuse, inert mass – even the fat woman endlessly singing a fatuous lyric with clothes pegs in her mouth is mere bourgeois furniture – perhaps the tyranny of *Nineteen Eighty-Four* would not seem so complete, or so irresistible. I am reminded, in this context, of an anecdote which Nadezhda Mandelstam recounts in her autobiography of the Stalin years, about a household in which she and her husband took refuge:

As we now discovered, people talked much more freely and openly in working class homes than in intellectual ones in those savage times . . . We had been conditioned to hold our tongues, and once, when M. had made some evasive remark, Tatiana Vasilievna looked at him pityingly and said: 'What can we do with you? You've all been scared out of your wits.'[58]

At a still deeper level, however, the stupor of the 'proles', as also their unassertive commitment to a vague 'decency', indicates the ideological difficulties Orwell himself was in as a consequence of the collapse of his wartime hopes. The stupor of the 'proles', perhaps, is not so much a class reflex as it is a reflection of Orwell's own political bemusement, and so of a piece with his affirmation, albeit hesitant, of the 'semi-anaesthesia' of ordinary people.

'If there was hope', Winston writes in his diary, 'it *must* lie in the proles' (*Nineteen Eighty-Four*, 73; italics in original). That stressed 'must' indicates of course an obvious ideological affiliation. However, it suggests also a kind of desperation:

if there was hope, it lay in the proles. You had to cling on to that. When you put it in words, it sounded reasonable: it was when you looked at the human beings passing you on the pavement that it became an act of faith.

(*Nineteen Eighty-Four*, 89)

Orwell, like Winston, returns repeatedly to the idea of salvation through the 'proles' but, recoiling from the idea of organisation, whether ideological or institutional, as being inherently 'totalitarian', he is forced into a mystification of the foundation on which that hope must rest. Echoing *Animal Farm*, Orwell writes:

the proles, if only they could somehow become conscious of their strength, would have no need to conspire. They needed only to rise up and shake themselves like a horse shaking off flies.

(*Nineteen Eighty-Four*, 73)

The evasiveness of that 'somehow' is not accidental, nor is the fact that, so soon after *Animal Farm*, Orwell is again driven to using the image, for a people becoming politically conscious, of 'a horse shaking off flies', without so much as a hint that his own imagination had, in a previous exploit, sent such horses to the knacker's.

Critics have remarked the perverseness of Orwell's dystopia. Orwell has been criticised for avoiding the crux of Dostoyevsky's question (posed by the Grand Inquisitor in *The Brothers Karamazov*) by projecting in *Nineteen Eighty-Four* a State which enforces unfreedom not to promote happiness, which raises all manner of difficult questions, but rather, and all too conveniently, to perpetuate unhappiness and suffering.[59] The reason for this simplifying perverseness again lies in the ideological readjustments which the disappointment of Orwell's wartime hopes in the reality of the post-war world entailed. The despair of *Nineteen Eighty-Four* and its perverse intensification is, in a sense, Orwell's punishment of himself for having entertained those hopes at all. He had already passed judgement on these in September 1944:

Since about 1930 the world has given no reason for optimism whatever. Nothing is in sight except a welter of lies, hatred, cruelty and ignorance . . . It is quite possible that man's major problems will *never* be solved. But it is also unthinkable! Who is there who dares to look at the world of today and say to himself, 'It will always be like this: even in a million years it cannot get appreciably better'?

(III, 243)

In 'Why I write' (1946) Orwell made the pregnant remark that *his* special gift lay in the power to face 'unpleasant facts', and moreover that, in some unspecified way, this enabled him to 'get his own back'. I suggest that the determined perverseness of *Nineteen Eighty-Four* (and the superficially cynical but equally rigorous perverseness of *Animal Farm*) is, precisely, an attempt to think the 'unthinkable', and thus recover an existential equipoise which the showing-up of his populist euphoria had wrecked.

In his populist phase, as we have seen, Orwell developed a sort of mysticism of war:

greatest of all agents of change. It speeds up all processes, wipes out minor distinctions, brings realities to the surface.

(II, 94)

In *Nineteen Eighty-Four*, war is the means for inhibiting all change:

The war is waged by each ruling class against its own subjects, and the object of the war is not to make or prevent conquests of territory, but to keep the structure of society intact.

(*Nineteen Eighty-Four*, 204–5)

In 1942, Orwell had written:

When it comes to the pinch, human beings are heroic. Women face childbed and the scrubbing brush, revolutionaries keep their mouths shut in the torture chamber.

(II, 164)

In the world of *Nineteen Eighty-Four* such courage is alien, and only the jingle of betrayal is heard: 'I sold you and you sold me' (*Nineteen Eighty-Four*, 300). The heroic willingness of ordinary people to put up with privations during the war, celebrated by Orwell in writings and broadcasts, is transformed into the joyless slavishness of the 'proles'. There is another, and deeply significant, reversal, similar in consequence to the one we have noted in connection with Newspeak. In earlier comments on the neo-pessimists (see III, 189–90) Orwell had argued against their assumption of the irredeemably corrupt nature of man and suggested instead that human nature was a function of circumstances and could therefore be modified, even made better. But in *Nineteen Eighty-Four* this humanist confidence has dwindled, and the infinitely corrupt human nature of the neo-pessimists reappears, now endowed with an infinite corruptibility. What was a resource has become a threat. Finally, in 1940, Orwell had written in affirmation:

Man is not an individual, he is only a cell in an everlasting body.

(II, 17)

This idea, again, has a horrific reincarnation in *Nineteen Eighty-Four*, in which 'the Party' is the 'everlasting body', sanctioning and enforcing the sacrifice of individualities. 'Can you not understand, Winston', O'Brien asks in the torture chamber:

that the individual is only a cell? The weariness of the cell is the vigour of the organism. Do you die when you cut your fingernails?

(*Nineteen Eighty-Four*, 270)

The paradox of the creative imagination, however, is such that despite the fact that, as I have tried to show, *Nineteen Eighty-Four* is an expression of and a projection from a mood of constriction and impotence, the articulation of Orwell's fantasy is characterised by what can only be described as zest. The descriptions of Julia's work on the 'novel-writing machines in the Fiction Department' show a pure creative exuberance:

She enjoyed her work, which consisted chiefly of running and servicing a powerful but tricky electric motor. She was 'not clever', but was fond of using her hands and felt at home with machinery. She could describe the whole process of composing a novel, from the general directive issued by the Planning Committee down to the final touching-up by the Rewrite Squad. But she was not interested in the finished product. She 'didn't much care for reading', she said.

(*Nineteen Eighty-Four*, 134)

Seeing Julia's arm in a sling, Winston assumes that:

probably she had crushed her hand while swinging round one of the big kaleidoscopes on which the plots of novels were 'roughed in'. It was a common accident in the Fiction Department.

(*Nineteen Eighty-Four*, 109)

The situations Orwell contrives in *Nineteen Eighty-Four* provide him ample opportunity to deploy his specific sensitivities, his sympathetic sense of disgust, of pain and of the infliction thereof. Whether it be Winston cowering in a smelly, glaringly lit cell, or O'Brien smilingly twisting the controls that regulate the quantum of Winston's torment, it is clear that Orwell is mining somewhere near the roots of his creative temperament. There are, indeed, hints enough in the body of the novel that *Nineteen Eighty-Four* is the working out of a pattern with which the author has an imaginative sympathy. Thus, it is repeatedly hinted that the apparent diachronic development from Winston's timid subversive beginnings through to the final 'conversion' to the 'love' of Big Brother is deceptive – that, underlying the diachronicity, there is a synchronic unity which the authorial imagination finds 'truthful'.

It is of course remarkable that every single one of Orwell's novels is about failed rebellions, secessions – from Flory, through Dorothy, Comstock and Bowling, to Winston Smith in *Nineteen Eighty-Four*. Finally, the weight of challenged reality is realised to be overwhelming and, barring Flory, who commits suicide, the others end up accommodating themselves, with varying degrees of relish, to the worlds from which they had fled. The earlier novels are, as we have noted, crucially incoherent, torn between subversive energy and conservative awe. This is clearly not the case with *Nineteen Eighty-Four*. The State of Big Brother is evil enough, and powerful enough, to produce and necessitate and justify *and sustain* endless rebellion. And Winston's defeat, far from being unprepared, and productive of aesthetic disequilibrium, is inevitable and necessary.

At what appears to be the beginning of his political odyssey, Winston muses:

Years ago – how long was it? Seven years it must be – he had dreamed that he was walking through a pitch-dark room. And someone sitting to one side of him had said as he passed: 'We shall meet in the place where there is no darkness.'

(*Nineteen Eighty-Four*, 28)

Winston is uncertain whether he dreamed this before or after he met O'Brien, but it is after exactly seven years that, finally, the Ministry of Love reveals that it has kept Winston under observation all along. The time shifts are confusing, but perhaps the point is that the notion of unidirectional time is itself alien when we are considering what appears to be the ideal realisation of a symbolic, synchronic pattern. Winston knows, and Orwell knows he knows, that:

what was happening was only the working out of a process that had started years ago . . . The end was contained in the beginning.

(*Nineteen Eighty-Four*, 164)

O'Brien tells Winston: 'This drama that I have played out with you during seven years will be played out over and over again generation after generation' (p. 274); and also that everything, the rebellion, the torture, the reconciliation and the despair, 'was all contained in that first act. Nothing has happened that you did not foresee' (p. 279).

Even Julia is anticipated, set in the larger pattern of necessity, as is the Golden Country:

It was an old, rabbit-bitten pasture, with a foot-track wandering across it and a molehill here and there. In the ragged hedge on the opposite side of the field the boughs of the elm trees were swaying very faintly in the breeze, their leaves just stirring in dense masses like women's hair. Somewhere, near at hand, though out of sight, there was a clear, slow-moving stream where dace were swimming in the pools under the willow trees.

The girl with dark hair was coming . . . What overwhelmed him in that instant was admiration for the gesture with which she had thrown her clothes aside. With its grace and carelessness it seemed to annihilate a whole culture.

(p. 34)

Confronted, much later, with the real thing, Winston 'underwent a curious, slow shock of recognition' (p. 127), as of course he must have with the rats in Room 101 because they too are, as O'Brien tells Winston, creatures of his imagination, the thing *he* most fears (p. 289). The Golden Country and the enormous, hungry rats with blunt, fierce muzzles are part of the same imaginative economy. Everything is simultaneously coexistent, bound by internal necessity, 'fixed', as Winston thinks, staring into the paperweight with the embedded coral, thinks of his life, and Julia's, of their world and its objects, its antecedents and its destiny, 'fixed in a sort of eternity at the heart of the crystal' (p. 151).

7

ORWELL'S TRUTH: CONCLUDING REMARKS

> Reflect a little as to what, in the language of the theatre, is *being true*. Is it showing things as they are in nature? Certainly not. Were it so the true would be the commonplace. What, then, is truth for stage purposes? It is the conforming of action, diction, face, voice, movement and gesture, to an ideal type invented by the poet, and frequently enhanced by the player.
>
> (Diderot, *The Paradox of Acting*)

A bestseller, it is said, is a successful sociological experiment: the simple and irreducible fact of its currency is an index of some truth, some fragment of verity, about its corresponding social order. Clearly, something similar might be maintained about an author whose works enjoy widespread currency, finding new readers in each successive generation;[1] whose expressions and conceptions have become, pursuing our metaphor, acceptable tender in the cultural marketplace; whose corpus or, more precisely, in Orwell's own metaphor, whose 'parabola'[2] – the thrusting away in an acute trajectory, the steady pull of gravitational forces, the eventual return to the plane of departure – represents a significant experience of our contemporary world in the social imagination, so that the adjective 'Orwellian' effortlessly connotes whole clusters of image and response, attitude and feeling. It seems reasonable to infer, therefore, that some *essential* structure of feeling and ideas, some *apt* pattern of experience and emotion is represented or enacted within Orwell's luminous trajectory. However, if one asks what this pattern or structure – Orwell's 'truth' – might be, one enters a zone of frequently acrimonious controversy. (The acrimony is an indication of the seriousness of the matters which he touches upon with such beguiling 'honesty'!) In the space that remains to me, I would like to take up some of the themes that were left in the air in the opening chapter of this study, and offer some speculations on the subject of Orwell's cultural resonance or 'plausibility', his puzzling but practically unanimous apotheosis as a hero of our times. For, after all, the widespread assent and admiration commanded by Orwell as man *and myth*, writer and 'exemplar' of a privileged mode of consciousness, suggests that he speaks to some essential distress, enacts with grace and insight some widely shared experience of impasse. As a truly *cultural* creation, however, the myth of George Orwell is no more to be identified exclusively with the utterances of the intelligentsia than folk art is reducible to artefacts in museums. Its presence is to be detected in casual remarks, in the contours of what is taken for granted, a phrase here, a flourish there. The 'texts' which a culture generates over time are, inevitably, sedimented accumulations, demanding patient archaeological labours merely for their reconstruction.[3] However, I would at the very outset like to recall Orwell's words about Kipling: 'It needs great vitality even to become a by-word, but to *remain* one . . . that is genius.'[4] It is precisely that *kind* of 'genius' which is our theme.

The major mythical function of Orwell, as I see it, relates to the ideological world of liberal social democracy, itself the post-war incarnation of the political tendency with which Orwell was proud to align himself – namely, 'democratic Socialism'.[5] However, before we can move on to a consideration of that, we must first dispose of what Bernard Crick identified as 'the *Time-Life* and *Encounter* view of Orwell'. This is the myth of Orwell the Cold War crusader, an early recruit to the armies of the Free World. In this construction, Orwell is the regenerate socialist, who returned from the Depression-struck coal mines of the North of England and the Republican trenches of Catalonia, and devoted the rest of his life to the struggle against 'totalitarianism'. In as much as it purports to offer an interpretation of Orwell's development, this myth is palpably ludicrous. So far from his being an early Cold Warrior, Orwell's post-war writings contain remarkably prescient anticipations of the Cold War world, including even the formidable propaganda apparatus that in time, and before his anguished eyes, engorged Orwell himself. It is worth noting, for instance, that in the imaginary world of *Nineteen Eighty-Four* – the classic text of this construction – 'totalitarianism' inherits the world

not through conquest, which has remained a durable feature of Cold
War rhetoric but is inconceivable between the States of *Nineteen
Eighty-Four* (pp. 190–1); it prevails instead by a form of induction,
across nominally hostile borders, its corruption deepened and per-
petuated by that nominal hostility.[6] This situation is, as it happens,
nearer the reality produced by the Cold War than the 'reality' that
haunted the rhetoric of the Cold War. Thus, the superstates of
Nineteen Eighty-Four, we are told, bolster each other up, like 'three
sheaves of corn' (p. 202). One may get a sense of the *real* project of
Nineteen Eighty-Four in Orwell's curiosity as to the 'ideological
implications' of Burnham's future projections, his curiosity as to:

the kind of world-view, the kind of beliefs, and the social structure that would
prevail in a state which was at once *unconquerable* and in a permanent state of
'cold war' with its neighbours.

(IV, 9)

In an essay written in early 1945, Orwell had already anticipated the
Cold War world and, indeed, its specific reactionary social function:

if the world does settle down into this pattern, it is likely that these vast states
will be permanently at war with one another, though it will not necessarily be
a very intensive or bloody kind of war. Their problems, both economic and
psychological, will be a lot simpler if the doodlebugs are more or less
constantly whizzing to and fro.

(III, 328)

There is sweet revenge in quoting Orwell back at his Cold War
appropriators. Thus, in 1946, Orwell wrote:

In five years it may be as dangerous to praise Stalin as it was to attack him two
years ago. But I should not regard this as an advance. Nothing is gained by
teaching a parrot a new word.[7]

In the desperate years after the war, Orwell had a sharp sense of the
fundamental realignments that were going on. In *Tribune*, on 12
October 1945, he wrote: 'And how many people have – *or had in the
summer of 1944* – the courage to utter genuine criticism of Soviet
Russia.'[8] On 26 January 1945, again in *Tribune*, Orwell had reported
meeting a journalist who 'thought it probable that British policy
would shortly take a violent anti-Russian swing, and that it would be
quite easy to manipulate public opinion in that direction if necessary'.
Orwell's comment on this can, in retrospect, only be read as deeply
ironic: 'For a number of reasons I don't believe he was right, but if he
does turn out to be right, then ultimately it is *our* fault and not that of

our adversaries' (III:91). *Animal Farm* was published on 17 August 1945.

Orwell was aware of the pressure of new conformities that was building up in the vaunted 'democracies':

For all I know, by the time the book *Animal Farm* is published my view of the Soviet regime may be the generally accepted one. But what use would that be in itself? To exchange one orthodoxy for another is not necessarily an advance. The enemy is the gramophone mind, whether or not one agrees with the record that is being played at the moment.[9]

One of these records, by now somewhat scratched and old-fashioned, happens to be a kind of 'Orwell'.

The ideologically staged confrontation between 'freedom' and 'totalitarianism' is central to the propaganda of the capitalist West. How else can the poor in the cardboard colonies, from Montevideo through Nairobi to Calcutta, be consoled for the avoidable misery that derives from the profitable persistence of traditional injustice, the cynical amalgam of feudal and capitalist exploitation – 'modernisation' with tears – other than by being told, often indeed by the native comprador elites that give Western imperialism its distinctive modern form, that they are being saved from a fate far worse? In this bizarre 'looking-glass' world of ideology, the hunger of children in 'democratic' Guatemala is 'justified' – balanced out – by the fact that in the suburbs of Prague police thugs beat up Professors of Philosophy. There is, alas, little human appeal – indeed, little humanity – in the barren world of glacial superpower blocs that corresponds to this ideological formation. And the appropriation of Orwell into this apparatus – the myth of the Cold War crusader – is simply a hijack, a desperate attempt to borrow some of his appeal, to plunder his socialist virtue for ends which must, of necessity, be disguised.[10]

However, the absorption of Orwell into the ideological apparatus of post-war social democracy provides one with an opportunity to observe the subtler processes that are implied in the notions of cultural resonance and plausibility, of a socially constructed 'coherence'.[11] In studying the transformation of 'democratic Socialism' into post-war liberal social democracy, one must give due and sympathetic consideration to the tremendous external pressures, the narrowing constraints, the overwhelming coercion of circumstance – along with, in my view, the inner *defect*, the ambivalence and the ambiguity. My account of this vast and profound historical process must, inevitably, be very sketchy. However, I offer it in the hope that not only is the transformation of 'democratic Socialism' in the post-war era relevant to an understanding of Orwell, but also that a sensitive reading of Orwell can illuminate certain features of the ideological crisis that underlay (and then was buried in) that transformation.

There is an obvious problem in discussing the emergence of post-war liberal social democracy in a context of difficulty and ideological distress. Because, of course, this was the period of its most remarkable electoral triumph, and of its attainment of political respectability. A deep historical divide separates the tragic social-democratic governments of the inter-war years from the social democracies of the period which starts with the ascension of Attlee's Labour Government of 1945. Further, critical as I am of several aspects of post-war liberal social democracy, I am also conscious of its very real achievements. The establishment of the Welfare State, despite its inadequacies and shortcomings, was, by any standards, a remarkable feat. However, the collapse of its supporting value structure and the recrudescence of unabashed illiberalism in the Thatcher era has revealed the weakness in the ideological foundations of that sadly dilapidated edifice with an irrefutability to which I can only aspire. Be that as it may, our concern here is with Orwell, and with the difficulty that attended the beginnings of social democracy's ambiguous triumph.

In broad terms, the difficulty of the immediate post-war years is easily described: between a narrow nationalistic self-interest masquerading as 'socialism' and a resurgent imperialism which adopted the mask of 'democracy', there wasn't much room for 'democratic Socialism' or, as it was then called, 'the Third Force'.[12] Orwell shared this moment of difficulty with his fellow-socialists, and his writings of these years contain numerous indications of it. The evidence of this difficulty must not be misinterpreted, however, to suggest, in Orwell, a turning away from 'democratic Socialism'. Though he was deeply critical of it in some respects, Orwell defended the Labour Government in words that will bear repetition: 'Looking on from outside and reading the British press, one might easily get the idea that the country is groaning beneath bureaucratic misrule and would be only too glad to return to the good old days of free enterprise; but this merely appears to be so because the big capitalists and the middling entrepreneur class are disproportionately vocal.'[13] However, the irreducible difficulty of the objective situation was compounded by the Attlee Government's economic dependence on the US. And the small hope that the 'Third Force' had of survival – through the agency of a Socialist United States of Europe – was killed by the conditionality which governed US assistance: assimilation into the anti-communist crusade.[14] Orwell himself described the situation as being, for socialists, comparable to that of 'a doctor treating an all but hopeless case' (IV, 370). And as the Attlee Government, hamstrung as much by its inhibitions as by the physical constraints of the actual situation, ground on to its sticky end, Orwell confessed to 'an all-prevailing sense of helplessness' (IV, 287, Penguin edition). This helplessness is not merely, I suggest, the generalised helplessness of the individual in the face of vast historical forces: it is a specific helplessness that goes to the heart of the ideological crisis of liberal social democracy. A *New Statesman* commentator in 1948 observed that the reason why the democratic Left was unable to offer constructive criticism of the Attlee–Bevin Government, which filled many of them with a sense of unease, was the fact that 'many of the ideas put forward by the Left have been accepted by the Government'.[15] After all, 'democratic Socialists' like Orwell, who had grown hoarse warning against having any truck with 'totalitarianism', had hardly any purchase – no foothold, no liberated zone either of ideology or imagination – wherefrom they could criticise the anti-totalitarian crusade in the name of which the socialism which they espoused was being traduced. They were, quite precisely, imprisoned in their rhetoric. There is thus an ironic appropriateness in the fact that the major underlying theme of Orwell's major work of these years, *Nineteen Eighty-Four*, should be that of conceptual imprisonment and embezzlement: the processes, crude and subtle, whereby oppression can be insidiously, inescapably, internalised, the love of Big Brother burned into the psyche so that the victim becomes his own executioner. (It is, incidentally, from this perspective that *Nineteen Eighty-Four* is truly original and powerful, and not from that of the long tradition of anti-socialist, anti-labour fantasy to which it might be construed to have a superficial affiliation.)[16] And there is a bitter analogy between Winston, struggling futilely for an appropriate language in which to criticise the tyranny of Big Brother, and Orwell himself, imprisoned in the rhetoric and images of 'totalitarianism', attempting to protest against the looming Cold War world.[17]

One can get a sense of the extraordinary pressures of the time, which drove many 'democratic Socialists' into uncharacteristic and ignoble positions, from looking at the extent to which even someone like Orwell was infected by those poisonous years. Thus, during the war, Orwell wrote of the communists: 'they do not seem to have attempted any definite sabotage of arms production, although the logic of Communist policy demanded this' (II, 47). But in the changed post-war climate, Orwell confidently accused the communists of 'trying' to 'disrupt the war effort' (IV, 320). The tone of Orwell's controversy with the subsequently 'purged' Labour MP, Konni Zilliacus, which took place during this time, is distinctly nasty. Replying to Zilliacus's rebuttal of Orwell's allegations that he was an 'underground Communist' (IV:49), which rebuttal included an account of his anti-communist positions of the past, Orwell wrote:

> he *says* he is not a 'crypto-Communist'. But of course he does! What else could he say? A pickpocket does not go to the races wearing a label 'pickpocket' . . . I do not think Mr Zilliacus's past record is evidence . . . let him show it by his actions.
>
> (IV:49)

Konni Zilliacus was later 'unmasked' as an agent of imperialism – this time by the Communists – but by then Orwell was dead.[18]

Orwell was sufficiently touched by the anti-communist fervour actually to join in the hunting of 'crypto-Communists', and even drew up a list of 'unreliable' elements. Thus, in an unpublished letter of 2 May 1949, Orwell wrote: 'I enclose a list with about 35 names . . . it isn't a bad idea to have the people who are probably unreliable listed'.[19] In a curious way Orwell manages, even during this period, to make his anti-communism sound like a minority creed.[20] Thus, in a controversy with the historian Geoffrey Barraclough about the rights and wrongs of the Warsaw Uprising, Orwell made a bluff avowal of ignorance, but still felt confident enough to be abusive about 'left-wing journalists and intellectuals generally': 'once a whore, always a whore' (III, 227). This undiplomatic roughness was, of course, part of Orwell's earlier attraction, but this attraction is now somewhat mitigated by the fact that anti-communism was fast becoming the official creed. Jeremiah sounds sinister as the mouthpiece of the official religion, inside the city walls.

It is possible that Orwell was, at some level, aware of the corruption caused by the tense, polarised situation. Indeed, it is precisely my point that Orwell was *coerced* by his language and his political conceptions; and also that he might even have been aware of this insidious coercion. Thus, in the essay 'Writers and Leviathan', Orwell takes time off from the anti-communist diatribe to lament the more general, undesirable effect 'on people of goodwill, of political thinking and the need to take sides politically' (IV, 408). Orwell's proposed solution is that while the citizen may (indeed, must, 'unless . . . armoured by old age or stupidity or hypocrisy') participate in the world of partisan loyalties and polemic, the writer –'inviolate' – must 'stand aside' (IV, 413–14).[21] Orwell's 'schizoid' strategy does not, however, work quite as simply as he suggests. The citizen participates enthusiastically in the polemic, but the attempt of the writer to 'stand aside' and be dispassionate, unaffected by the heat and dust, the cries of battle, has ambiguous consequences. The phantoms refuse to lie down – indeed, as we have seen, their horror is magnified and *compounded* by the tactical 'marginality' of the writers: the marginality, like the pressure to align that necessitated the strategy, itself becomes a factor in the making of the 'truth' which the writer can tell.

A critique of capitalism is fundamental to the very idea of socialism – a sort of *sine qua non*. Orwell certainly believed this at *all* times in his career, and in 1939, in the context of Spain, he expressed the view that while parliamentary democracy was adequate for 'family quarrels' between 'liberals and conservatives', it was clearly inadequate 'when the issue is, for instance, between capitalism and socialism'.[22] An avowed 'democratic Socialist', Orwell believed that there was a contradiction between capitalism and democracy, and pointedly rebuked the American ambassador in wartime London, Joseph P. Kennedy, for blandly assuming that the two were the same (II:17). However, in the post-war period, democratic socialists like Orwell were driven into a compromise with the capitalism that they had believed was antithetical to both socialism and democracy. Such a compromise could hardly be inconsequential. We have already observed, in the context of *Nineteen Eighty-Four*, the dialectic of the notions of 'democratic Socialism' and 'totalitarianism' in the case of Orwell (see pp. 141–2). The idea of 'totalitarianism' had, even in the pre-war period, defined a kind of *external* limit for 'democratic Socialism': it identified that domain of 'undemocratic Socialism' in relation to which 'democratic Socialists' defined their distinctive identity. However, in the tense post-war years, as 'democratic Socialism' was forced into a compromise with capitalism, liberal social democracy was *forced* to evacuate its left positions, leading to a kind of vacuum, a space, an 'absent centre'.[23] And the space, lately vacated by its socialist principles, came to be occupied by the arid theology of 'anti-totalitarianism'. The rhetoric of 'anti-totalitarianism', grown strong by feeding on the indubitable malignancy of Hitler and Stalin, proved an irresistible attraction for liberal social democracy. And increasingly, 'totalitarianism', which had earlier defined the external limit of 'democratic Socialism', came to define also, if only by sterile negation, the inner space of liberal social democracy. Thus, the American political scientist Samuel P. Huntington called upon liberals, in the name of the defence of liberal institutions against the threat of 'totalitarianism', 'to lay aside their liberal ideology and to accept the values of conservatism for the duration of the threat . . . To continue to expound the philosophy of liberalism simply gives the enemy a weapon with which to attack the society of liberalism.'[24]

Under the pressure of ideological necessity (over and above the pressure of historical necessity) post-war capitalism itself was perceived as having been transformed. The 'managerialist' thesis of the transformation of capitalism is central to the conception of liberal social democracy. What is visualised within it – and one can see how Fabianism and other tributary streams of social democracy feed into this – is the emergence of a 'managerial' class which dispossesses the owners of capital and, incidentally, subjugates the working class, thus freeing itself from the fatal Marxist dialectic of class conflict and ensuring its permanent dominance. And the end of history. There are positive and negative variants of this idea. Burnham himself, for instance, started out being critical of the idea but found it possible, in the changed post-war world, to celebrate it as 'democracy'.[25] C. A. R. Crosland's *The Future of Socialism* (1956), a key document of this ideological formation, contains a chapter whose triumphant title betrays its managerialist orientation: 'The loss of power by the business to the State'. This State, in turn, although it is debarred from radical intervention by the fear of 'totalitarianism' on which rests its own possibility, developed a pragmatic philosophy of technocratic manipulation that goes by the name of 'social engineering'. In the words of one commentator: 'Social democracy . . . is the application through social engineering of the findings of the social sciences.'[26] It is an inevitable consequence of the dependence on the theory of totalitarianism that the category of the social totality itself should pass out of recognition and out of the reach of political intervention.

Where, one asks, does Orwell fit into this development? It might be suggested, with some justification, that through the 'anti-totalitarian' polemic of *Nineteen Eighty-Four* and his other late writings, Orwell assisted the process whereby fundamental social thinking became vulnerable to the charge of 'totalitarianism', and thus strengthened the smug, anti-political and even anti-critical tendency that found expression in Daniel Bell's famous thesis in *The End of Ideology* (1960).[27] However, it might equally be argued that *Nineteen Eighty-Four* is a polemic *against* this development wherein fundamental political ideas yield place to a regime of technocratic options and 'social engineering'; *against* such a brutish condition in which the goals and bases of a society can never be subjected to examination because the relevant conceptual language has been inhibited and suppressed, and the only questions that can be raised concern the administrative achievement of predetermined ends. This is how Orwell describes the 'proles' of Airstrip One:

> even when they became discontented, as they sometimes did, their discontent led nowhere, because being without general ideas, they could only focus it on petty specific grievances. The larger ends invariably escaped their notice.
>
> (*Nineteen Eighty-Four*, 61, Penguin edition)

'I would not deny', Orwell wrote in January 1944, 'that the "managerial class" *might* get control of our society, and that if they did they would lead us into some hellish places before they have destroyed themselves. Where Burnham and his fellow-thinkers are wrong is in trying to spread the idea that totalitarianism is *unavoidable* and that we must therefore do nothing to oppose it.'[28] Here 'totalitarianism' is identified, specifically, with 'managerial' control: the essential development around which post-war liberal social democracy defines itself.[29] (This article has, in fact, been republished in *CEJL* (III:14). However, for some reason, *these sentences have been excised from it.*)

It is remarkable that Orwell had visualised, as early as July–August 1947, a situation in which: 'As the struggle between East and West becomes more naked, there is a danger that democratic Socialists and mere reactionaries will be driven into combining in a sort of Popular Front' (IV, 374). Ironically, however, Orwell had imagined that the ideological cement of this 'Popular Front' would be provided by the Catholic Church. Little could he have imagined that that function would be performed by the theory of totalitarianism to which he gave such a powerful boost; and that he, too, would be one of the icons in *that* church.

While one must, in honesty, distance Orwell from the optimistic variant of 'high' social democracy, it seems to me that a particular, plausible construction of Orwell *is* almost uniquely suited to the mythical needs of liberal social democracy. This is the myth of Orwell as the 'honest witness': not the Cold War crusader, which he never was, but the man with the wound in his throat, who spoke the bitter truth in a flat, level voice; told, even against his own activist grain, of the searing ambiguities of radical political intervention; and maintained, through the vicissitudes of his difficult career, a kind of bleak, lonely integrity. This myth, it will be seen, employs rather than suppresses Orwell's characteristic strengths. Orwell's activism, his commitment to socialism, far from being awkward and irrelevant, lends substance and conviction to his terminal vision of futility. Such a construction of Orwell also, I believe, helps us to understand the ideological development, in the larger culture, from the 'committed' thirties to the 'less deceived' fifties: the development whereby the criterion of political virtue itself got internalised, from the activism of the pre-war period to the existential 'honesty' of the grey post-war world. Consider, by way of illustration, Blake Morrison's description of the form in which 'the Movement' of the fifties appropriated Orwell:

Orwell's advocacy of quietism, his disillusion with the Left, his determination to be 'less deceived', his growing fear of totalitarianism: these played a crucial part in shaping the Movement's political identity . . . To be politically astute in the 1950s, the Movement implied, was to be politically inactive.[30]

In her brilliant account of the contemporary ideological predicament, *After Utopia: The Decline of Political Faith* (1957), Judith Shklar described the situation in these words: 'We are left with a romanticism deprived of all its positive aspirations, wallowing in its own futility' (p. 108). As for 'democratic Socialism', 'if it exists at all as a systematic theory, [it] has become purely defensive' (p. 219). Another commentator, Irving Howe, is perceptive about the plight of the liberal social democracy that formed in the era of the Cold War: 'It becomes a loose shelter, a poncho rather than a programme . . . the dominance of liberalism contributes heavily to the intellectual's conformity. Liberalism dominates, but without confidence or security . . . and for the *élan* it cannot summon, it substitutes a blend of complacence and anxiety.'[31] The abbreviation of the 'socialism' to 'social' in 'social democracy' is not, I suggest, incidental. One recalls Orwell's observation about the term *Comintern*: 'in thus abbreviating a name one narrowed and subtly altered its meaning, by cutting out most of the associations that would otherwise cling to it' (*Nineteen Eighty-Four*, 'Appendix: the principles of newspeak'). 'Socialism', like Orwell's 'Communist International', conjures up 'a composite picture of universal human brotherhood, red flags, barricades'. 'Social', on the other hand, as in 'social democracy' evokes, well . . .

In an essay on Jack London's dystopian fantasy, *The Iron Heel*, Orwell observed that London's strength lay in his recognition that an indulgent hedonism was insufficient as a self-justification for a ruling class. Even a dystopian ruling elite needed an ideology, a morality and a principle of legitimacy (see II: 11, 'Prophecies of fascism'). However, it is remarkable in the light of this observation that, in fact, there is no hint of such a ruling class ideology in Orwell's own *Nineteen Eighty-Four*. Winston's question: 'I understand HOW: I do not understand WHY' (p. 83), remains unanswered. The *technique* of domination is carefully rendered, but the ideology is a significant absence, a vacuous circularity:

> The object of persecution is persecution.
> The object of torture is torture.
> The object of power is power.

> (p. 269)

Orwell could hardly have foreseen that he would himself, along with his legitimate 'democratic Socialist' anxieties, be absorbed into the black hole of an analogous ideological absence, albeit in the name of social democracy.

Writing in 1955, Arthur Koestler complained:

The pressure of totalitarian forces from outside and inside our Western civilisation has led to a tendency among liberals . . . to call any attitude of non-complacency 'totalitarian' . . . A certain amount of administrative muddle, a margin of tolerated confusion are indeed essential to the functioning of a democratic society as lubricants and safety valves are to be machine. But the harsh, inhuman precision of totalitarian ideologies makes the liberal mind inclined to believe that the safety valves are all that matter, whereas pistons, pressure and energy are totalitarian as such.[32]

Koestler's exasperation is comic – and no doubt exaggerated – but it seems nevertheless to bring to light an aspect of post-war social democracy that is likely to remain unnoticed amidst the flurry of its managerial innovation. At a deeper level, it appears, social democracy in this period *was* defined by a failure of nerve, a kind of timidity, an

accommodation to the given social order with rapidly fading reluctance. And the root cause of this failure was (and in my view is), in the
main, ideological. Post-war social democracy lacked an adequate
theory of itself and of society, of the limits and possibilities of political
intervention.[33]

It is in the process of consequent ideological regrouping that the
myth of Orwell the 'honest witness', the seer into the evils of
'totalitarianism', becomes relevant. 'Totalitarianism' legitimises the
despair that follows the realisation of the missed historical opportunity: the crutch of despair stabilises the stricken ideology of social
democracy. All the unresolved anxieties, the problems endlessly
deferred, pertaining to the future, to technology, to the shape of
industrial societies – matters which the ideology is increasingly ill-
equipped even to *think* about, let alone handle – all these are projected
on to an Other, given a name and a comfortingly distant location.[34]

Myths need to be understood in terms of their functions, in the
contexts of the problems in relation to which they offer, in one way
and another, strategies of *coping*. Myth *does*: 'myth helps people
"understand" social and political reality that is at once mysterious
and threatening'.[35] The Orwell myth, I suggest, derives from, and
derives its continued purchase from, the persistence of certain
features that are best described in Orwell's own words: 'This is the age
of the unresolved dilemma, of the struggle which never slows down
and never leads to a decision. It is as though the world were suffering
from a disease which is simultaneously acute, chronic, and not fatal
. . . a state of almost continuous crisis, like one of those radio serials,
in which the hero falls over a precipice at the end of each
instalment.'[36] It is to such a hysterical world, or, alternatively, a world
perceived in such hysterical terms, that the Orwell myth speaks, then
as now. It engages across a wide range – through the famous
multivocality that transcends the paradox and the contradiction –
and, crucially, *reconciles* in one unlikely harmony the emotions of a
corrosive resentment against such a world, a despairing sense of the
density and opacity of historical process, and an exhausted but
virtuous passivity.[37] I have argued that the suppression of politics is
an essential part of the ineluctable project of post-war liberal social
democracy. However, even after the end of ideology and the dawn of
the managerial utopia, recalcitrant human beings refuse to be
reconciled to various aspects of the socio-economic order – refuse,
that is, to love Big Brother. This recalcitrance, this amorphous and

promiscuous *unease* with the way things are, can be a potential focus for political mobilisation, a trauma waiting to be inflamed. Despair, too, must be managed, apathy produced.[38] The Orwell myth permits the engagement – even, be it said, the arousal – of these 'proto-political' impulses and emotions, and neutralises them by bringing them in conjunction with the absolute Negative of 'totalitarianism'.[39]

A close examination of Orwell's writings in this period, I suggest, helps one to *diagnose*, beneath the electoral triumph, the real situation of difficulty and arrest in which democratic socialism found itself in this period. But social democracy, which is a product of this moment of arrest and difficulty, is enamoured of and dependent upon the ideological 'forms' in which this difficulty is rationalised. It seeks through the ritual invocation of the heroic and futile passion of St George – a mythical construction – not diagnosis, but extenuation: extenuation, be it noted, not for irresponsibility, or the barely disguised inhumanity of the Right, but rather, for its stance of conscientious impotence, agonised ineffectuality . . .

It would be unfortunate, however, if the appropriation of Orwell by social democracy for *its* ideological needs – the absolution of its radical apathy – were taken to be the 'real' Orwell. Whereas we may, happily, leave that question to the metaphysicians and the mantle-snatchers, we can only note with admiration the manner in which, despite the extraordinary pressures of the time, Orwell still managed to distance himself, not only from the English Tories who were eager to use him (see IV:8), and from the American Republicans who had pounced upon *Nineteen Eighty-Four* (see IV:160), but also from the 'democratic Socialists' who were soon to be transformed into the social democrats we know and love. To take one last example, in a critical account of the first three years of the Labour Government, published in 1948, Orwell drew attention to 'the still unresolved contradiction that dwells at the heart of the Socialist movement. Socialism, a creed which grew up in the industrialised Western countries, means better material conditions for the white proletariat; it also means liberation for the coloured peoples. But the two aims, at least temporarily, are incompatible.'[40] Orwell had an acute sense that democratic socialism would have problems in generating a *democratic* mandate for something that was essential in terms of its *socialist* principles. In the *only* 'As I please' column from the entire run of fifty-seven that the editors of *CEJL* chose to omit from volume III, Orwell wrote about the treatment of blacks in the USA, and about the fact that Asia and Africa are used as a bottomless reserve of cheap labour, exploited alike by 'white' capitalists *and* 'white' workers. He concluded: 'There is no solution until the living-standards of the thousand million people who are not "white" can be forced up to the same level as our own. But as this might mean temporarily *lowering* our own standards the subject is systematically avoided by Left and Right alike.'[41]

Social democrats, in office and out of it, have sought refuge from this contradiction in the simplifying polarities of the Cold War, and have gratefully accepted the implicit absolution they offer from the guilt of empires both old and new. There is a little-remarked feature of the world of *Nineteen Eighty-Four*, the 'rough quadrilateral' over which the superpowers are 'constantly struggling': 'a bottomless reserve of cheap labour . . . The inhabitants of these areas, reduced more or less openly to the status of slaves, pass continually from conqueror to conqueror, and are expended like so much coal and oil' (*Nineteen Eighty-Four*, 152, Penguin edition). It sounds familiar.

In trying to distinguish between Orwell and the myths of Orwell, I am not suggesting that the latter are false. Indeed, if these myths did not incorporate some aspect of the truth about Orwell – and also about the social order in which they have their being – they would not have the necessary purchase. However, one must also recognise that Orwell, ultimately, escapes the myths – even, perhaps, his myth of himself. What seems to emerge out of my account of Orwell's career is a sort of unfinished radicalism: unfinished not only in the sense that it is incomplete, being bounded and constrained by a conservative awe, but also in the sense that it is unextinguished, that it is present even in the intensity of his final despair. I have remarked, apropos *Nineteen Eighty-Four*, a crucial ambiguity as to whether the State of Big Brother represents a freak of irrationalism or, more unnervingly, a hyper-trophied rationalism. The former possibility, for all its unpleasantness, leaves one with the consolation of a known, knowable world. The despair consequent upon the latter, however, engulfs not merely socialism but also capitalism; not merely capitalism but the entire rationalist project itself, the history of confident humanist assertion which derives from the Enlightenment.[42] It is perhaps the tension between this radical despair and the activism of the dying writer, his heroic and humane vulnerability to the shifting nuances of history, that is, finally, what is most characteristically Orwellian.

I have discussed the myth of 'Orwell' from the perspective of its function: in terms, that is, of the social experience that it articulates and processes in particular ways and to particular ends. If, however, we turn our attention away from function towards the *etiology* of the myth, and ponder not merely upon its ideological consequences but also upon its ontological and epistemological status, we enter a zone of almost impenetrable difficulty. From one perspective, as I have argued, the Orwell myth is a creation of liberal social democracy: a sort of in-house projection of its ideal self. From another perspective, 'Orwell' is the creation of immense historical factors impinging on an individual and his experience; these factors, at another level, 'produce' in the crucible of a specific conjuncture the ideological formation 'liberal social democracy'. And from this second perspective, the myth of Orwell – a pattern of 'instress' in the evolution of a historically unique individual; a matrix or grid through which that evolution might be 'read' – is also a 'crystallisation' of macro-historical factors through the mediation of an evolving individual consciousness, and can be used as such to *decode* the relatively amorphous ideological formation which is also shaped by that larger history. Summarising, therefore, it appears from one perspective that liberal social democracy is 'expressed' in the myth of Orwell; from the other, the larger historical conjuncture is 'expressed' in liberal social democracy as well as in the myth which both *informs* the development of and enables the cultural appropriation of George Orwell.

The dialectic of mind and reality is an endlessly puzzling phenomenon, a phantasmagoric regress in which the organising oppositions of the commonsensical world appear to dissolve. At the level of popular metaphor, of course, the mind 'reflects' reality. Somewhat more rigorously, one might say that reality 'structures' the mind, reads itself into the forms of consciousness: *informs* consciousness. One might even say that the mind 'crystallises' reality. There is, however, a residual passivity in the foregoing, perhaps unavoidably obscure, formulations. Because, of course, the mind doesn't only reflect, crystallise, process or in other ways *reproduce* reality: it also creates, impinges and acts upon reality. If reality reads itself into the forms of mentality, mentality in turn, in both its individual and collective modes, reads itself into the changing structures of reality.

We have had occasion to observe the pressure of narrative modes – patterns of expectation, the 'forms' in which mind recognises reality – in the case of particular Orwell texts. And at the level of the career as a whole: Orwell's absorption into the larger cultural narrative of liberal social democracy.[43] There is, however, another message there, in the

NOTES AND REFERENCES

(Unless otherwise specified, Orwell references throughout are to the Uniform Edition published by Secker and Warburg. There are a few residual references, clearly identified as such, to the (Penguin) paperback editions, which have had to be retained due to the local unavailability of the Uniform Edition. References to Orwell's writings which have been included in the Uniform Edition are incorporated in the text itself. References to writings which have *not* been included in the Uniform Edition are given, along with references to the other writings that I have quoted from, in the following pages. The four-volume *The Collected Essays, Journalism and Letters* of George Orwell is identified as *CEJL*, and for the references to these volumes I have followed this convention: a roman numeral by itself identifies the volume number of *CEJL*; a comma after that denotes that what follows is a page number, a colon that it is an *item* number. Unless otherwise specified, Archive is the Orwell Archive at University College London.)

1 INTRODUCTION: THE ORWELL PROBLEM

1 George Woodcock, *The Writer and Politics* (London, 1948; edition used, 1967 reissue), p. 124. See also Eric Bentley in Jeffrey Meyers, ed., *George Orwell: The Critical Heritage* (London, 1975), p. 220.

2 'Revolt in the urban desert', *Observer*, 10 Oct. 1943. See also Conor Cruise O'Brien, *Writers and Politics* (London, 1965), Introduction.

3 'The faith of Thomas Mann', *Tribune*, 10 Sept. 1943. See also Christopher Norris, 'Language, truth and ideology: Orwell and the post-war Left', in C. Norris, ed., *Inside the Myth: Orwell: Views from the Left* (London, 1984), esp. p. 245.

4 C. B. Macpherson, 'Politics: post-liberal democracy?', in R. Blackburn, ed., *Ideology in Social Science* (London, 1972). See also J. Dunn, *Western Political Theory in the Face of the Future* (Cambridge, 1979), esp. pp. 49–50; A. Arblaster, *The Rise and Decline of Western Liberalism* (Oxford, 1984), esp. chapters 17 and 18.

5 Michael Walzer, 'Nervous liberals', *New York Review of Books*, 26:15, 11 Oct. 1979.

6 J. P. O'Flinn, 'Orwell on literature and society', *College English*, 31:6 (March 1970), 612. The reference is to Perry Anderson's thesis of an 'absence' at the centre of the British Left. See also Anderson's essay, 'Components of the national culture', in A. Cockburn and R. Blackburn, eds., *Student Power* (London, 1969).

7 Cited in David Rankin, 'The critical reception of the art and thought of George Orwell', unpublished London University Ph.D. thesis, 1965, p. 265. On this diversity

of interpretation, see also George Woodcock, *The Crystal Spirit* (London, 1967; edition used, Penguin 1970), p.49; Raymond Williams, *Orwell* (London, 1971), pp.83–5; R. Heppenstall, 'Orwell intermittent', *The Twentieth Century*, 157 (May 1945), 481.

8 J. V. Knapp, 'Orwell's fiction: funny, but not vulgar', *Modern Fiction Studies*, 27:2 (Summer 1981), 294–301; David Ehrenfeld, 'The roots of prophecy: Orwell and nature', *Hudson Review*, 38:2 (Summer 1985), 193–213; Norman Podhoretz, 'If Orwell were alive today', *Harper's* (January 1983), p.37.

9 See Richard J. Voorhees, *The Paradox of George Orwell* (West Lafayette, Indiana, 1961).

10 Bernard Crick, *George Orwell: A Life* (London, 1980), p.385; hereafter simply *Life*.

11 See Wayne Burns, 'George Orwell: our "responsible" Quixote', *West Coast Review*, 2 (1967), 19; George Woodcock, 'Recollections of George Orwell', *Northern Review*, 6:3, 26; David Kubal, *Outside the Whale: George Orwell's Art and Politics* (London, 1972), p.141. J. MacNamara and D. J. O'Keeffe, writing in *Encounter* in December 1982 are emphatic: 'Professor Crick is . . . misleading when he asserts that *Nineteen Eighty-Four* is simply a great book that Orwell wrote just before he happened to die. It is very clearly his *summa*' (vol. 59, no.6, p.46).

12 See V. S. Pritchett's review of *Nineteen Eighty-Four* in *New Statesman*, 18 June 1949.

13 Peter Keating's review of Crick's *Life*, *Financial Times*, 6 Dec. 1980.

14 See Donald Crompton, 'False maps of the world – George Orwell's autobiographical writings and the early novels', *Critical Quarterly*, 16:2 (Summer 1974), 149–69; Howard Wolf, 'George Orwell and the problematics of non-fiction', *Critical Quarterly*, 27:2 (Summer 1985), 23–30. See also Cleo McNelly, 'On not teaching Orwell', *College English*, 38 (1977), 553–66.

15 Isaac Rosenfeld, in Jeffrey Meyers, ed. *George Orwell: The Critical Heritage* (London, 1975), p.170. See also Irving Howe: 'Like all critics who are also significant writers themselves, Orwell developed standards that were largely self-justifying: he liked the prose that's like a window-pane because that's the kind of prose he wrote' *Harper's* (January 1969), in Meyers, *Critical Heritage*, p.357.

16 Richard Rovere, 'The importance of George Orwell', in *The Orwell Reader* (New York, 1956).

17 See Adorno's remark about Kafka: 'Through the power with which Kafka commands interpretation, he collapses aesthetic distance. He demands a desperate effort of the allegedly "disinterested" observer of an earlier time, overwhelms him, suggesting that far more than his intellectual equilibrium depends on whether he truly understands; life and death are at stake', *Prisms*, trans. S. Weber (London, 1967), p.246.

18 See Fredric Jameson, *Marxism and Form: Twentieth-Century Dialectical Theories of Literature* (Princeton, NJ, 1971), p.315.

19 See Gerald Graff, *Literature Against Itself: Literary Ideas in Modern Society* (London, 1979), particularly 'What was New Criticism?'. Graff cites Robert Scholes on 'The fictional criticism of the future': 'criticism is about the impossibility of anything being about life, really, or even about fiction, or, finally, about anything. Criticism has taken the very idea of "aboutness" away from us. It has taught us that language is tautological, if it is not nonsense, and to the extent that it is about anything it is about itself' (p.60). On the surprising return of New Critical autonomism, in radical guise, see also Frank Lentricchia, *After the New Criticism* (Chicago, 1980) and Edward Said, *The World, The Text and the Critic* (Harvard, 1983).

20 See Richard Hoggart, 'Contemporary cultural studies: an approach to the study of literature and society', in Malcolm Bradbury and David Palmer, eds., *Contemporary Criticism* (London, 1970): 'It is important that some critics continue to insist that a work of literature is an autonomous artefact. This reminds us that the "coherent universe" of a work is, first and foremost, itself and not something else to be used for other purposes. It underlines the singularity of each work of art and the sense in which the expressive arts are free, pointless acts. The claim for autonomy has a heuristic value and in the last decade or two has done a great deal to sharpen and make more subtle our understanding of literature. But it is at bottom a limited and mistaken claim. A work of art, no matter how much it rejects or ignores its society, is deeply rooted within it. It has massive cultural meanings. There is no such thing as "a work of art in itself"' (p. 163).

21 In Raymond Williams, ed., *George Orwell: A Collection of Critical Essays* (Englewood Cliffs, NJ, 1974), p. 79.

22 Irving Howe, *Politics and the Novel* (New York, 1957), p. 17.

23 George Woodcock, 'Orwell, Blair and the critics', *Sewanee Review*, 83 (1975), 524.

24 *Fiction and the Shapes of Belief* (Berkeley, 1964), pp. 233–4.

25 See Arnold Rattenbury, 'Total attainder and the helots', *Renaissance and Modern Studies*, 20 (1976). See also John Wain, 'George Orwell', in *Essays on Literature and Ideas* (London, 1963): 'Orwell was, in fact, very close in spirit to the other writers of his generation, though the closeness has been obscured by the different turn he took after 1945, and by his habit during the 'thirties of referring to his fellow-writers in rather disdainful terms' (p. 209).

26 See Jeremy Hawthorn, *Identity and Relationship: A Contribution to the Marxist Theory of Literary Criticism* (London, 1973), pp. 94–6.

27 See James Walsh, 'George Orwell', *Marxist Quarterly*, 3 (1956), 25–39; also, Samuel Sillen's review of *Nineteen Eighty-Four* in *Masses and Mainstream*, August 1949, pp. 79–81. For a pleasant contrast to Walsh and Sillen, see Peter Thirlby, 'Orwell as a liberal', *Marxist Quarterly*, October 1956, pp. 239–47.

28 John Wain, 'George Orwell'.

29 Howe, *Politics*, p. 24.

30 The phrase is from V. S. Pritchett's obituary notice on Orwell, *New Statesman and Nation*, 28 Jan. 1950.

31 John Mander, *The Writer and Commitment* (London, 1961), p. 16.

32 'Orwell's bad good books', *Twentieth Century*, April 1955, p. 359. See also Orwell's remark in the *Observer*, 12 November 1944, while reviewing a biography of Gerard Manley Hopkins: 'criticism and hagiography are different things'.

33 Adams, 'Authenticity-codes and sincerity-formulas', in Leonard Michaels and Christopher Ricks, eds., *The State of the Language* (London, 1980), p. 589. Italics added.

34 'The fictions of factual representation', in Angus Fletcher, ed., *The Literature of Fact* (New York, 1976).

35 It might be helpful to bear in mind John Goode's remark about Dickens's 'effectivity': 'a function of his ideological organicism, his subordination to the intellectual needs of the class for whom he writes' (in *George Gissing: Ideology and Fiction*, London, 1978, p. 30). Goode cites Gissing on Dickens's 'understanding' with his public which permitted him 'to say aloud with impunity that which all his hearers say within themselves dumbly, inarticulately'. See also Barthes's notion of 'white writing' which, in Jameson's words, attempts 'to efface itself in . . . socially motivated

transparency' (*Marxism and Form*, p. 397). Professor Wayne Booth's *Modern Dogma and the Rhetoric of Assent* (London, 1974) contains interesting and valuable insights into many of these questions.

36 Robert McCormack, 'Orwell', *Tamarack Review*, 58 (1971).

37 R. Gotesky, 'The nature of myth and society', *American Anthropologist*, 54 (1952), 523–31; cited in Gregor Sebba, 'Symbol and myth in modern rationalistic societies', in Thomas J. J. Altizer, ed., *Truth, Myth and Symbol* (Englewood Cliffs, NJ, 1962).

38 Cited in Sebba, *ibid*.

39 Frank Kermode, *The Sense of an Ending* (New York, 1967), p. 164.

40 Fredric Jameson, *The Political Unconscious: Narrative as a Socially Symbolic Act* (London, 1981), p. 287.

41 Sebba, 'Symbol and myth'.

42 *Time and Tide*, 5 July 1941.

43 Cited in Robert Hewison, *Under Siege: Literary Life in London 1939–1945* (London, 1977), p. 48.

44 See Daphne Patai, *The Orwell Mystique: A Study in Male Ideology* (Amherst, Mass., 1984): 'both Orwell and the cult that arose around him in the mid-twentieth century will eventually be viewed as a problem in intellectual history and intellectual consumption. In the future, I think, interest in Orwell will focus not on his work but on the phenomenon of his fame and what it reveals about our own civilisation' (p. x).

45 Raymond Williams, *Politics and Letters* (London, 1979), p. 389.

46 *Ibid*., p. 388.

2 TOTALITARIANISM, ETC.

1 Conor Cruise O'Brien, *Writers and Politics*, p. 174.

2 *Dictionary of the History of Ideas*, ed. Philip S. Wiener (New York, 1973), p. 408.

3 Franz Borkenau, *The Totalitarian Enemy* (London, 1940), p. 13.

4 Martin Kitchen, *Fascism* (London, 1976), p. 26.

5 O'Brien, *Writers*, p. 168.

6 On the anti-statist dimension of the theory of totalitarianism, see Gordon K. Lewis, 'Twentieth-century capitalism and society: the present state of the Anglo-American debate' (first published 1959), in W. E. Stankiewicz, ed., *Political Thought Since World War II* (London, 1964), p. 303. More generally, on the role of totalitarianism in the ideological support system of contemporary capitalism, see Ralph Miliband, *The State in Capitalist Society* (London, 1969), chapters 7 and 8, entitled, jointly, 'The process of legitimation'.

7 See entry on 'totalitarianism' in A. Bullock and O. Stallybrass, eds., *The Fontana Dictionary of Modern Thought* (London, 1977).

8 Joyce and Gabriel Kolko, *The Limits of Power: The World and U.S. Foreign Policy 1945–1964* (London, 1972), p. 31.

9 *Dictionary of the History of Ideas*, p. 410.

10 Kitchen, *Fascism*, p. 25.

11 See Arblaster, *Rise and Decline of Western Liberalism*, chapter 18, entitled 'Cold war liberalism', esp. sub-section on 'Totalitarianism'.

12 Benjamin R. Barber, 'Conceptual foundations of totalitarianism', in *Totalitarianism in Perspective: Three Views* (London, 1969), p. 19.

13 Kitchen, *Fascism*, p. 26.

14 Cited in *ibid.*, p. 26.

15 *Ibid.*, pp. 32–4.

16 Mander, *The Writer and Commitment*, p. 101.

17 D. A. N. Jones, 'Arguments against Orwell', in Miriam Gross, ed., *The World of George Orwell* (London, 1971) pp. 160–1.

18 Bullock and Stallybrass, *Dictionary of Modern Thought*.

19 S. Andreski, 'Is totalitarianism a meaningful concept?', in *A Dictionary of the Social Sciences* (1964). Cited in Paul T. Mason, ed., *Totalitarianism: Temporary Madness or Permanent Danger?* (Boston, 1967), pp. 31–2.

20 Walter Laqueur, *The Fate of the Revolution: Interpretations of Soviet History* (London, 1967), p. 200.

21 In the 1980s, in Reagan's America, the term has been rehabilitated, particularly among intellectuals of a neo-conservative stripe, to distinguish the empire of Unfreedom from the 'authoritarian' regimes that are vital to the survival of 'democracy' in our time. On this distinction, and its role in reviving the spirit of the Cold War, see Michael Walzer, 'On failed totalitarianism', *Dissent*, 30 (Summer 1983), 297–306.

22 *London Review of Books*, 3:3, February 1981.

23 William Steinhoff, *The Road to 1984* (London, 1975), p. 3.

24 Hannah Arendt, *The Origins of Totalitarianism* (London, 1951), p. ix.

25 *Ibid.*, p. 432.

3 INVENTING A FORM

1 See John Wain, 'George Orwell' (see note 25 to chapter 1).

2 John Lehmann, *The Whispering Gallery* (London, 1955), pp. 115–16.

3 *Winds of Change* (London, 1963), p. 283; cited in Noreen Branson and Margot Heinemann, *Britain in the 1930s*, (London, 1971), p. 6.

4 'The education of a communist', *Left Review*, 1:3 (December 1934), 63.

5 'Straws for the wary: antecedents to fascism', *Left Review*, 1:1 (October 1934), 19–21.

6 Page 11.

7 Branson and Heinemann, *Britain in the 1930s*, p. 257.

8 'James Joyce: the meaning of *Ulysses*', *Calendar of Modern Letters*, 1:5 (July 1925), p. 355.

9 *Ibid.*, 1:6 (August 1925), 473–4. Italics added.

10 *Adelphi*, 2:1 (1930). 71.

11 *New Country* (1933), p. 17.

12 1:1 (October 1930), 2.

13 1:1 (Summer 1933).

14 Peter Stansky and William Abrahams, *The Unknown Orwell* vol. 1 (London, 1972; edition used, Paladin 1974), p. 240.

15 *Ulysses*, Penguin Modern Classics, p.47.

16 'The Twenties', in Cyril Connolly, *The Evening Colonnade* (London, 1973), p.23.

17 Cf. 'The outsider', in Gilbert Highet, *A Clerk of Oxenford: Essays on Literature and Life* (London, 1954), pp.62–8; see also Stansky and Abrahams, *The Unknown Orwell*, p.246.

18 1:1 (Summer 1933), 10.

19 See Jeremy Hawthorn, *Identity and Relationship*, p.19. Hawthorn cites opinion to the effect that what is recognised as 'real' is determined by the 'whole cultural orientation'.

20 Christopher Isherwood, *Lions and Shadows* (London, 1938), pp.128–9.

21 'Poverty – plain and coloured', by Eric Blair, *Adelphi* (April 1931): 'Most fiction is written by the well-fed, about the well-fed, for the well-fed.'

22 'By-words', *New Statesman and Nation*, 16 Nov. 1940; see also 'New novels', *ibid.*, 22 Feb. 1941.

23 'From Bloomsbury to the Bowery', *Tribune*, 12 April 1940.

24 'Sunday', in *New Country* (1933), p.188.

25 'Letter to a young revolutionary', in *ibid.*, p.28.

26 Edmund Wilson has written about a minor skirmish in the attempt of the American Left – circa 1932 – to overcome its minority status and achieve critical recognition. Michael Gold of *New Masses* charged Thornton Wilder with being 'bourgeois': 'Where are the cotton mills, and the murder of Ella May and her songs? Where are the child slaves of the beet fields? Where are the stockbroker suicides, the labour racketeers or the passion and death of the coal miners?' Later, when Gold published his novel *Jews Without Money, he* was attacked by Melvin Levy for being insufficiently proletarian because he had included no references to 'the Triangle fire and the great garment strikes'. Gold defended himself thus: 'I could do nothing else honestly and emotionally at the time . . . It is difficult to write proletarian literature in this country because all the critics are bourgeois. If a Thornton Wilder writes books in praise of the Catholic theology or if a Robinson Jeffers preaches universal pessimism and mass-suicide, that is art. But if a revolutionary writer, even by implication, shows the social ideals that are stirring in the heart of the working class he is called a propagandist. This taunt which one meets on every side creates a powerful psychic force which proletarian writers will have to ignore.' See 'The literary class war', in Edmund Wilson's *The Shores of Light* (1952), esp. pp.537–8; see also Malcolm Cowley, *Exile's Return: A Literary Odyssey of the 1920s* (London, 1961), p.303.

27 In Archive.

28 J. K. Stanford, *Ladies in the Sun: The Memsahib's India, 1790–1860* (London, 1962); cited in Allen J. Greenberger, *The British Image of India: A Study of the Literature of Imperialism 1880–1960* (London, 1969), p.2.

29 Terry Eagleton, *Exiles and Emigrés: Studies in Modern Literature* (London, 1970), p.85.

30 For further evidence on this point, see Greenberger, *British Image of India*, p.110.

31 Bhupal Singh, *A Survey of Anglo-Indian Literature* (London, 1934), p.167. The following account relies largely upon Singh.

32 Kenneth Ballhatchet, *Race, Sex and Class under the Raj: Imperial Attitudes and Policies and their Critics, 1793–1905* (London, 1980), p.96.

33 See also 'A tale told by moonlight', in Leonard Woolf, *Diaries in Ceylon 1908–1911* (London, 1963).

34 'George Orwell and Burma', in Gross, ed., *The World of George Orwell*, p. 24.

35 In Meyers, ed., *Critical Heritage*, p. 83.

36 See *CEJL* 1:52. See also Crompton, 'False maps of the world'.

37 For similar perceptions put to widely different uses, see Mander, *The Writer and Commitment*, p. 80; Edward M. Thomas, *Orwell* (London, 1965), p. 28; Keith Aldritt, *The Making of George Orwell: An Essay in Literary History* (London, 1969), p. 102.

38 See George Woodcock, 'Orwell, Blair and the critics', and the two-volume biography of Orwell by Stansky and Abrahams, *The Unknown Orwell* (1972) and *Orwell: The Transformation* (1979).

39 See Crick, *Life*, pp. 187–8.

40 Avril Dunn, 'My brother, George Orwell', *Twentieth Century*, 169 (March 1961).

41 See Edward M. Thomas, *Orwell*, p. 96.

42 See Orwell's remark: 'Unwilling witnesses are generally accounted the most reliable', in 'Spanish prison', *Observer*, 24 December 1944. See Robert M. Adams, 'Authenticity-codes and sincerity-formulas', p. 588: 'Overcoming obstacles, real or apparent, is a way of seeming to guarantee authenticity . . . By confessing to transgressions which his readers have themselves committed in thought or deed, the confessor establishes bonds of sympathy with them; if, in addition, he invites or challenges punishment in their stead, he offers them the agreeable experience of vicarious atonement.' Paul Fussell, 'The critics who made us – George Orwell', *Sewanee Review*, 93:2 (Spring 1985), 232–43, makes some acute observations about the rhetoric of Orwell's 'honesty'. Also, on this theme, see Hugh Kenner, 'The politics of the plain style', in Robert Mulvihill, ed., *Reflections on America, 1984: An Orwell Symposium* (Athens, Ga., 1986).

43 In Archive.

44 John Bayley, *The Uses of Division: Unity and Disharmony in Literature* (London, 1976), p. 56.

45 See Patricia Meyer Spacks, *Imagining a Self* (London, 1976), pp. 2–3.

46 Rattenbury, 'Total attainder'.

47 Yvonne Cloud, 'Criticising the Left', *New Verse*, n.s.1 (January 1939).

48 Raymond Williams, *Orwell*, p. 90.

49 Jonah Raskin, 'Imperialism: Conrad's *Heart of Darkness*', *Journal of Contemporary History*, 2:2 (April 1967), 115.

50 See H. R. Fink's unpublished 1968 London University Ph.D. thesis, 'George Orwell's novels in relation to his social and literary theory', p. 61. Fink's source is Victor Gollancz.

51 Cited in A. Zhdanov *et al.*, *Problems of Soviet Literature* (1935), p. 179.

4 A KIND OF SOCIALISM

1 Cited in William H. Pritchard, *Seeing Through Everything: English Writers 1918–1940* (London, 1977), p. 198.

2 Stephen Ingle, 'The politics of George Orwell: a reappraisal', *Queen's Quarterly*, 80 (1973).

3 Alexander Trocchi's review of *The Road to Wigan Pier* in *Evergreen Review*, 2:6 (Autumn 1958).

4 'If Orwell were alive today', *Harper's*, January 1983.

5 Leopold Labedz, 'Will George Orwell survive 1984?', *Encounter*, June 1984, p. 13.

6 Rattenbury, 'Total attainder'.

7 *Friends Apart: A Memoir of Esmond Romilly and Jasper Ridley in the Thirties* (London, 1954), p. 18.

8 Crick, *Life*, p. xxii.

9 See Woodcock on Orwell's intellectual 'opportunism' in Meyers, ed., *Critical Heritage*, p. 245.

10 The expression is used by Jameson in *Marxism and Form* to describe the kind of undogmatic Marxism of which he approves.

11 From the first part, 'Unemployment', published on 29 December 1928, of a three-part article in *Le Progrès Civique* collectively entitled 'The great misery of the British worker'.

12 See Jenni Calder, *Chronicles of Conscience: A Study of George Orwell and Arthur Koestler* (London, 1968), p. 33; also Stansky and Abrahams, *The Transformation*, p. 16.

13 Book review entitled 'Life in London's underworld', *Tribune*, 23 August 1940.

14 A letter from one L. I. Bailey, an early advisor to the apprentice writer, suggests that the inhibition of political interest in Orwell's 'Tramps and beggars book' might, in part, have been due to Mr Bailey's counsel: 'of course, if it is political, that would be rather against it'. See Crick, *Life*, p. 117.

15 'The burial of the dead', from *The Waste Land*, in *Collected Poems 1909–1962* (London, 1963), p. 65.

16 Lawrence Ferlinghetti, 'Autobiography', in *A Coney Island of the Mind* (New York, 1958), p. 61.

17 See John Stevenson, *Social Conditions in Britain Between the Wars* (Harmondsworth, 1977), p. 20; see also Eric Hobsbawm, *Industry and Empire* (Harmondsworth, 1969), p. 220; and Branson and Heinemann, p. 12.

18 The Independent Labour Party's summer camp was held at Letchworth, the *Adelphi*'s at Langham in Essex. See Crick, *Life*, p. 201; Stansky and Abrahams, *The Transformation*, p. 188; J. Middleton Murry, 'The Adelphi Centre', *Adelphi*, 2 (1936).

19 A. C. Pointon, *The Bombay Burmah Trading Corporation Ltd 1863–1963* (Southampton, 1964), p. 65. See also Carlyle King, 'The politics of George Orwell', *University of Toronto Quarterly*, 26 (October 1956), 79–91.

20 Report of the Burma Police Enquiry Committee, p. 10.

21 Report of the Standing Committee for the Imperial Idea, p. (i).

22 D. G. E. Hall, *Imperialism in Modern History* (Rangoon, 1923).

23 *Report*, p. 12. See also Appendix G of the *Report*, p. 85.

24 Roger Beadon, 'With Orwell in Burma', *The Listener*, 81 (29 May 1969), 755.

25 Maung Htin Aung, 'Orwell of the Burma Police', *Asian Affairs*, 60 (1973), 181–6.

26 Source: Reports of the Prison Administration of Burma for the relevant years. These reports have now disappeared from the British Library. However, they are still available at the India Office Library in London – including the report for 1926 which is said to be unavailable in Crick, *Life*, p. 423. My figures are at variance with those cited by Prof. Crick on p. 85 but I have double-checked and so stand by mine.

27 Aung, 'Orwell', pp. 181–6.

28 Beadon, 'With Orwell', p. 755.

29 The information is derived from Aung, 'Orwell', pp. 181–6, but the inference is mine.

30 *Rangoon Gazette Weekly Budget*, passenger list, 18 July 1927.

31 Review by Eric Blair of E. R. Curtius's *The Civilisation of France*, *Adelphi*, May 1932.

32 Aung, 'Orwell', pp. 181–6.

33 The *Rangoon Gazette Weekly Budget* noted on 20 June 1927 that 'Leave on average pay for a period of eight months is granted to Mr E. A. Blair, Asst. Supdt. of Police.'

34 In the *New York Daily Tribune*, 8 August 1853; cited from the collection *On Colonialism* (London, 1960), p. 81.

35 Leonard Woolf, *Growing: An Autobiography of the Years 1904–1911* (London, 1961), p. 159.

36 G. Aubry, ed., *Joseph Conrad: Life and Letters* (London, 1927), vol. II, p. 142.

37 'British Empire' section, p. x. The main body of the paper carried details pertaining to the Amritsar massacre – the necessary counterpoint to Thomas's bland pomposity. Thomas, incidentally, is reported to have been willing to bring libel actions against people who so much as suggested that he was a socialist. See David Coates, *The Labour Party and the Struggle for Socialism* (London, 1975), p. 24. On this theme generally, see Parthasarathy Gupta, *The Labour Movement and Imperialism 1914–64* (London, 1965).

38 Alex Zwerdling, *Orwell and the Left* (London, 1974), p. 31.

39 E. P. Thompson, *The Poverty of Theory* (London, 1978), p. 68.

40 Broadcast, 5 March 1943; transcript in Archive.

41 See Raghavan Iyer, 'Utilitarianism and all that', *St Antony's Papers*, 8 (1960), 29.

42 Arendt, *The Origins of Totalitarianism*, p. 185.

43 Bernard Semmel, *The Governor Eyre Controversy* (London, 1962), pp. 178–9.

44 Alan Sandison, *The Wheel of Empire* (London, 1967), p. 76.

45 Report by the District Commissioner, Sandoway (Burma), Annual Police Report, 1927.

46 Francis Odle, 'Orwell in Burma', *Twentieth Century*, 179 (1972), 38–9.

47 See Leonard Woolf's description of his response to the colonial situation: 'as time went on, I became more and more ambivalent, politically schizophrenic', *Growing*, p. 159.

48 John Lewis, *The Left Book Club* (London, 1970), p. 36.

49 *Left News*, June 1937, p. 393.

50 Richard Wollheim, 'Orwell reconsidered', *Partisan Review*, 27:1 (Winter 1960), 82–97; see also I. R. Willison, 'Orwell's bad good books', p. 361: '[his] ambiance was Fleet Street rather than Bloomsbury'.

51 *New Society*, 27 January 1977.

52 The chapter on Orwell in Paul Potts's *Dante Called You Beatrice* (London, 1960) is entitled 'Don Quixote on a bicycle'.

53 *Left News*, March 1937, pp. 275–6.

54 'George Orwell and *The Road to Wigan Pier*', *Critical Quarterly*, 7:1 (Spring 1965), 72–85.

55 In Meyers, ed., *Critical Heritage*, p. 117.

56 In Meyers, ed., *Critical Heritage*, p. 187.

57 *Left Review* 2:9 (June 1936), 468.

58 Review of Alec Brown's *The Fate of the Middle Classes*, *Adelphi*, May 1936.

59 In Meyers, ed., *Critical Heritage*, p. 118.

60 Wollheim, 'Orwell reconsidered', pp. 90–1.

61 See George Woodcock: 'however strongly the conservatism that dominated one side of his nature might draw him toward a kind of patriotic social democracy, the radicalism that was its other made him perpetually susceptible to the appeal of the sectarian personality', *Commentary*, June 1969.

62 Robert E. Dowse, *Left in the Centre: The Independent Labour Party 1893–1940* (London, 1966), p. 193.

63 *Inprecorr*, 18 April 1936; cited in James Jupp, 'The Left in Britain: 1931 to 1941', unpublished London University M.Sc. thesis, 1956, p. 490.

64 *New Leader*, 12 March 1937.

65 See Peter Stansky and William Abrahams, *Journey to the Frontier* (London, 1966), p. 316.

5 WAR AND REVOLUTION

1 Cyril Connolly, *The Condemned Playground* (London, 1945), pp. 186–7; from 'Barcelona', written in November 1936.

2 *New Statesman*, 20 April 1962, p. 568.

3 Raymond Williams, 'George Orwell', *Essays in Criticism*, 5 (1955), 46.

4 *Horizon*, 69 (September 1945), 215; see also Cyril Connolly, *Previous Convictions* (London, 1963), p. 318.

5 Cited in Eric Homberger, *The Art of the Real* (London, 1977), p. 22.

6 In Archive.

7 See article by Dr C. A. Smith of the Independent Labour Party in *Left News*, May 1940.

8 I, 357. An unpublished letter from Richard Rees to Orwell, dated 25 May 1938, from Paris, also contains a reference to such a pamphlet: 'Eileen tells me you have written a Peace pamphlet.' In Archive.

9 'Political reflections on the crisis', *Adelphi*, December 1938.

10 Diary and letters in Archive.

11 'We are observed!', *Time and Tide*, 2 March 1940.

12 See Paul Addison, *The Road to 1945: British Politics and the Second World War* (London, 1975), p. 145.

13 See Stephen Lutman, 'Orwell's patriotism', *Journal of Contemporary History*, 2:2 (April 1967), 149–58, for a somewhat different account of Orwell's patriotic affirmation and its connections with his Spanish experience. See also Gregory Claeys, 'The Lion and the Unicorn, patriotism, and Orwell's politics', *Review of Politics*, 47 (April 1985), 186–211.

14 Angus Calder, *The People's War: Britain 1939–1945* (London, 1969), p. 34.

15 Julian Symons, *Notes From Another Country* (London, 1972), pp. 92–3.

16 Cited in Calder, *People's War*, p. 163.

17 Ralph Miliband, *Parliamentary Socialism: A Study in the Politics of Labour* (London, 1961), p. 274. See also Addison, *Road to 1945*, p. 15: Calder, *People's War*, p. 17: *Times* leader, 1 July 1940, cited in Calder, *ibid.*, p. 137; Mass Observation Report no. 496, 'Popular attitudes to wartime politics', cited in Calder, *ibid.*, p. 139.

18 *Postcripts* (London, 1940), p. 12.

19 'Weekly news review', 18 April 1942. In the BBC Written Archives Centre (BBC WAC) in Caversham, near Reading.

20 Crick, *Life*, pp. 238–41; BBC WAC ref. File No. E2/361/2 'Foreign Gen': Acc. No. 90.

21 'Weekly news review', 7 March 1942. Source: BBC WAC.

22 'Weekly news review', 14 March 1942. Clearly, Orwell's masochistic ardour was felt to be excessive, because the entire paragraph was deleted. Source: BBC WAC.

23 'Through Eastern eyes', 20 January 1942. Source: BBC WAC.

24 See Philip Toynbee, *Friends Apart*, p. 91: 'it was against our principles to *want* a war of the old kind, and only a "people's war" could mark an occasion for disclosing our secret, unadmitted longings'.

25 'Outside and inside views', *New English Weekly*, 8 June 1939.

26 Laqueur, *Fate of the Revolution*, p. 180.

27 See Jack Lindsay, *After the Thirties: The Novel in Britain and its Future* (London, 1956), p. 93 footnote.

28 'Our opportunity', *Left News*, January 1941.

29 'Fascism and democracy', *Left News*, February 1941.

30 Second part of the three-part 'The great misery of the British worker', *Le Progrès Civique*, 1 January 1929.

31 F. Neumann, *Behemoth: The Structure and Practice of National Socialism 1933–1944* (edition used, Harper and Row, 1966), pp. 98–101.

32 See David Kubal, 'Freud, Orwell and the bourgeois interior', *Yale Review*, 67 (Spring 1978), 389–403.

33 Orwell's blindness with respect to the question of feminism is a large theme on which I must content myself with giving a few bibliographical references: see Daphne Patai, *The Orwell Mystique*; Deirdre Beddoe, 'Hindrances and help-meets: women in the writings of George Orwell', in Norris, ed., *Inside the Myth* (see chapter 1, note 3); Beatrix Campbell, 'Orwell – paterfamilias or Big Brother?', in *ibid.*, and 'Wigan Pier and beyond', *New Statesman*, 106 (16/23 Dec. 1983). In the last-mentioned article Campbell writes: 'Feminism is Orwell's Achilles' heel, and he pays dearly for it. For he is left without those ingredients which do transform limited economic objectives into radical aspirations . . . What Orwell offers instead is a radical repossession of key words in consensus politics – patriotism, decency and justice.'

34 Letter to the Editor, *Tribune*, 16 February 1945.

35 Letter to the Editor, *Tribune*, 1 February 1946.

36 'Mr Joad's point of view', *Time and Tide*, 8 June 1940. It is interesting to note that, 'anachronism' as he was, C. E. M. Joad was generous in his praise of Orwell's projection of the 'fanatical' future, *Nineteen Eighty-Four*. Thus, in a letter to Orwell dated 8 September 1949, he wrote: 'Of its kind this is a masterpiece, and it's churlish not to say so.' In Archive.

37 See II, 116. See also 'The Home Guard and you'. *Tribune*, 20 December 1940; as well as 'Our opportunity', *Left News*, January 1941. Further, in this context, see Stuart Hall, 'The social eye of *Picture Post*', *Working Papers in Cultural Studies*, 2 (Spring 1972), 93. According to Stephen Spender. *The Thirties and After* (London, 1978), Wintringham and Slater were described by the American authorities as 'premature anti-fascists' (p. 85)!

38 I am indebted, during the following discussion, to Raymond Williams's *Orwell*, chapter 2, 'England whose England?' See also Angus Calder, 'The myth of the Blitz', *Cencrastus* (Edinburgh), Spring 1984. pp. 18–24: 'The "gentleness" extolled by Orwell, the "kindness" emphasised by Strachey were hardly compatible with revolutionary action or even with rough measures in Parliament. They implied mutual compromise between class interests; they pointed towards the "Butskellite"

consensus of the 1950s.' See also Stuart Hall on *Picture Post* (note 37 above) and Out of the people: the politics of containment 1935–45', *Working Papers in Cultural Studies*, 9 (Spring 1976), 29–50, by the Cultural History Group of Birmingham University's Centre for Contemporary Cultural Studies.

39 See 'The Home Guard and you', pp. 8–9.

40 *Ibid.*

41 'Home Guard lessons for the future', *Observer*, 15 October 1944.

42 Background note to Robert Duval's 'Whitehall's road to Mandalay', *Tribune*, 2 April 1943.

43 *Tribune*, 16 April 1943.

44 Letter to the Editor, *Tribune*, 23 April 1943. For an interesting historical resonance, see J. M. Winter, 'The Webbs and the non-white world: a case of socialist racialism', *Journal of Contemporary History*, 9:1 (1974), 181–92. Winter quotes the Webbs on 'The guardianship of the non-adult races': 'These weaker races are, at least in respect of power to defend themselves, virtually in the position of children in a universe of grown men; and in such a position the grown men have duties and responsibilities towards the children which they ought not to ignore' (*New Statesman*, 2 Aug. 1913).

45 *Tribune*, 20 November 1942.

46 'Democrats and dictators', *Time and Tide*, 17 February 1940.

47 See John Gross, 'Imperial attitudes', in M. Gross, ed., *The World of George Orwell*, p. 38.

48 Film Review in *Time and Tide*, 31 May 1941.

49 Letter to the Editor, *Tribune*, 7 May 1943.

50 Letter to the Editor, *Tribune*, 14 May 1943.

6 THE ROADS TO AIRSTRIP ONE

1 'Weekly news review' of 20 Feb. 1943 and 27 Feb. 1943. Source: BBC WAC.

2 'Weekly news review' of 20 Feb. 1943. Source: BBC WAC.

3 'Weekly news review' of 13 June 1943. Source: BBC WAC.

4 Probably written for the projected broadsheet edition, the preface was not, eventually, used since Secker and Warburg decided finally to publish *Animal Farm*. 'The freedom of the press' was first published in the *Times Literary Supplement* on 15 Sept. 1972.

5 Otto Friedrich, 'George Orwell', *Points*, 19 (1954), 25–36.

6 Cited in David Patrick Buckley, 'The novels of George Orwell', unpublished Columbia University Ph.D. thesis, 1952, p. 153.

7 E. P. Thompson, *Out of Apathy* (London, 1960), p. 171.

8 Alan Dutscher, 'Orwell and the crisis of responsibility', *Contemporary Issues*, 8 (1956), 308–16.

9 Jeffrey Meyers, 'The evolution of *Nineteen Eighty-Four*', English Miscellany, 23 (1972), 247–61.

10 See Irving Howe, *Politics and the Novel*, p. 237.

11 Jennifer McDowell, '*Nineteen Eighty-Four* and Soviet reality', *University of California Graduate Journal*, 1 (1962), 12–19.

12 Matthew Hodgart, 'From *Animal Farm* to *Nineteen Eighty-Four*', in Gross, ed., *The World of George Orwell*.

13 A. Calder-Marshall, 'The case of Comrade Orwell and Mr Blair', *Reynold's News*, 12 June 1949.

14 'George Orwell', *Marxist Quarterly*, 3 (1956), 25–39.

15 Cited by David Pryce-Jones in 'Orwell's reputation', Gross, ed. *The World of George Orwell*, p. 152.

16 George Steiner, 'The writer and communism', in *Language and Silence: Essays and Notes, 1958–66* (London, 1967), p. 392. See also Erich Fromm, Afterword to the Signet edition of *Nineteen Eighty-Four* (New York, 1962); Golo Mann in Meyers, ed., *Critical Heritage*; Greenblatt, *Three Modern Satirists*; F. Lewis, '1984: the meaning of porn', *North American Review*, 268:4 (1983), 69–72; Mark Crispin Miller, 'Big Brother is you, watching', in Mulvihill, ed., *Reflections on America, 1984*. Finally see Conor Cruise O'Brien's remark: 'If *Nineteen Eighty-Four* is even partially any kind of satire on our western way of life, I'm a Chinaman' ('Stranger than fiction', *Observer*, 18 December 1983).

17 See Hobsbawm, *Industry and Empire*, p. 245; Coates, *The Labour Party*, pp. 44–5.

18 See A. C. H. Smith (with E. Immirzi and T. Blackwell), *Paper Voices: The Popular Press and Social Change 1935–1965* (London, 1975), p. 159; R. H. S. Crossman, 'The lessons of 1945', in Perry Anderson, ed., *Towards Socialism* (London, 1966).

19 See 'An old man interviewed', in Anthony Burgess, *1985* (London, 1978); Susan Cooper, 'Snoek Piquante', in M. Sissons and P. French, eds., *The Age of Austerity* (London, 1963); Frank W. Wadsworth, 'Orwell's later work', *University of Kansas City Review*, 22 (June 1956), 285–90.

20 *The Captive Mind* (1953), cited in Meyers, ed., *Critical Heritage*, p. 286.

21 See Richard Crossman, ed., *The God That Failed: Six Studies in Communism* (London, 1950).

22 Meyers, 'Evolution of Nineteen Eighty-Four'.

23 *Times Literary Supplement*, 10 June 1949.

24 See William Gaunt, *The Aesthetic Adventure* (London, 1945), pp. 89–90. For a sophisticated 'generic' version of the argument that *Nineteen Eighty-Four* is 'the culmination of Orwell's literary career', see Carl Freedman, 'Antinomies of *Nineteen Eighty-Four*', *Modern Fiction Studies*, 30:4 (Winter 1984), 601–20.

25 File ref.: 'KKArdaschir, File 1, 1941–43'. Source: BBC WAC.

26 'The end of Henry Miller', *Tribune*, 4 December 1942.

27 Hodge and Fowler *et al.*, *Language and Control* (London, 1979), p. 20.

28 See H. R. Fink, 'Newspeak: the epitome of parody techniques in *Nineteen Eighty-Four*', *Critical Survey*, 5 (1971), 155–63.

29 Fink, 'Newspeak'. Fink also suggests Hayek's *The Road to Serfdom* (London, 1944) as a source of influence, but language plays only a minor part in Hayek's dire prognostications. Moreover, as we shall see, Newspeak is really an ironic extension of Orwell's own ideas on language which antedate Hayek's book.

30 Broadcast talk entitled 'Have we too many words?' (3 June 1937). Source: BBC WAC.

31 In Meyers, ed., *Critical Heritage*, p. 370.

32 See Walzer, 'On failed totalitarianism', pp. 303–4.

33 See George Steiner, 'The hollow miracle', in *Language and Silence*, p. 118 footnote; see also 'Orwellian linguistics', and *passim*, in Fowler, *Language and Control*.

34 Fowler, *ibid.*, p. 190.

35 'Orwellian linguistics', in *ibid.*, pp. 14–15. See also Robert Martin Adams,

'Authenticity-codes'; Carl Freedman, 'Writing, ideology, and politics: Orwell's "Politics and the English language" and English composition', *College English*, 43:4 (April 1981), 327–40; Christopher Norris, 'Language, truth and ideology: Orwell and the post-war Left', in Norris, ed., *Inside the Myth*, pp. 242–62; Roy Harris, 'The misunderstanding of Newspeak', *Times Literary Supplement*, 6 January 1984. For a technical discussion of Orwell's views on language (and much else besides) by a linguist, see W. F. Bolton, *The Language of 1984: Orwell's English and Ours* (Oxford, 1984).

36 The 'break' between 'the Orwell of *Nineteen Eighty-Four*' and 'the Orwell of "Politics and the English language"' was noted by Randolph Quirk in '1984 and "1984"', *London Review of Books*, 6:3 (February 1984), 10–11.

37 See Michael Wilding, *Political Fictions* (London, 1980), p. 223: 'Orwell's patriotism . . . is the base from which a frisson of horror can be squeezed – how can Englishmen surrender the name of their land? "This was London, chief city of Airstrip One . . ."'

38 Cited in Steinhoff, *The Road to 1984*, p. 211.

39 Peter Davison, ed., *Nineteen Eighty-Four: The Facsimile Edition* (London, 1984): deleted portion from ms page 174 corresponding to Davison edn, p. 161.

40 'The Cold War revisited', *New York Review of Books*, 26:16 (25 October 1979).

41 Isaac Deutscher, '*Nineteen Eighty-Four* – the mysticism of cruelty', in Raymond Williams, ed., *George Orwell: A Collection of Critical Essays*, pp. 119–32.

42 For a more technical discussion of *Nineteen Eighty-Four* and paranoia, see Murray Sperber, '"Gazing into the glass paperweight": the structure and psychology of Orwell's *Nineteen Eighty-Four*', *Modern Fiction Studies*, 26:2 (summer 1980), 213–26.

43 Ellen Douglass Leyburn, *Satiric Allegory: Mirror of Man* (New Haven, Conn., 1956), p. 128.

44 *Times Literary Supplement*, 10 June 1949.

45 The idea is endorsed by Stephen Spender in *The Creative Element* (London, 1953): 'where good is impossible, the sins of the senses can be used as a moral weapon against abstract evil' (p. 130). See also Reimut Reiche, *Sexuality and Class Struggle* (London, 1970).

46 See P. Reilly, '*Nineteen Eighty-Four*: the failure of humanism', *Critical Quarterly*, 24:3 (August 1982), 19–30. See also Reilly's *George Orwell: The Age's Adversary* (London, 1986).

47 See David Kubal, 'Freud, Orwell and the bourgeois interior', p. 391: 'If it were not for his uncontrollable unconscious – his "ancestral memory" as he calls it – which first haunts him in the form of dreams, he may indeed have been a model member of the Inner Party. It is this which explains O'Brien's extraordinary concern for Winston; not only is Winston a mutant in the whole process, but he also represents a substantial loss to the Party.'

48 'The last happy writer', in Roland Barthes, *Critical Essays* (Evanston, Ill., 1972), p. 85.

49 See John Lewis Gaddis, *The United States and the Origins of the Cold War 1941–1947* (London, 1972), p. 355 footnote.

50 Cited in David Horowitz, *From Yalta to Vietnam* (London, 1965; edition used, Pelican 1967), p. 21.

51 *Ibid.*

52 Joyce and Gabriel Kolko, *The Limits of Power* (see note 8 to chapter 2), pp. 11–14. 68, and *passim*. See also Gaddis, *The United States*, p. 357.

53 The term was proposed by the historian Herbert Butterfield in an essay entitled 'The tragic element in modern international conflict', in *History and Human Relations* (London, 1951).

54 See note 40 above.

55 Joyce and Gabriel Kolko, *The Limits of Power*, pp. 33 and 499. See also David Horowitz, ed., *Containment and Revolution: Western Policy Towards Social Revolution: 1917 to Vietnam* (London, 1967), Introduction.

56 See Mark W. Gregory, '"An act of faith": George Orwell's socialist thought and 1984', *South Atlantic Quarterly*, 84:4 (1985), 368–78.

57 Raymond Williams, *Orwell*, p. 79; see also Samuel Hynes, ed., *20th Century Interpretations of 'Nineteen Eighty-Four'* (Englewood Cliffs, NJ, 1971), p. 11; and Crompton, 'False maps'.

58 Nadezhda Mandelstam, *Hope Against Hope: A Memoir* (London, 1971), p. 336.

59 Robert C. Elliott, *The Shape of Utopia: Studies in a Literary Genre* (London, 1970), p. 98. For an account of Orwell's perverse exploitation of the utopian and dystopian traditions, see Michael Wilding, *Political Fictions* (London, 1980) esp. chapter 7; Steinhoff, *The Road to 1984*, is a more general exploration of Orwell's literary sources.

7 ORWELL'S TRUTH: CONCLUDING REMARKS

1 See John Sutherland, *Bestsellers* (London, 1981), p. 5. Sales information derived from a private interview with David Farrer of the firm of Secker and Warburg, Orwell's publishers.

2 See John Lehmann, *The Whispering Gallery* (London, 1955), p. 275: 'From Auden's *Spain* to George Orwell's *Homage to Catalonia*: the same parabola had been described.'

3 See Alan Brown's careful examination of the ways in which 'Orwell' is constructed for schoolchildren: 'Examining Orwell: political and literary values in education', in Christopher Norris, ed., *Inside the Myth: Orwell: Views from the Left* (London, 1984).

4 Unsigned review of Edward Shanks's *Rudyard Kipling* in *The Listener*, 25 April 1940.

5 See Anthony Arblaster's account of 'Cold War liberalism' in *The Rise and Decline of Western Liberalism* (Oxford, 1984).

6 See transcript of conversation with Fredric Warburg re *Nineteen Eighty-Four*, cited in Crick, *Life*, p. 395. See also James R. Bennett, 'Oceania and the United States in 1984: the selling of the Soviet threat', *Social Theory and Practice*, 10:3, (Autumn 1984); Alan Wolfe, *The Rise and Fall of the 'Soviet Threat': Domestic Sources of the Cold War Consensus* (Washington, DC, 1979); Murray N. Rothbard, 'George Orwell and the Cold War: a reconsideration', in Robert Mulvihill, ed., *Reflections on America, 1984*.

7 Orwell's annotation of Randall Swingler's 'The right to free expression', *Polemic*, 5 (Sept.–Oct. 1946).

8 'Milton in striped trousers', *Tribune*, 12 Oct. 1945; italics added.

9 *Times Literary Supplement*, 15 Sept. 1972. See note 4 to chapter 6.

10 See Michael Maddison, 'Nineteen Eighty-Four: a Burnhamite fantasy?', *Political Quarterly*, 32 (1961), 71–9.

11 See above, chapter 1, pp. 9–10.

12 A. Werth, 'Is the Third Force defeated?', *New Statesman and Nation*, 3 Sept. 1949.

13 'Britain's struggle for survival: the Labour Government after three years', *Commentary*, Oct. 1948, pp. 343-9.

14 'Uncle Sam's poor relation', *New Statesman and Nation*, 10 Jan. 1948. See also Orwell's 'Towards European unity' (IV:88).

15 'Socialists and Western Union', *New Statesman and Nation*, 21 Feb. 1948.

16 See I. F. Clarke's *Voices Prophesying War 1763-1984* (London, 1966).

17 See Wilding, *Political Fictions*, esp. pp. 216-17 and 232-3.

18 E. P. Thompson, *Exterminism and Cold War* (London, 1982), p. 338.

19 In Archive. See also Crick's *Life*, p. 388. Two letters to Sir Richard Rees, dated 17.4.49 and 2.5.49, are also of interest in this context. In the first, Orwell writes: 'Re. the cryptos and fellow-travellers . . . Cole I think should probably not be on the list, but I would be less certain of him than of Laski in case of a war. Martin of course is far too dishonest to be outright a crypto or a fellow-traveller, but his main influence is pro-Russian and is certainly intended to be so, and I feel reasonably sure he would quislingise in the case of a Russian occupation, if he had not managed to get away on the last plane . . . The whole business is very tricky.' In the second: 'it seems to me very important to attempt to gauge people's subjective feelings, because otherwise one can't predict their behaviour . . . The whole difficulty is to decide where each person stands, and one has to treat each case individually . . . A. J. P. Taylor, the chap who turned traitor at the Wroclaw conference. I gather from her [his wife] that Taylor has since turned a good deal more anti-C.P.' (Letters in Orwell Archive.) Whatever one may think of all this, Orwell would certainly have made an unlikely political commissar!

20 In his 1946 set-to with Orwell (see note 7 above) Randall Swingler complained with some justification: 'Orwell's posture of a lonely rebel hounded by monstrous pro-Soviet monopolists has a somewhat crocodile appearance.'

21 See Michael Roberts's distinction in the 'Preface' to *New Country* (1933) between 'the necessary anarchy of thought and the essential dictatorship of action'. See also MacNeice on propaganda and art in the 'Commitments' number of *New Verse*, Autumn 1938.

22 'Caesarean section in Spain', *The Highway*, 31 (March 1939), 145-7.

23 See David Caute, *The Great Fear: The Anti-Communist Purge Under Truman and Eisenhower* (London, 1978), p. 51.

24 'Conservatism as an ideology', in W. J. Stankiewicz, ed., *Political Thought Since World War II* (London, 1964), p. 372.

25 Consider the trajectory from *The Managerial Revolution* (1942) through *The Machiavellians* (1943) and *The Struggle for the World* (1947) to *The Coming Defeat of Communism* (1950). Burnham's celebration of the world of monopoly capitalism and gigantic corporations, in the last-named book, rises to a kind of bizarre poetry: 'Overhead the bright plane, sheathed by the Aluminum Company of America, powered by Pratt and Whitney, braked by Borg-Warner, supercharged by General Electric, tyred by Goodrich, held to course by the Sperry Foundation, follows the airways which, marked by radio beam and searchlight, now tie together the air of the nation as the ground was earlier tied by rails. Wherever he goes, he will see and hear and touch the material extensions of the mills and assembly plants and lathes and presses of Pittsburgh, Detroit, Chicago, Schenectady, Bridgeport, Youngstown, Birmingham, Beaumont. In whatever town he enters, there in the windows he will find spread before him the brand names that are his litany: Del Monte, Frigidaire,

Parker, Remington, Duz, Birdseye, Wearever, Silvertone, Ford, Hotpoint, Bandaid, Arrow, Nylon, Singer, Kodak, Calverts, Sunkist' (p. 259).

26 John Vaizey, *Revolutions of Our Time: Social Democracy* (London, 1971), p. 213.

27 See 'The end of the end of ideology', in Alasdair Macintyre, *Against the Self-Images of the Age* (London, 1971), pp. 3–11. See also Christopher Lasch, *The Agony of the American Left* (London, 1970).

28 'As I Please', *Tribune*, 14 Jan. 1944.

29 See Noam Chomsky, *American Power and the New Mandarins* (Harmondsworth, 1969), esp. p. 104. See also Michael Walzer's review, 'The new masters', of Alvin Gouldner's *The Future of Intellectuals and the Rise of the New Class*, *New York Review of Books*, 27:4 (20 March 1980).

30 Blake Morrison, *The Movement: English Poetry and Fiction of the 1950s* (Oxford, 1980), p. 94. See also Anthony Hartley, *A State of England* (London, 1963), pp. 55–7.

31 'This age of conformity', in *The Partisan Review Anthology*, ed. William Phillips and Philip Rahv (London, 1962), pp. 151–2. Howe's essay was first published in 1954.

32 'Judah at the crossroads', in *The Trail of the Dinosaur*, pp. 138–9; cited in Jenni Calder, *Chronicles of Conscience: A Study of George Orwell and Arthur Koestler* (London, 1968), p. 201.

33 See Ralph Miliband, *Parliamentary Socialism: A Study in the Politics of Labour* (London, 1961).

34 I have already referred to I. F. Clarke's excellent *Voices Prophesying War* (note 16 above). See also his *The Pattern of Expectation 1644–2001* (London, 1979), and *The Tale of the Future (an annotated bibliography 1644–1970)* (London, 1972); Erich Fromm, Afterword to the Signet edition of *Nineteen Eighty-Four* (New York, 1962); Brian W. Aldiss, 'The downward journey: Orwell's *1984*', *Extrapolation*, 25 (1984). In a recent article, '1948 and not *Nineteen Eighty-Four*' (*Futures*, 16 Feb. 1984), I. F. Clarke quotes Paul Valéry's rueful/cynical observation: 'The future is not what it used to be.'

35 Sebba, 'Symbol and myth', p. 152: 'Another, equally important function of myth consists in producing and maintaining homogeneity of feeling and solidarity within the body politic.' For a more conventionally 'mythic' reading, see Patricia Hill, 'Religion and myth in Orwell's *1984*', *Social Theory and Practice*, 10:3 (Autumn 1984), Orwell Special Number.

36 'Britain's struggle for survival' (see note 13 above).

37 See Fritz Stern, *The Politics of Cultural Despair: A Study in the Rise of Germanic Ideology* (Berkeley, 1961): 'description will show these men [i.e. the conservatives who are Stern's subject: Paul de Lagarde, Julius Langbehn, Moeller van den Bruck] to have been a complex instance of the search for salvation, by a type of mind that can neither endure nor overcome the conditions of modern life' (p. 269).

38 My debt to E. P. Thompson's seminal 'Outside the whale' (1960) in this entire section is too great to be discharged by a mere attribution.

39 See chapter 1, p. 11 above.

40 'Britain's struggle for survival', see note 13 above.

41 'As I please', *Tribune*, 10 Dec. 1943.

42 This despair of 'reason' as being potentially 'totalitarian' (with specific references to Orwell and Koestler) turns up in a Mass Observation study of 1947: *Puzzled People: A Study in Popular Attitudes to Religion, Ethics, Progress and Politics in a London Borough* (London, 1947). See also Mark Crispin Miller, 'Big Brother is you, watching', *Georgia*

Review, 38 (winter 1984), 695–719; P. Reilly, '*Nineteen Eighty-Four*: the failure of humanism', *Critical Quarterly*, 24:3 (Aug. 1982), 19–30; Sheldon Wolin, 'Counter-Enlightenment: Orwell's *Nineteen Eighty-Four*', in Mulvihill, ed., *Reflections on America* (see note 6 above). For an opposite account, see Mike W. Martin, 'Demystifying doublethink: self-deception, truth and freedom in *1984*', *Social Theory and Practice*, 10:3 (Autumn 1984).

43 See Paul Fussell's *The Great War and Modern Memory* (London, 1975), *passim*; George Steiner, 'Killing time', *New Yorker*, 59 (12 Dec. 1983), esp. p. 171. See also 'E.L.''s introduction to J.-P. Faye's 'The critique of language and its economy', *Economy and Society*, 5 (1976), 52–73: 'what are the conditions for which stated ideologies will be acceptable? And from this unfolds another question: how, starting from those conditions, is the acceptability of an action constructed? This is the basis for an analysis of *ideology*, that is to say, the complex of narrations through which a society reveals itself and hides from itself and which becomes, in turn, a material force acting upon the society which it expresses.'

44 See J. B. Elshtain, 'The relationship between political language and political reality', *PS*, 18:20–6 (winter 1985). Elshtain enquires into the 'habits of mind, [the] epistemological and political commitments, [the] structural features of our contemporary world [which] promote the ends of Orwell's Syme, working to narrow the range of thought, oversimplifying and making crude our moral sensibilities and our capacities to perceive reality' (p. 21). And warns that 'Mobilised language, wartime's rhetoric of binary deadlock, may persist and do much of our thinking for us' (p. 25).

45 See Orwell: 'The movement towards collectivism goes on all the time, though it takes varying forms, some hopeful, others horrible', 'Will freedom die with capitalism?', *Left News*, April 1941. Orwell's contribution was a reply to a 'criticism of socialism from what may be called the liberal angle' by one Douglas Ede in a letter to the Editor of *Left News*.

INDEX